SCORING HIGH ON
BAR EXAM
ESSAYS

SCORING HIGH ON
BAR EXAM
ESSAYS

Mary Campbell Gallagher, J.D., Ph.D.

New York

The bar examiners of California, Colorado, Connecticut, Michigan, Montana, Nebraska, New Jersey, New York, Oregon, Utah, and Vermont have allowed reprinting of bar examination materials.

Sulzburger & Graham Publishing, Ltd.
New York, NY

CONTENTS

Acknowledgments

I am indebted to my earliest students of writing for the bar examination, including especially Valerie von Bleichert Wolfman, Mark Jacobson, Susan Helman, and Karel Karpe. It was Karel Karpe's introduction to Diane Eisenberg, then an editor at Arco, that ultimately led to the publication of this book, and I thank them both. Each of the many students who have followed them has also contributed to my understanding of the exam writing process and of how lawyers learn to write. I am grateful to them all.

Among the students of the Mary Gallagher Legal Writing Classes who have read and commented on drafts of portions of this book, special thanks goes to Joseph Scantlebury, Theresa Ciccotto, and Lisa Evans. Sharon Day's excellent answer to one question formed the basis for one of the answers printed in this book.

Professor Leslie Newman, Head of the Legal Writing Program in the Benjamin N. Cardozo School of Law of Yeshiva University, read a draft of Parts I and II, as did Sanford Jorgensen, a member of the New York Bar. They both have my gratitude. I must also express my thanks to the energetic staff of the Columbia Law School Library for assistance while I was doing research. David Brockett, a member of the New York Bar, read Part III and gave me the benefit of his knowledge of civil procedure and of his ability to argue both sides of every case, including bar examination hypotheticals. My students Lisa Evans and Michael Samuels provided able cite checking.

I have taken the principal bar review courses, preparing to take the Massachusetts, California, and New York Bars. All were excellent. I must, however, specifically acknowledge the excellence of the Pieper Bar Review Course, which prepares students for the New York Bar. I have learned a great deal from J. Gardiner ("John") Pieper's instruction, and I hope it shows.

If I am now myself a good writer, it is in part because lucky stars gave me good teachers, from my parents on. I learned logic from a master teacher, Professor Emeritus Joseph G. Brennan of Barnard College, now a member of the faculty of the Naval War College in Newport, Rhode Island. For legal writing, I am particularly indebted to my former colleague in the Appellate Section of the Civil Division of the United States Department of Justice, John K. Villa, now a member of the Washington, D.C., firm of Williams & Connolly.

Without the insights, efforts, and encouragement of one member of the New York Bar, Joan H. Donnelly, I would not have started working with bar candidates nor have published this book. She deserves particular thanks.

Mary Campbell Gallagher

Part I
About the Bar Examination

Introduction to the Bar Examination

Every jurisdiction in the United States has its own court system, its own judiciary, and its own bar, that is, the body of attorneys admitted to practice before its highest court. The courts may govern the process of admission to the bar, or the legislature may govern it, or both. In every state, however, there is now, as there always has been, a specified route for qualification, a rite of passage. Being "admitted" to the bar has always been a privilege for which a candidate has had to prove himself qualified,* not a choice that was his alone. In some manner, the candidate had to prove that he had the requisite knowledge of the law, skill, and good character to deserve admission. In the days when most candidates for the bar learned law as clerks in the law offices of experienced practitioners, the rite of passage was simpler. Indeed, in his years as a successful private practitioner in Springfield, Illinois, Abraham Lincoln served the Illinois Bar by examining the qualifications of character of some of those who applied. Committees on character still play a role, but now, in addition, we have the **bar exam**.

While most state bar exams now include multiple-choice questions for ease of scoring, the backbone of the exam is the essays. All state bar exams use essay questions to measure the candidate's use of his legal knowledge. An essay question can pose a fact pattern similar to one a practicing lawyer might encounter in actual practice. Writing a good essay answer requires a mastery of law and the skills of issue analysis, application of law to facts, and deduction of logical conclusions. These are the legal, logical, and writing skills that a lawyer needs in practice.

Every jurisdiction that administers a bar examination includes essay questions in the examination. However state bar examinations may differ, essay questions remain essentially the same. They require the same skills. Essay questions range from short paragraphs to the extended forty-minute to one-hour questions of the New York and California bars. All essay questions, however, require mastery of law, application of law to facts, and the drawing of logical conclusions.

The national multiple-choice bar examination, the Multistate Bar Examination ("MBE"), introduced in July 1972 in a few states, is now administered in all but five jurisdictions (Indiana, Iowa, Louisiana, Puerto Rico, and Washington State).† The six subjects the MBE tests are Contracts and Sales, Constitutional Law, Criminal Law and Procedure, Evidence, Real Property, and Torts. Originally introduced as a means of simplifying the examination-grading process with computer scoring, the Multi-

---

* The masculine pronoun is used throughout, for simplicity.

† The information in this section comes from the *Comprehensive Guide to Bar Admission Requirements, 1989*, American Bar Association Section of Legal Education and Admissions to the Bar and the National Conference of Bar Examiners (American Bar Association, Chicago, Il: 1989), and from the publications supplied to candidates in the various jurisdictions.

state has assumed a power of its own. Although it must test only on "majority rules," since it is administered in so many jurisdictions, it must somehow distinguish among candidates and create a range of final scores. There has accordingly been a progressive increase in the reading difficulty of the MBE questions. Many ask not for the "correct" answer or even for the "best" answer but, for example, for the "least likely to be useful" answer. (The state of California has just announced that it will eliminate the MBE and introduce its own multiple-choice test starting in 1993. The California Bar Exam will still include a high proportion of essay questions; you must still learn to write good bar exam essay answers.)

States administering the MBE must somehow weight the MBE scores against the scores on the essay examination. They do this in a wide variety of ways. For example, California, New York, Massachusetts, and some other states have devised formulas for weighting the MBE and essay scores. In Maine the MBE counts for four-elevenths of the total score, and the essay for seven-elevenths. In Tennessee, each essay has a predetermined "passing" score. With a 125 scaled on the MBE, the candidate must pass 9 of 12 essay questions; with 135, he need pass only 7 of 12. In New Jersey, a scaled score on the MBE of 125 or above is "passing," and the candidate must also achieve 8 out of 15 points on the essays. With an MBE score of 120–124, the New Jersey candidate can pass by achieving 9 out of 15 points on the essays. Some states provide for automatic admittance where the MBE score is sufficiently high. These states include Michigan (150) and Colorado (152).

The most common subjects on the essay part of the state bar examination include, again, the six basic subjects that appear on the Multistate: Contracts and Sales, Constitutional Law, Criminal Law and Procedure, Evidence, Real Property, and Torts. In addition, states frequently test on the staples of daily sole practice, particularly trusts and estates, and domestic relations. Although the law differs from state to state, the legal skills required to write the essays remain the same: knowledge of law, application of law to facts, and drawing of logical conclusions.

Unlike the homogenized United States of the Multistate—commercial, rarefied, and so abstract that even the curriculum of a so-called national law school looks earthy by contrast—the world of state bar examination essay questions is down-to-earth. Shopkeepers, housewives, and ranchers abound. People own used-car lots in small towns and deal at the bank with fellows with whom they went to high school. In Texas, candidates must know the law of oil and gas. Montana requires knowledge of Montana water law. In Vermont, candidates are tested on contracts and property law in essay fact patterns that may involve one farmer leasing logging rights to his timber to another farmer. In the farm states of the Middle West, secured transactions is a staple of state bar examinations. A lawyer has to know how to make sure that his tractor-dealer clients become secured creditors. On the California Bar, community property law looms large, both as the key to trusts and estates and, there is no escaping it, to that high-profile standard of California law practice, the law of divorce. Even local customs for *taking* the bar examination differ. While taking the California Bar the author of this book was surrounded by San Diegans wearing shorts, T-shirts, and flip-flops. The rules in Virginia, by contrast, require candidates to appear for the examination dressed as they would be for an appearance in court: men in coat and tie, women in suits or dresses suitable for trying a case. Anyone who believes that television has leveled regional differences entirely has not been reading instructions to state bar applicants and essay questions for state bar examinations.

With a good knowledge of the law taught in a bar review course, and with the essay-writing skills this book teaches, any candidate for the bar can pass the bar examination on the first attempt. The pass rates for the various bar examinations in 1988, just to touch base with reality, ranged from lows of 46% in the Virgin Islands, 49% in the District of Columbia, and 50% in California, to highs of 71% in Michigan, 73% in Florida, and 81% in Illinois. In New York, the pass rate was 60%. In most jurisdictions that administer the test twice yearly, let it be noted that the pass rate is higher in the summer than in the winter, possibly because repeaters have a lower pass rate than first-time takers, and there are more repeaters in the winter.

Whether out of simple curiosity or a readiness to pack their bags and move to a more agreeable jurisdiction, students frequently ask which bar examination is the easiest to pass. If there is an answer to that question, it is not the same as the jurisdiction with the highest pass rate. The presence of repeaters, the inclusion of special areas of law (Remember your Indian reservation law? Your oil and gas law? Your state Administrative Procedure Act?), and the match between the candidate's relative skills on the MBE and in essay writing all influence the outcome.

Making the Transition from Law School to the Bar Examination

Of all the professional schools preparing students to practice the various professions, none has a curriculum so hazily related to the daily practice of the profession as does the average law school. As a first-year student in a prestigious law school, the author of this book took a course in civil procedure in which students were never shown so much as a single pleading, nay, not even a complaint.

Walk into any civil procedure class in any law school in the United States and try to find any evidence of what the course is supposed to be about. You will see, instead, casebooks of legal decisions *about* complaints, interrogatories, motions, and the like. A modern Diogenes might search a long time before the light from his lantern fell on a law student who possessed the basic lawyering skill of drafting a complaint. Dentists learn to drill teeth in dental school. Physicians learn to tell a patient with acne from a patient with measles. Only the law schools have moved so far from the task of preparing students for the real tasks of daily professional practice.

Where, then, do students learn how to practice law? Apart from the few who had jobs or supervised clinical experience where they were taught basic lawyering skills during law school, new lawyers usually learn on the job. In a peculiar return to the system of clerking in someone else's office that predated the establishment of the great law schools, students learn in their first legal positions, after admission to the bar, by working for large law firms, corporations, or government agencies, or by clerking for a judge. In all of these training grounds, the new lawyer gets paid to do the apprentice work that he did learn a *little* about in law school, namely, legal research and memo writing. He learns by observing real lawyers doing the real things that he did not learn how to do in school.

As the law schools increasingly march to the beat of their own drummer, diverging more and more from the old objective of educating students for practice, another kind of school, the commercial bar review course, has arisen to fill another part of the void. The bar examination *is* related to practice, and since law schools do not train students for it, the commercial bar review courses have assumed that task. Law schools do not protest.* On the contrary, the law school and the bar review course now lie down together in happy complementarity, each doing its quite separate

---

* This phenomenon was pointed out, very amusingly, by Jeffrey M. Duban, in his piece "Rethinking the Exam: The Case for Fundamental Change," *Manhattan Lawyer*, June 1990, 16 at 24. He argues that the existence of bar review courses has become a disincentive for the law schools to start preparing students for the bar examination.

thing.* But even the bar review courses do not devote much time to legal writing or to the bar examination essays.

Do, in fact, newly graduated lawyers know how to write a good memorandum of law? Can they write a good brief? Do they have the essay-writing skills that the bar exam requires, which is to say, the legal writing skills that even an apprentice position in a law firm requires? If the answers to those questions were an unqualified "yes," there would be little need for the present book. This brings us to our present topic, namely, how to write the essay part of the state bar examination.

Most law schools have courses in which students learn the skills of legal research and in which they do some legal writing. However, most students enter law school with very little training in formal logic or in writing. These students are products of mass education. They attended large high schools and gigantic universities in which they took lecture courses with hundreds of other students. They need a lot of training, and very few law schools make serious attempts to teach writing or specific legal writing skills.

Writing, in any event, is not a mass subject. It is not like basic physics or calisthenics. It can really only be taught to one person at a time, over a period of time. Just as no one teaches music by lecturing to a hundred people at once, then expecting them all to be able to play the cello, no one teaches writing, or reasonably expects good writing, with mass methods. Teacher and student must sit down and work together. The teacher corrects the student, showing where he needs improvement and where he has improved already, and points out the features of good performers that the student should strive to emulate.

We will be teaching you a simple format, called the Model Paragraph, for legal writing. This format is based solidly on the logic of legal argument. We have included enough models, examples of corrected and annotated essays, and practice materials so that you, the student, can learn the simple format by using it. This format is specifically designed for use in the high-pressure situation of a state bar examination. If you study it carefully, learn the unique outlining system, use it, and do the exercises faithfully, you will learn a great deal about legal writing and will learn how to do legal writing.

If your thinking, organizing, and writing habits are already good, you will discipline them further and hone your skills for the particular requirements of the essay examination. If your habits are less well developed, you will improve them. In either event, in the end you will not only do a good job on the essay part of your bar examination, you will also become a better lawyer.

How to Study for the Bar Examination

Studying for the bar examination is the final step in your years of studying and working to become a member of the legal profession. It is an opportunity not only to prepare to pass a formal licensing examination but to solidify legal knowledge and polish legal skills before your entry into the profession. If you take this opportunity seriously, it will enrich your experience in the practice of law.

---

* Some critics of bar examinations argue that they are too little like law school examinations. One would think that was, if anything, given their practical purpose, a virtue.

Use Your Bar Review Course to the Full

There is no substitute for a bar review course. Whether you are taking your state's bar examination for the first time or are a repeater, a bar review course is essential. A bar review course will teach you areas of law you did not study in law school. It will keep you on schedule in your studying. It will show you the simple basic outlines of your subjects. It will give you human contact during a period when isolation can make you slightly insane. A bar review course will also give you some information about the examination that you would not otherwise have. It will give you encouragement from teachers who have a stake in your passing the bar.

To your surprise, in addition you will learn things in your bar review course that will be helpful to you when you practice law, after you pass the bar.

Start Early, and Start with an Overview of your Bar Review Course

In an ideal world, everyone who decided to go to law school would take a bar review course in the summer before entering law school or, in any event, before entering the third year. That way, before beginning the race, every runner would have the final hurdle plainly in view. Since bar review courses inevitably simplify, every student would have an overview of his law school courses before beginning to study law. Failure to provide that overview is one of the common defects of legal education.

Look over the bar review course materials early. Even if the course you are taking consists only of lectures, go over the course outline several times. See which subjects come first: Are they the ones most heavily emphasized in your state's bar examination? Are they on the Multistate?

Be an Active, not Passive, Learner

To make learning active, not passive, write down two or three questions you have on the basics of each subject. When you attend lectures on that subject, make sure you get answers to your questions.

Review your lecture notes immediately. Sit down right away and read through your notes. Make sure that you write down any new questions. Ask those questions of your instructor, your friends, your own lawyer—anyone who will answer them. Be active in going over your lecture notes. Review each subject another four or five times. Just casting your eyes over the notes quickly will eventually enable you to bring the whole subject to mind.

Master the Fundamentals of Each Subject

There is a well-known rule that applies to economics, to business, and to preparation for the bar examination. It states that eighty percent of the result flows from twenty percent of the raw material. In business, for example, sales managers find that eighty percent of the sales come from twenty percent of their salesmen.

You will find that eighty percent of the bar examination comes from twenty percent of the legal material you must study. You must be in full control of the fundamentals of torts, contracts, and the other Multistate subjects as well as of the fundamentals of the subjects covered in the essay part of the bar examination. You must also be familiar with the rest of the subjects. You cannot begin to understand the more complex areas, however, until you master the fundamentals.

Know the basic definitions in each field. What is a contract? What is consideration? What is the difference between an offer and negotiation? What is the difference between acceptance and a counteroffer? If you managed to make it through law school by using these terms in context without thorough understanding, fill in the gaps right now.

Memorize the Basic Rules and Mnemonics

Memorization is an inevitable component of mastery in any field. Once you really "know" a subject, it becomes part of your memory. A conscious effort to memorize will make your life simpler, both on the bar examination and in legal practice. If you have memorized the elements of negligence or the definition of a contract, you will never have the queasy feeling of not having "covered" a subject properly. You will be certain that you have covered it, because you know it.

Concentrate on the fundamental rules of every subject and memorize them. Do not waste time; go straight to the essentials and learn them. Will you understand what you are memorizing, for example, about state rules of civil procedure? Absolutely. The point is obvious: Memorizing and understanding are not mutually exclusive events. Some students have misguidedly been taught *not* to memorize, but they have not been given any substitute.

Face the facts. Put the basic rules and definitions of each subject on index cards, or buy commercial flash cards. Highly recommended are the flash cards published by Professional Flash Cards, Ltd. [Law in a Flash, telephone number: (800) 233-5274; in Connecticut, (203) 838-5806]. Memorize. If your bar review course provides mnemonics, memorize as many of them as you can. The outstanding Pieper Bar Review course, taught entirely by J. Gardiner ("John") Pieper, prepares candidates for the New York Bar Examination and provides Pieper students with approximately 150 mnemonics. These cover topics from the elements of jurisdiction to the exceptions to the warrant requirement. They are invaluable aids. They help in answering the Multistate and give students material to write on the essay part of the New York State Bar Examination. In whatever form you can learn the basics of each subject—in definitions, in lists, by way of mnemonics—put them on flash cards. Memorize them.

Master the Basic Rules by Using Hypotheticals

Use hypotheticals to learn how the rules apply to facts. Associate a set of example situations with every rule you learn. Test yourself on your mastery of the rules by trying the rules out on hypothetical examples. This is the only sure way to learn the meanings of the rules.

In each subject, say to yourself: "Here is a situation in which this rule should apply. Does it apply and, if so, how?" When you are studying contracts, say to yourself: "Suppose I enter into an oral contract with my father (or law school dean or a stranger) to perform services for six months: is it an enforceable contract? What if the period is eighteen months?" And so on for each of the subjects you are studying for the bar examination.

Form a Picture in Your Mind of Each Subject's Outline

We will soon be teaching you to use the basic outlines of your subjects to write successful essay examinations. One of your tasks as a candidate for the bar is to discover and learn the essential structure of every one of the subjects included in your state's bar examination. Once you have the basic outline, together with the definitions of the basic terms, you not only have an overview of the subject, but an outline of every essay you may be called upon to write on that subject. Know that outline, both verbally and visually. It will serve you well.

Master the Basic Vocabulary of Each Subject

Nothing is more important to sounding like a lawyer than using words like a lawyer. As you study each subject for the bar examination, pay the closest attention to discovering and defining the crucial basic terms. The word "deal" is ordinary English, or slang. The word "agreement" is sometimes but not always a legal term. The word "contract" is a legal term. Use it. Similarly, the word "widow" is correct in daily speech. A lawyer talking about wills, however, speaks of the "surviving spouse's right of election." That is the way to talk on the bar examination.

Learn the limitations of legal terms. Devote the extra effort to memorize definitions of terms so as to use them correctly. The time limit for filing an answer is a time limit; it is not a "statute of limitations." The bank on which a negotiable instrument is drawn is the payor bank, not a "holder in due course." Be able to demonstrate to the bar examiners your active mastery of the terms of art of the profession for which you are applying for membership. Sound like a lawyer.

Remember that the Essay Part of the Bar Examination Tests Your Ability to Write Like a Lawyer

To be examined on writing like a lawyer is to be put through a sort of slalom course. The object is not merely to get to the bottom of the hill (that is, to get the right answer), but to go through all of the zigzag gates without knocking them over.

What are the required moves? Regrettably, too few law schools make it their business to teach their students how to write like lawyers, moving smoothly from first legal principles through facts to legal conclusions.

That is what this book promises to do. Use it.

Preparing for the bar examination is both an opportunity and a challenge. Looked at as an opportunity, it permits the law school graduate to bring together a great deal of law. It enables him to get a firmer grip on the law than his law school may have required. It is an opportunity to improve the quality of the bar candidate's legal writing. This book prepares the bar candidate to take the essay part of the state bar examination with confidence. These writing lessons do not stop bearing fruit when the last bluebook is closed. These lessons bear directly on law practice. Solid work with the methods this book teaches and daily practice until the bar examination will result in better memoranda of law, better client letters, and better appellate briefs.

How to Use This Book

What the Task of Writing the Bar Examination Really Is

The bar examiners look for the following when grading the essay part of the bar examination:

1. Statement of the rules of law: analysis of the issues
2. Application of law to facts
3. Demonstration of a logical conclusion

The primary task is not to find the right answer. On the contrary, the primary task is to show that you can write and think like a lawyer.

It helps to compare this task with tennis. In most matches, it is the player who makes fewer unforced errors—the one who hits the ball into the net fewer times and who hits the ball out of the court fewer times—who wins. In general, it is the player who retains better control over himself who wins.

One of your main tasks in writing the bar examination essay part is to avoid hampering yourself with faults and unnecessary errors. If you can maintain self-control, you will do far better than if you commit a great many faults, no matter how much law you know.

If you insist on starting to write your essay before you prepare an outline, you are displaying lack of self-discipline. If you ramble off on the first issue in the question that strikes your eye, you are displaying lack of self-discipline. If you permit your concentration to lapse in the all-important analysis of the interrogatory (the so-called call of the question) before you write your outline, you are displaying lack of self-discipline. If you fail to discriminate between facts in the fact pattern that are relevant to the answer and those that are irrelevant, you are, again, without self-discipline.

Legal writing is an exercise in self-discipline. It is the mastery of certain skills of analysis and thinking and the mastery of certain patterns of logic and presentation. It is a clarity that comes with not yielding blindly to one's first impulses. It is a discipline in the best and highest sense.

Success on the bar examination essay part requires mastery of self-discipline before all else. It then requires a disciplined application of certain specialized skills, which we will soon be discussing in great detail.

What Students Worry About,
Although They Do Not Need To

Displaying a Wide Knowledge of Legal Rules Tangentially Related to the Question

One of the questions bar candidates most frequently ask is, "Should I add . . .?" Students do not know where to begin and where to end, what to include and what to omit.

The bar examination is a forum for the display of lawyer-like conduct in solving problems. It is not an invitation for you to display your erudition. The Model Paragraph format, taught in Part II, helps to simplify the task. You must state the applicable rules of law, clearly and simply. You should state any higher-order rules, for example, constitutional principles, on which the applicable rules of law rely. You should define terms of art. If the question requires application of one of the seller's remedies under the U.C.C., and you know the whole list of seller's remedies, you should write out the list, succinctly. Keep it simple!

Impressing the Grader

The grader in many states will devote two minutes or less to reading a bar examination essay. He already knows the answers to the questions. You cannot impress him. Give him just exactly what he is looking for: a competent job of analysis and argument.

Avoiding the Obvious

Misplaced modesty is the downfall of many a candidate for the bar. To write a successful essay, you must embrace the obvious.

You must state all of the applicable law. Much of it will be pedestrian. If the question turns on whether there is a case in negligence, you must state the five elements of negligence: "The elements of negligence are duty of care, breach of duty, cause-in-fact, proximate cause, and harm." You must state any ambiguities or contradictions in the fact pattern: "The fact pattern does not make it clear whether Able negotiated the contract on his own behalf or as agent for Baker." You must be explicit in stating your assumptions: "Assuming that the date by which the answer was due was not a Saturday, Sunday, or holiday, . . ." or "Assuming that the written document contained the same terms as the oral agreement, ..." A good lawyer sets out clear premises, some of which are obvious. To write a successful bar examination essay, you must conduct yourself like a good lawyer.

Figuring Out What They Want

What the question *seems* to be asking is what the question is *really* asking. Read the interrogatory with care. Read it several times. Examine the parts of the fact pattern to which the interrogatory explicitly refers. Understanding the question is a large part of writing the answer. The question is straightforward. All the examiners want is an answer to the question.

Preparing for Success on the Essay Part

The finest legal writing takes into account and incorporates a vast knowledge of law and history. This book does not pretend to be an instruction manual on the highest types of legal writing or on the most profound types of legal analysis. The objective is a far simpler one: to teach you to produce lawyer-like essay answers and to succeed under the time constraints of the essay part of the bar examination.

You will learn a unique and very simple method of *paragraph structure*, called the model paragraph. Your first task is to master the writing of clear and lawyer-like paragraphs under time pressure. If you can write such paragraphs, you can succeed on the essay part.

Second, you will learn a unique and very simple method of *outlining* your bar examination essay. One of the keys to success on the essay part is focusing your attention on rules of law and their application to facts. This book will teach you an outlining technique that focuses your attention on rules of law, allows you to control your time, and provides a basis for the paragraphing technique you will need to apply in writing your essay.

You, however, must do your part. To get the greatest benefit from this book, you must practice. Writing well is not solely a matter of thinking well, nor is knowing the law enough. Good writing results from good habits. Habits are developed in only one way, by repetition. Therefore, you must set aside time every day to practice writing bar exam essays.

First, practice the techniques of paragraph composition. You can compose paragraphs in your head while traveling; also use part of your daily study time to write out paragraphs on paper. Regular daily practice is a must. The simple structure of the model paragraph, which you will learn in Part II, must become part of your automatic response to a legal question.

Second, outline at least two bar examination essays every day for at least two months before the bar examination.

The more practice you get, the better. Outline all of the sample bar examination questions in Part III. Answer all the essay questions whether they come from your own state or not, whether or not they are in exactly the same form or of the same length as the bar examination questions in your state. The techniques and methods outlined in this book are applicable regardless of variations in question content, length, or format. Practice with another state's questions is directly transferable practice. Simply practice the outlining technique, one essay outline after another. You must practice, practice, practice.

Learn to overcome the temptation to look at an essay question, cover your eyes, and say, ''I don't know the law!'' or ''I can't do it!''

Use this book to support you in the habit of outlining essays whether you think you know all of the law or not. That habit may come in handy on the bar examination, where you must answer even when unsure of the law.

The bar examination requires you to produce lawyer-like analysis under time pressure. Practice in using the techniques this book teaches trains you to behave like a lawyer in situations where undisciplined instinct, especially under pressure, would tell you to panic and run.

Set aside time every day to practice outlining. Supplement the practice essays in this book with those your state bar examining committee supplies and with those your bar review course supplies. You will be building good habits and learning to write like a lawyer. At the end of two months of outlining two bar examination essays per day, you will have developed the competence and the confidence that you will need to succeed on the essay part of the bar examination.

How Bar Examination Essay Questions Are Graded

What the Bar Examiners Say

Whether in directions to applicants or in state publications, whether in the publications of the National Conference of Bar Examiners or in commentaries for examination graders, the bar examiners say the same thing. They are looking not for long answers or for erudition, but for clear, logical writing. Logic requires stating (1) legal rules, (2) application of the legal rules to the facts in the fact pattern, and (3) conclusions.

Standard 16 of the Code for Bar Examiners is, in effect, a definition of "writing like a lawyer":

> The bar examination should test the ability of the applicant to identify legal issues in a statement of facts, such as may be encountered in the practice of law, to present a reasoned analysis of the issues and to arrive at a logical solution by the application of fundamental legal principles, in a manner that demonstrates a thorough understanding of these principles.*

Standard 16 states that the examination should test the ability to:

1. Identify the legal issues in a statement of facts, and present a reasoned analysis of the issues;

2. Apply fundamental legal principles [to the facts];

3. Arrive at a logical solution.

The Connecticut Bar Examining Committee follows these principles in its directions to applicants:

> The *line of reasoning* adopted by the applicant should be clear and consistent without gaps or disgressions. This is the most important element in the applicant's answer, and, therefore, carries the most weight in the grading process. (Italics added.)

---

* For further treatment of the grading of bar examinations, see *The Bar Examiners Handbook*, 2d ed., Stuart Duhl, ed. (The National Conference of Bar Examiners, Chicago, IL: 1980).

Again stressing the importance of *logic*, the Committee of Bar Examiners of the State of California writes to the candidate, in the "Essay Examination Instructions":

> Your answer should evidence your ability to apply the law to the given facts and to *reason in a logical, lawyer-like manner* from the premises you adopt to a sound conclusion. . . . (Italics added.)

Good *logic* is more important than reaching the right conclusion. Thus, the New York State Board of Law Examiners writes that credit is given for clarity and logic, even where the answers are incorrect:

> Appropriate credit will be given . . . for well-reasoned analyses of the issues and legal principles involved, even though the final conclusion may be incorrect. . . .*

So important is logical reasoning that even an answer that is correct by itself will receive little credit without a clear statement of the reasoning that suggests it. The Connecticut Bar Examining Committee writes:

> An answer which consists entirely of mere conclusion unsupported by any statements or discussion of the rules or reasoning on which it is based is entitled to little credit.

The first premise of the candidate's presentation of legal reasoning is the rule of law. The examiners stress the importance of stating the rule of law clearly. The Connecticut Bar Examining Committee writes:

> The answer should demonstrate the applicant's knowledge of legal rules and principles and his ability to repeat them accurately on the examination as they relate to the problem presented by the question. The principles and rules governing the issues presented by the question should be stated concisely and succinctly. . . .

We will now review and analyze three sample bar examination essay answers written by actual candidates in response to the same question on a recent Connecticut Bar Examination. One received the lowest possible grade (1), one received the highest possible grade (7), and one received the grade in between (4).

We will then go on to discuss graders' scoring sheets and present a question from a Colorado Bar Examination together with the model answer and the *grader's scoring sheet*. While the most important element in the essay is the application of law to facts through logical reasoning, the scoring sheets that graders actually use dramatically illustrate the importance of clear statements of black-letter law.

---

* *New York State Bar Examination: Handbook of Information for Applicants*, New York State Board of Law Examiners.

Three Answers to the Same Question: What Makes the Difference Between a Low Grade and a High Grade?

All of the sample essays in answer to the following question have drawn, in general, the "right conclusions." The difference between a "1" and a "7" is not that the latter is "right" but rather that it displays better legal reasoning.

Following is Question 10 from the February 1989 Connecticut Bar Examination:

Question 10 (thirty minutes)

Under a contract with Utopia Marathon Organizers, *Pizzeria* agreed (with respect to both females and males) to pay the winner of the upcoming Utopia Marathon $15,000 and the second place finisher $10,000 (if the first and second males finished in two hours fifteen minutes and the first and second females finished in two hours forty-five minutes).

The contract required each finisher to be drug-tested immediately after the race, and positive results disqualified the finisher from any payment by *Pizzeria*.

Pizzeria wrote to reigning champions Walter Fitzgerald and Eleanor Rigby promising that if each took part in the upcoming Utopia Marathon, *Pizzeria* would pay each $20,000 for participating. Eleanor received her letter and decided to participate. Walter was on tour and did not receive his letter, which was sent to his home address. He took part in the race without knowing of *Pizzeria's* letter.

The marathon took place as scheduled. Walter won in two hours ten minutes. Eleanor won among the females in two hours twenty minutes. Both their post-race drug tests were negative.

John Doe finished in two hours eleven minutes, but his post-race drug test was positive for a disqualifying drug.

Bernadette Carnegie finished second among the females in two hours fifty minutes, and her post-race drug test was negative.

Pizzeria refused to pay any finishers.

With respect to each finisher, discuss whether each has any:

(a) Contracts with *Pizzeria*.

(b) Claims against *Pizzeria*.

Give reasons as to each.

Legally, this is a simple question. *Pizzeria* has a (bilateral) contract with Utopia Marathon Organizers regarding awards to finishers in the race who meet certain conditions precedent regarding finishing times and drug tests. The entrants in the race are intended third-party beneficiaries of that contract. The entrants have in turn, therefore, assented to a unilateral contract rewarding finishers who meet the stated conditions precedent. In addition, *Pizzeria* has offered unilateral contracts to both Walter Fitzgerald and Eleanor Rigby to induce them to take part in the race. Of the finishers, only Walter and Eleanor meet the conditions precedent and qualify for the top prizes. As to the special inducements to Walter and Eleanor to participate, only Eleanor qualifies because Walter never found out about the offer.

The interrogatory invites answers in terms of each finisher and what he wins.

The Connecticut Bar examiners gave the lowest possible grade ("1") to the following answer. Notice that this answer comes to the "right conclusions," but as the Connecticut Bar Examining Committee has already stated, "the line of reasoning adopted by the applicant should be clear and consistent without gaps or digressions." This is what will carry the most weight.

Question 10, Benchmark 1

The Utopia Marathon prizes given by Pizzeria are offers to a unilateral contract. They request that a certain act be performed and that in return they (Pizzeria) promises to pay. The offer, will not fail for indefiniteness only 4 people fit the description and therefore only 4 can accept. However, the offeree must have knowledge of the offer. The offeror will be estopped from denying payment should somebody who detrimentally relies on the promise to pay by fully performing the requested for act.

Essay starts with application of law to facts, then states a conclusion, then a rule ("offeree must have knowledge. . ."), concludes with incomplete sentence.

The offer to be valid must be communicated to an intended offeree. Since Walter performed the required act if he knew of the offer would take $15,000. However, we are told whether he did or did not know of the prize whether he, therefore, recieved communication of the offer. The offer to participate.

Misreads facts: Walter did not *know of the offer.*

Eleanor would take the $20,000 offered to participate. The consideration is found in her attending for publicity purposes.

As to the prize she may be found to have already had a pre-existing legal duty. The contract to participate was not binding until she accepted by her performance. She was then under legal duty to participate however she was not required to win under the time limit her satisfying both offers would entitle her to $35,000. The new consideration found in the detriment of her winning in her time.

Misapplies law to facts: Eleanor did not have a "pre-existing legal duty" at all. Facts and conclusions are jumbled together.

John Doe will not take his prize; substantial performance will not do. He failed to satisfy a condition subsequent by having used drugs.

Bernadette also failed to satisfy the condition in the offer that the offeree must finish within a specified time limit. Bernadette will have failed to do this.

Conclusions are confused. "Substantial performance" does not apply. The conditions are "conditions precedent," not "conditions subsequent."

This paper fails to exhibit a "clear and consistent" line of reasoning and contains numerous "gaps or digressions."

It is extremely repetitive. It states, "the offeree must have knowledge" in the first paragraph, and that the offer "must be communicated to an intended offeree" in the second paragraph. The second paragraph further states: "However, we are [sic] told whether he did or did not know of the prize [sic] whether he, therefore, recieved communication of the offer. The offer to participate."

The applicant uses a great many terms that bear no relationship to the fact pattern, and of whose meaning he is clearly ignorant. "Fail for indefiniteness," "pre-existing legal duty," "legal duty to participate," "substantial performance," and "condition subsequent," are not only misused, but are used where the applicant in fact had no need to use legal terms at all.

Notice, again, that although the candidate reached the "right conclusions," he received a low grade because he failed to exhibit a "clear and consistent line of reasoning."

The following paper received a "4," which is an average grade. It is extremely well organized. Notice that one conclusion is in error: Walter is, in fact, not entitled to collect special inducements to participate, because the offer was never communicated to him.

Question 10, Benchmark 4

Eleanor has two possible claims against Pizzeria for money that is due to her. First, Eleanor participated in the race and did so in reliance upon the letter that Pizzeria sent to Eleanor promising to pay her $20,000 for participating. Once Eleanor began to participate a contract was formed as the two parties and Eleanor acted in reliance on that information. As such Eleanor is entitled to the $20,000 Pizzeria had promised to her. In addition a contract was also made between Pizzeria and the organizers to pay $15,000 for the first finisher of the marathon. Eleanor finished first among the women and she can claim a right to the $15,000 first place prize being offered to the winner. In the contract for her appearance there was no limiting language as to whether Eleanor could be eligible for both monetary amounts ($20,000 and $15,000) and having won, it is due her.

> Essay has clear pattern of organization; takes one finisher at a time. Then takes one contract at a time: the participation contract, then the offer to finishers.

Walter Fitzgerald should also be able to sue Pizzeria to recover money due him for the marathon. While it is true that Walter did not know of the offer to appear and be compensated until after he completed the race he should not be estopped from begin able to institute a contract action once he became aware of the matter since by appearing in the race he accepted. If the court would be hard pressed to find a contract actually existed as to Walter's appearance, then Walter should still make a claim under the contract that was in existence as far as winning the marathon since Walter did finish first and did not fail the drug test. Walter should be successful in his $15,000 claim.

> Misstates law regarding knowledge of unilateral offer. Uses "estopped" where the term is not relevant.

John Doe would not be able to successfully litigate his claim against Pizzeria. Pizzeria specifically made a negative drug test a condition of the contract and as such John Doe would be estopped from pursuing his claim. John Doe never had a one-on-one contract with Pizzeria but would have had a unilateral contract action if he had performed according to the specified conditions called for.

> The essay reaches correct conclusions about Bernadette Carnegie and John Doe. It does not state a rule of law underlying the right of a qualifying finisher to recover. It misapplies the word "estopped." The treatment is jumbled.

Bernadette also would not be able to successfully pursue a claim against Pizzeria. She completed the race in two hours and 50 minutes when the conditions called for two hours and forty five minutes. She would also be estopped from asserting any claim against Pizzeria due to her failure to finish within the time limit. By entering the race Bernadette could have instituted unilateral contract action had she completed the race within the time limits.

The following received a grade of "7," the highest grade. Clearly, organization, more than anything else, makes the difference between this paper and the others.

Question 10, Benchmark 7

All participants in the race are intended third-party beneficiaries of Pizzeria's contract with Utopia Marathon Organizers and their contract rights vested as soon as they learned of the contract. Moreover, they have a valid unilateral contract with Pizzeria assuming they satisfy the conditions specified. Thus, Walter, Eleanor, John and Bernadette all had contract rights against Pizzeria, but they were all subject to the contract's conditions.

In addition to the original contract, <u>Eleanor</u> has a valid contract with Pizzeria for her $20,000 appearance fee. Pizzeria's letter to Eleanor was an offer for a unilateral contract. Eleanor accepted the offer on its terms by participating in the race.

<u>Walter</u> on the other hand has no contract with Pizzeria other than the general contract, because he never received Pizzeria's offer. For there to be a valid contract, the offer must induce a detriment in the offeree. While Walter's participation in the race is a detriment it was not induced by Pizzeria's offer. Walter cannot accept an offer of which he was unaware.

Thus under the various contracts, Eleanor is entitled to $35,000 from Pizzeria $20,000 for participating and $15,000 for winning the race in less than two hours forty-five minutes and testing negative on the drug test. Walter has a valid claim merely for the $15,000 because he too satisfied the conditions precedent. He won the race in less than two hours fifteen minutes and he tested negative on his drug test.

Neither <u>Bernadette</u> nor <u>John</u> has any valid claim against Pizzeria because each failed to meet a condition precedent to Pizzeria's duty to pay. John failed the drug test and Bernadette's time was too slow to meet the terms of the offer. Because John and Bernadette failed to meet all the conditions precedent, Pizzeria duty to pay them is excused.

Sidebar notes:

Essay begins with clear statements of two basic rules of law, applied to facts here. Next, applies these rules efficiently to all four finishers.

Essay then takes each finisher in turn, states conclusion, supports conclusion with application of law to facts.

Before going on to the other finishers, essay summarizes rights of Eleanor and Walter.

Final paragraph treats other two finishers, starts with conclusion, supports conclusion with application of law to facts.

Bar Examination Graders' Answer Guides

In most states, the graders of bar examination essays work from a simple checklist of issues and points, from a schematic model answer, or from both.

The fact that the grader works from a simple device, whether a checklist or schematic model answer, and that he normally has two minutes or less in which to grade each essay, means that the candidate must write clearly and simply in order to succeed. Knowing that the grader has a checklist of one sort or another, the candidate must be especially mindful of discussing all the issues the question presents. As the Board of Law Examiners of Tennessee puts it:

> Almost all essay questions will raise more than one issue. . . . The fewer
> issues you discuss, the less your chances. . . .*

---

* *Tennessee Bar Examination: Information Booklet*, Board of Law Examiners of Tennessee, Nashville, TN, p. 23.

The graders' score sheets made available for the preparation of this book include specific point credit for rules of law, issues, application of law to facts, and conclusions. Question 4 of the July 1989 Colorado Bar Examination (a contracts question) and its accompanying scoresheet checklist make very clear the assignment of specific point credit for application of law to facts (see item 6) and, separately, credit for correct statement of the conclusion (item 7).

Question 4, Colorado, July 1989

Seller and Buyer discussed for months the possibility of Seller selling Buyer his farm known as Greenacre. Finally on Wednesday morning, May 3, Buyer received the following telegram from Seller: "Will sell Greenacre for $250,000. Offer is irrevocable. Reply by wire at once." In response Buyer sent a letter to Seller stating: "I accept your offer to sell Greenacre for $250,000. Let's close the deal next week." Buyer's letter was mailed Wednesday afternoon, May 3. On Thursday, May 4, before Buyer's letter arrived, Seller sent the following telegram to Buyer: "My offer is revoked. Greenacre is no longer for sale." Buyer received the second telegram on Thursday, May 4. Seller received Buyer's letter Friday morning May 5.

Question: Buyer retains you to advise him whether he has an enforceable contract to purchase Greenacre from Seller. State your advice and the reasons for it.

Examinee #_____
Final score _____

Scoresheet for Question 4, Colorado, July 1989

Instructions: Assign one (1) point for each issue as indicated.

1. Seller's first telegram is an offer.

2. The offer was revocable in absence of consideration supporting such irrevocability. _____

3. Acceptance will not be valid upon dispatch because it is not in the manner invited by the offer. _____

4. Acceptance will be valid upon receipt on Friday, May 5. _____

5. Seller's second telegram is a valid revocation. _____

6. The revocation is valid upon receipt on Thursday, May 4. _____

7. Revocation is effective before the acceptance, so no contract is formed. _____

8. Writings here are probably sufficient to satisfy Statute of Frauds challenge. _____

Bar Examiners' Discussion for Question 4, Colorado, July 1989

This question requires an analysis of offer and acceptance when the contract negotiating process is carried out through correspondence of the parties. For a good general discussion of the problem in this area *see* Farnsworth, *Contracts* sec. 3.22 and 1 *Williston on Contracts* sec. 81.

In this particular case, the first telegram is clearly an offer, since it is clear, definite, and unequivocal. Farnsworth, *Contracts* sec. 3.10. An offer can be generally revoked by the offeror at any time prior to acceptance. Farnsworth, *Contracts* sec. 3.17. This is true even when the offer says it is irrevocable unless consideration was given in exchange for the offeror's promise not to revoke. Farnsworth, *Contracts* sec. 3.23. A letter response which is definite and does not vary the terms of the offer will constitute a valid acceptance if the offer has not been revoked at the time the acceptance takes place. Farnsworth, *Contracts* sec. 3.13.

A key problem in this case is when the acceptance will be valid. The acceptance will not be valid upon dispatch because it is not in the manner and means invited by the offer. *Restatement (Second) of Contracts* sec. 63. As such it is valid, if at all, upon receipt. 1 *Williston on Contracts* sec. 87. Because the offer expressly stated that the acceptance had to be by wire in order to be valid, it will operate as an acceptance only upon receipt. *Restatement (Second) of Contracts* sec. 60.

The second telegram is a revocation that is valid upon receipt. Farnsworth, *Contracts* sec. 3.17. In this case, the revocation is effective upon its receipt on Thursday as the acceptance would not be valid until receipt on Friday and no contract is formed.

• • •

The type of question and the legal area to be discussed play a role in determining the relative amount of credit the candidate will receive for stating the law, as against applying the law to the facts or drawing the right conclusion. In a torts question, for example, the greatest credit will often go to applying the law to the facts. The law is simple, and the conclusion, once the law is rightly applied, is obvious. In an evidence question, by contrast, the strongest emphasis is normally on spotting the issue and giving the correct rule of law.

Thus, for example, in an evidence question on the February 1990 Montana Bar, the case was a murder in which the murder weapon was never found. The prosecution sought to enter into evidence the testimony of a pawnbroker who said that the defendant had previously pawned and redeemed a twenty-five caliber revolver. The scoresheet assigned three times as much credit to the fact that this testimony is "relevant circumstantial evidence," under Montana Rules of Evidence 402 and 403, as to the "right answer," namely, that the testimony is admissible.

In a question on commercial paper, on the other hand, a higher number of points might go to the application of law to facts, for example, to a demonstration that a particular party is or is not a holder in due course. In this respect, the scoring of a commercial paper essay may closely parallel the scoring of a torts essay.

The Two Main Types of State Bar Essay Questions

The two main types of bar examination essay questions are what we will call brief-writing questions and memo-writing questions.* In a brief-writing question you are asked to come to one and only one conclusion: *Did the court correctly rule?* In a memo-writing question you are asked to consider several conclusions or several alternative courses of action and to weigh each one: *Discuss what actions your clients can take, and the likely results of each one.* Many law school examinations are of this latter type.

Brief-Writing Questions

In New York and many other states, the great majority of questions are brief-writing questions. You are asked whether the court ruled correctly, or what the rights of the landlord are, or whether the plaintiff can recover damages. These essay answers must have the logical form of an appellate brief or a judicial decision; they are linear. The principal feature of this type of answer is that it reaches one set of conclusions. It moves surely and securely from first legal principles to the demonstration of one set of conclusions.

The following short essay question from the 1990 Nebraska Bar Examination is a typical brief-writing question in its logical form.

Nebraska Second Series no. V, March 1990

Tony, a resident of Nebraska, opened a new pizza restaurant in Purdum, Nebraska. Tony purchased a pizza oven from Specialty Ovens, a Nebraska corporation, with its main place of business in Omaha, Nebraska. Specialty Ovens custom builds and installs its ovens for its customers. When built, the oven was installed in Tony's place of business. Problems immediately ensued. The oven did not properly bake pizzas because of uneven heating. Specialty Ovens employees attempted to correct the problem to no avail. Tony hired extra employees to monitor the oven and to follow the recommendations of Specialty Ovens' employees exactly. Customers were displeased and voiced their opinions to Tony.

---

* Some bar examinations, notably those in California and Colorado, feature a "practical" component that may require, for example, writing an appellate brief based on trial exhibits and pages of trial transcript. The principles set out here apply to the writing of that type of examination, in which, again, you are being asked either to write a brief-like document or a memo-like document.

Tony purchased and installed a new pizza oven from a different company. This oven worked perfectly. Tony notified Specialty Ovens of the purchase and installation of the new pizza oven.

May Tony recover from Specialty Ovens:

A) the amount of the purchase price and installation expense of the new pizza oven, and

B) the amount paid for the extra labor to monitor the Specialty Ovens pizza oven? Discuss

There are only two questions: each concerns whether Tony can recover one of two types of damages. The following answer moves from legal principles in the Uniform Commercial Code to legal conclusions:

Tony may recover the amount of the purchase price and installation expense of the new pizza oven. Under Section 2-314 of the U.C.C., there is an implied warranty that goods shall be merchantible if the seller is a merchant in goods of that kind. This means that the goods are at least such as are fit for the ordinary purposes for which such goods are used. Here, Specialty Ovens either knew or should have known the purpose for which the pizza oven was intended. Therefore, Tony may recover the purchase price of the new oven.

Under Section 2-715(2)(a) of the U.C.C., consequential damages may include loss resulting from buyer's needs of which seller at the time of contracting had reason to know. Here, Specialty Ovens had reason to know that Tony would have to pay for additional labor if he had a new oven installed. Therefore, Tony may recover the amount paid for additional labor as consequential damages.

This is a classical answer to a brief-writing question in that the writer moves from the basic principles (recovery of the price under the U.C.C.; recovery of consequential damages under the U.C.C.), to application of law to facts, to conclusion. The question does not require discussion of alternative scenarios. It does not require analysis of alternative lines of reasoning. It does not require discussion of alternative results under different legal hypotheses.

Notice that each paragraph contains one or more rules of law, application of law to facts, and a conclusion. Notice, too, that the rules of law begin with the word "Under," the application of law to facts begins with the word "Here," and the conclusion begins with the word "Therefore." That is the core of the system for writing a successful paragraph on the bar examination.

Memo-Writing Questions

In Connecticut, New Jersey, and some other states, many bar examination questions are memo-writing questions. The bar examiners may ask the candidate to place himself in the shoes of a junior attorney or law clerk and to write a memo to a senior attorney or judge setting out the alternatives possible under a given fact pattern. Alternatively, the bar examiners may provide a hypothetical case and ask for discussion of the constitutional issues.

For example, the fact pattern may present the candidate with a situation in which there is disharmony among the family members who own shares in the family corporation. The call of the question may be: *You are the attorney for the majority shareholders. What advice do you give your clients?*

Notice, first, that this memo-writing question is a multiple of the brief-writing question. The candidate must deal with alternative scenarios, or with arguments first on one side of the question and then on the other side of the question. The candidate will advise his clients on what to do in each of several situations. Or, he will decide among competing arguments. He will give the rules of law applicable to each one.

The following is an interesting question of the memo-writing type from the February 1989 Michigan Bar Examination. The model answer accompanying it is an edited and rearranged version of the discussion of the question the Michigan bar examiners provide to bar candidates. The model answer uses the format this book teaches: Rule—Application—Conclusion. The model answer begins with a two-sentence restatement of the conclusion. The restatement at the beginning of the essay serves as a short answer to the interrogatory in the essay question. In answering bar exam essay questions, it is wise to leave space at the front of the bluebook and write the bulk of the essay (i.e., Rule, Application, Conclusion), then return to the beginning and fill in the answer to the interrogatory.

We close this chapter with a commentary on the model answer as an example of memo-writing.

1989 Michigan Constitutional Law Question

In 1964 the Surgeon General released his findings on the health dangers of cigarette smoking. Since that time, numerous studies have linked cigarette smoking to cancer, lung disease, heart disease, pregnancy complications, etc. It is reported that 350,000 Americans die annually from cigarette-related disease, and the medical care and lost productivity costs associated with cigarette smoking have been estimated to run $15 billion per year.

The R.J. Morris Tobacco Company, Inc. paid a number of newspapers and news magazines to publish an advertisement titled "Of Cigarettes and Science." The ad was an example of what is sometimes referred to as an "advertorial," "advocacy advertising," or "editorial advertising." The advertisement stated in part:

Of Cigarettes and Science

This is the way science is supposed to work. A scientist observes a certain set of facts. To explain these facts, the scientist comes up with a theory. Then to check the validity of the theory, the scientist performs an experiment. If the experiment produces negative results, the theory is re-examined, modified or discarded. But, to a scientist, both positive and negative results should be important. Because both produce valuable learning.

Now, let's talk about cigarettes . . . .

The "advertorial" goes on to describe research that fails to support a direct link between cigarette smoking and heart disease and concludes as follows:

We at R.J. Morris do not claim this study proves that smoking doesn't cause heart disease. But we do wish to make a point. Despite the results of MR. FIT and other experiments like it, many scientists have not abandoned or modified their original theory, or re-examined its assumptions. They continue to believe these factors cause heart disease. But it is important to label their beliefs accurately. It is an opinion. A judgment. But no scientific fact. We believe in science. That is why we continue to provide funding for independent research into smoking and health. But we do not believe there should be one set of scientific principles for the whole world and a different set for experiments involving cigarettes. Science is science. Proof is proof. That is why the controversy over smoking and health remains an open one.

Assume that the advertisement is commercial speech, but is not false and misleading. Discuss whether the commercial ad could be banned by the federal government consistent with the first amendment. Limit your discussion to first amendment issues.

Model Answer to 1989 Michigan Constitutional Law Question

A total ban on all advertising for cigarettes might survive constitutional challenge. A ban only on "advertorials" like the one in issue here would be more vulnerable to challenge on first amendment grounds.

1. Under the first amendment as applied by the Supreme Court in such cases as *Central Hudson Gas & Elec. Corp. v. Public Serv. Comm'n.*, 477 U.S. 557 (1980), when the government seeks to regulate truthful commercial speech, (i) the government interest asserted must be "substantial," (ii) the regulation must "directly advance" that interest, and (iii) the regulation must be no more extensive than necessary to serve that interest. The burden of justifying a restriction on commercial speech is on the government. *Bolger v. Youngs Drug Prods. Corp.*, 463 U.S. 60 (1983). Employing this test, the Court has generally held unconstitutional bans on truthful commercial speech involving legal activity. However, in *Posadas de Puerto Rico Assocs. v. Tourism Co. of P.R.*, 478 U.S. 328 (1986), the Court upheld a Puerto Rican ban on casino gambling advertising aimed at Puerto Rican residents, even though gambling was legal in Puerto Rico. The Court reasoned that the fact that an activity is legal does not prevent the legislature from attempting to reduce the demand for it.

2. Here, it is not clear whether the question presented is a proposed legislative ban on all cigarette advertising, on the one hand or, on the other, a regulatory ban solely affecting this or similar "advertorials."

3. Assuming it to be a ban on all cigarette advertising that is at issue, the applicability of the Supreme Court rulings cited above is as follows.

4. First, given the well-documented evidence of the health hazards of cigarette smoking, the ban on advertising promotes a "substantial" government interest in public health.

5. The principal issue is the government's choice of means, i.e., whether the regulation "directly advances" the government's interest. In other words: Is the order "narrowly tailored" to the objective proposed? Morris will contend that the proper response to a supposed public health danger is public education or increased counter-advertising, not government regulation. Assuming that it would be legal to ban cigarettes from the marketplace, however, then it should also be legal to ban cigarette advertising. In *Posadas*, the Court said that it was for the legislature to decide whether a counter-speech policy would suffice. The Court indicated that if the legislature has the power to ban the activity, it follows that the legislature may take the less-restrictive step of banning advertising for the activity.

6. Morris can argue that in fact, unlike gambling, cigarette sales and smoking are generally legal. A legislative censorship of truthful information relating to

such legal behavior should not enjoy the same legal deference as censorship of information regarding behavior that is generally illegal.

7. Perhaps most important, Morris can argue that the law in *Posadas* was limited to advertising "addressed" to Puerto Rican residents. It was not a complete ban on advertising. In fact, the *Posadas* ruling was not so narrow. It gave great deference to the power of the government to use a ban on advertising to advance "substantial" government interests.

8. If in fact the government can ban cigarettes entirely, as appears to be the case, then the *Posadas* reasoning will also apply in this case and will be dispositive. A total legislative ban on cigarette advertising would, under this reasoning, be constitutional.

9. If the question is whether "advertorials" alone can be banned, the result is the contrary. Nothing in the fact pattern distinguishes advertorials as in their nature more pernicious than other cigarette advertising. The rule in *Central Hudson* would probably defeat the government's claims.

Commentary on the Model Answer as an Example of Memo-Writing

The first numbered paragraph of the model answer sets out the applicable rules of law. The second paragraph points out the ambiguity in the question (discussed below). Paragraph 3 states the writer's assumption about the issue, namely, that it is whether a legislative ban on all cigarette advertising would be constitutional.

In paragraph 4, the essay starts applying the law to the facts. Part of the three-part test for governmental regulation of commercial speech is that the government interest must be "substantial." In paragraph 4, it is pointed out that there is well-documented evidence of the health hazards of cigarette smoking. Protecting health is a "substantial" government interest.

Paragraph 5, similarly, applies the facts to another part of the test for governmental regulation of commercial speech: whether the regulation "directly advances" the government's interest and is "narrowly tailored" to the objective proposed.

So far, so good. By the end of paragraph 5, the essay has reached the conclusion that under the *Posadas* case the courts might permit the proposed ban on cigarette advertising.

The first five paragraphs of the model answer are the same as they would be if this were simply a brief-writing exercise, not a memo-writing question, i.e., Rule—Application—Conclusion.

In paragraph 6, however, the model answer begins a presentation of arguments counter to the first set of conclusions. In paragraph 7, the answer discusses further arguments counter to the first set of conclusions. It also disposes of the counterarguments. It leads, again, to the same conclusion as that drawn in paragraph 5. In paragraph 8, the model answer firmly ties up the conclusion.

This is a familiar pattern in memo-writing essays. First, the candidate should set out all of the arguments in favor of one conclusion. Next, he should set out all of the arguments for the opposite conclusion. Finally, he decides between the two.

A Further Note on Writing This Essay

This essay presents several instructive challenges. First, it is not clear whether the examiners are positing a complete legislative ban on cigarette advertising or a more limited ban (legislative or regulatory) on cigarette "advertorials." Indeed, even the state bar examiners' discussion of the answer is ambiguous on this point. The candidate must therefore point out the ambiguity in the question and make his own assumptions clear. (The model answer assumes, explicitly, that the question concerns a complete ban on cigarette advertising.)

Second, in writing an effective essay the candidate must reach for good arguments when there is not a great deal to say. As is so often the case, writing an effective essay turns out to require taking each one of the elements stated in the original rule and painstakingly applying it to the facts in the fact pattern. In this case, the elements come from the three-part test in *Central Hudson Gas & Elec. Corp.*

The candidate may wisely ask what he should do in case he does not remember all three parts of the test. The answer is that he should sound reasonable and behave in a lawyer-like way. Most law students know that commercial speech is less protected than other speech. Put that down first, if all else fails. Most law students also know that the state must meet a heavy burden to regulate commercial speech. Put that down. Then try to figure out just what the burden is. If the candidate takes things slowly, he will write a creditable answer, whether or not *Central Hudson Gas & Elec. Corp.* is a household case for him.

First Rules for Writing Successful Answers

1. Know the law.

It may seem unlikely that students who have spent three years in law school and many hours in a bar review course still go into a bar examination without knowing basic law. It may also seem unlikely that the British had to take their infantrymen off the beach at Dunkirk in civilian rowboats.

Unfortunately, both are true. Students do emerge from law school without having learned the legal analysis and legal theory their professors had hoped to teach and without the fundamentals of black-letter law. Worse still, just as the British were not equipped to evacuate the beach at Dunkirk, so the law students are not equipped with skills for studying law. They must approach the bar review course with solid determination in order to learn the law. And so must you.

You will never know enough law to pass the bar examination if you do not take it seriously. Take it seriously.

Pay attention in your bar review course. Make (or buy) flash cards for the basic definitions in each area of law on which you will be tested. Burrow in and master the fundamental definitions in each area of law, even if the fine points momentarily escape you. For "issue spotting" there is an excellent series of books prepared by Beatrice Taines, available either from law book stores or from Prima Facie Press (P.O. Box 82, Walnut Creek, CA 94597-0082).

2. Use words like a lawyer.

To sound like a lawyer you must call things by their legal names. You have to use the right "buzzwords" as my Navy friends say. Avoid sounding like someone giving kitchen table advice and sound like the person the community looks up to, a person with professional competence. Would you want to go to a doctor who always called the abdomen the "tummy"? The same consideration applies to lawyers, except possibly more strongly, since the lawyer's craft is primarily one of words.

Using lawyer-like language will help you to study for the bar examination. And it will help you to write successful essays on the bar examination. Vocabulary exists in a web, not a vacuum. Every word is tied by association to hundreds of other words. The legal terms in a lawyer's vocabulary are tied to other words in the same field of law and to related ideas in other fields of law. Once you become accustomed to using legal vocabulary in your own thinking and writing, you will find that it enriches your access to the law. It will do so even while you are studying. It will also do so when you sit down to write the bar examination.

3. Write a slow, deliberate, full, and lawyer-like answer.

Anxiety and impulsiveness often act as stumbling blocks to the production of a professional essay. They lead the writer to go straight for "the answer," instead of going through all the steps in a lawyer-like way.

Suppose, for example, that the question concerns a will. One of the legatees renounces his bequest, but he has issue who may (or may not) be entitled to inherit, given the conditions set out in the fact pattern.

Many students will go straight to that difficult issue and spend all of their time on it, even though, or especially when, that is an issue on which they are insecure. Such Anxious Andys are moths drawn to the flame of difficult issues. They burn themselves up on the hot spots in the questions. When I ask them why, they always say, "That's what I thought the question was about."

Now hear this. The question is always "about" one thing: whether you, the exam taker, can reason and write like a lawyer. The question is never, not even once, about whether you know the "right answer" to the most difficult and challenging issue raised by the essay fact pattern.

Every single wills question begins with one issue: Is there a valid will? (I assume there is no question as to whether the testator is in fact dead. That issue, of course, precedes the question of whether his will is valid.) So you start out by writing: "Under the law of [your state], the requirements for a validly executed will are as follows:" and you spell out those requirements. You go on: "Here, . . . "and you show that this will has (or does not have) each of those elements. Then you draw your conclusion: "Therefore, this will is/is not valid." THAT IS WHAT THE QUESTION IS "ABOUT": LAWYER-LIKE ANALYSIS.

4. Display the logical structure of the answer.

Because many students aim straight for the part of the question that they know least about, they never go through the lawyer-like motions that display not only their own mastery of the subject matter, but the logical structure of the answer.

Other students take more time and set out an impressive number of the fundamental principles of that area of law, but their answers, too, fail to set out the logical structure of the subject. They twist the law and the fact together. They put the conclusion in the middle of the paragraph instead of at the beginning or at the end. They are full of the words "because" and "although," and their clauses are heaped upon each other so profusely that it would take a patient reader days to disentangle their work. Needless to say, the bar examination grader does not have days to spend. He may only have a minute or two for the full answer. By not displaying the logical structure of his answer, the student forfeits the grade he could have achieved.

5. Finish within the time allowed.

Part of doing a job in a lawyer-like way is finishing it within the time allowed. The practice of law is full of time limitations. There are periods of time for the return of service and responses to motions. There are statutes of limitations within which actions must be filed. There are periods for the response to interrogatories and the production of documents. There are tax-filing dates. There are dates for the probate of wills. No matter what type of law the practitioner practices, he is always in the midst of a busy calendar. He must always do things within a time limit. He must always cut short his research, draft his document to size, produce his complaint on time.

So it is with the bar examination.

Many bar candidates, however, launch themselves into writing an answer to a question for which they have between thirty minutes and an hour with no idea at all where their answer is going nor how much time and space their first paragraph ought to occupy. They do not plan. They have, indeed, no visualization or idea of what that whole is of which their first paragraph will be but one part. They have no idea how many parts of that kind the whole will require.

Naturally, not having divided the answer to the question into time segments, they have no idea they are behind on time until the gong sounds, the gate comes down, and it is too late to add more.

6. Organize by rules of law.

Because many students read the questions looking for "the answer" they begin their essay answers with "the answer" and don't know where to go from there.

Other students, those who start with the part of the question they know least about, begin writing in the hope that "the answer" will somehow occur to them while they are writing.

Still other students are trained in "issue spotting." They are ahead of those poking around looking for "the answer," if only because they are likely to find more than one issue and so have rather more to say than the others. However, far too many of them can spot an issue and start a sentence that begins with "The issue is," but do not know where to go from there. They cannot integrate a statement of issues into a lawyer-like treatment of the law, with the application of the law to the facts.

7. Use separate paragraphs for each major rule of law.

The paragraph is the principal unit of writing. In general, each major rule of law becomes the major building block of one paragraph. This helps the grader to grade your paper and makes your paper easier to read. However, related rules of law leading to one conclusion may all go in one paragraph.

8. Leave ample white space between paragraphs.

Unless there is a great paper shortage in your state, ask for plenty of bluebooks at the beginning of the examination. Begin every paragraph on a new page, not at the top, but in the middle of the page. That way you will have space to add new rules of law and new conclusions. You will not have to write in tiny, cramped script, with complex sets of directional arrows that confuse the grader. Chances are good that you will wish to add something to your essay after you have written it. Be prepared. Leave plenty of white space. No one ever lost points on a bar examination because there were large white spaces between his paragraphs.

If you are leaving a large white space at the bottom of a page, it is wise to write "continues" in the lower right corner so as to alert the grader to turn the page and continue reading.

9. Use section headings to guide your reader.

Label your paragraphs and put the label at the top of the page. *Negligence* might be the label on one paragraph. *Strict Product Liability* might be the label on another paragraph in the same essay.

Likewise, where two or more paragraphs deal with the same topic, label each section. *Smith's Case Against Jones* may be the label on one section. The next section may read: *Counterclaims*. The third section may be labeled *Defenses*. You are helping the grader while helping yourself to keep organized and on track. And your headings will help you to confirm that you have covered all the points on your outline.

10. Use short declarative sentences.

There will be time to work on your legal style after you become a member of the bar. You will be able, then, to cultivate the flowing prose of Benjamin Cardozo. In the meantime, aim for simplicity. The grader of the bar examination simply may not have the time to interpret a complex sentence. Write in crisp, clear, simple sentences. Not complex sentences, not compound sentences, but simple sentences (e.g., "The five elements of negligence are duty of care, breach of duty, cause in fact, legal cause, and harm."). Avoid "because," "although," and other inducements to put the principal idea into a subordinate clause. Always keep the horse before the cart. Simple sentences are key.

11. State your conclusions in short, numbered sentences on the first page of your bluebook.

Placing all of your conclusions on the first page of your bluebook simplifies life for the grader. Do it. Your first page will look something like this, depending on the number of major issues in each essay in your state:

1. Jones is liable in negligence;
2. Mighty Widget Co. is liable in strict product liability;
3. Mighty Widget Co. will fail in its attempt to assert the statute of limitations as a defense.

12. Go for every single part of a point of credit.

Is there a definition of a term of art that you can add? Is there an exception to a rule that you should note? Would service in fact have been within the statute of limitations had the statute run on a holiday or Sunday? Do not add irrelevant or superfluous material. Do add those refinements that a good lawyer would add to a brief. They can raise your grade.

13. Do not be intimidated or discouraged; handle every single issue of law, whether or not you are expert in it.

The chances are that most students begin their bar review courses with much the same knowledge. All have an equal opportunity to learn about new fields of law during the bar review course. Trusts and estates, for example, and domestic relations are major areas covered in many state bar examinations. Many law school graduates have never set eyes on those fields of law, however, before they start learning them for the bar examination. If you do not know those fields, you are just like thousands of others. If you do know those fields, you are starting out ahead.

You are in full charge of your own skills of legal analysis as you write the bar examination essays. Take each issue, find the law, apply the law to the facts, then draw a conclusion. Keep doing that, one issue after the other, omitting no issues, and you will do at least as well as the other candidates. Just keep applying your skills. Do not worry about what anyone else is doing. Handle every issue in a lawyer-like way and you will inevitably surpass the performance of those who know exactly as much law as you do, but who become panicky and confused.

14. Be courteous to the bar examiners: Do not indicate that it is more important to you to know the law of jurisdictions other than this one.

A bar candidate who writes, "Some jurisdictions have a rule on third-party beneficiaries, and some do not" is behaving more courteously than the candidate who shows that the law of the local jurisdiction is irrelevant to him. "In my home jurisdiction, we have such a rule, but I don't know how it is done here," simply throws sand in the eyes of the local bar examiners. You are, after all, applying to practice law in their jurisdiction. Show respect.

15. Spend half of your time reading and outlining the question.

It is impossible to overemphasize the importance of practice. In the bar examination you are under time pressure and psychological stress. If you do not practice restraining yourself, if you do not practice the skills of outlining, you will want to start writing your essay answer as soon as you have read the question once. The man on your left may be packing up to go, having finished the entire examination. The woman on your right may be noisily crumpling up the pages of her unfortunate first draft. Your heart will be beating crazily, and every nerve in your body will be screaming "Write!" Train yourself to spend half of your time reading and outlining. Many points are lost on careless reading. Careful outlining allows you to pace your writing. Take the time. It leads to success.

16. Do not discuss what the bar examiners tell you not to discuss.

If the question says that the will was "validly executed," it is telling you not to put down the requirements for a validly executed will. If the question says that the complaint was "duly served," do not write down the due process requirements for service. Take advantage of what is given you as the basis upon which to plan your essay. Do not waste time telling the examiners what they have already told to you.

17. Do discuss what the bar examiners tell you to discuss.

If the interrogatory asks which causes of action in tort the plaintiff has, do not tell the examiners that there are no causes of action in tort, but only in contract. One of the late Professor Irving Younger's famous rules for cross-examination was, "Don't quarrel with the witness." A similar rule applies here: Don't quarrel with the bar examiners.

18. When you make an assumption not stated in the fact pattern, explain what you are doing.

Fact patterns sometimes suggest more than they state. Do not make an assumption about the facts without saying what you are doing. "Assuming that the will was validly executed," or "On the assumption that New York is also a race-notice jurisdiction," are ways to make clear your premises. Clarity shows thoughtfulness for the reader; it also helps to explain the reasoning behind your answer. It may gain you valuable points. And it may save you when your thoughtfully reasoned conclusion is incorrect because it was based on a well-articulated, though erroneous, assumption.

19. Once you have spent the allotted time on a question, whether or not you are finished, STOP.

In few bar examinations will you find the essay questions rigidly timed, question by question. Rather, you are required to write the answers to a certain number of questions within a given period of time. You will find a statement of "suggested time" or even "time allotted" either at the beginning of the essay question section, if all are to be treated equally, or at the beginning of each question. Treat "suggested time" as if it read "time allowed." Act as if there were a bell at the end of the allotted time and as if bluebooks were to be collected. Do not go over the time suggested.

An extra five or ten minutes will not substantially improve one essay; a missing five or ten minutes may destroy another essay. You should devote only the full suggested time to each essay. The last essay is just as important as the first.

Part II
The Method

Reading a Bar Examination Essay Question

Good reading is a prerequisite to good writing. Half the mistakes bar candidates make result from faulty reading of the question. Study this chapter with care. Apply its lessons faithfully to your practice essay questions and finally to the essay questions on your bar exam.

1. Read every question from the bottom up.

Read the call of the question, the so-called interrogatory, first. It will tell you what sorts of information you must look for in the fact pattern. It will, in effect, structure your reading and writing task for you. It will give you information. If the call of the question refers to one or more judicial rulings, find those rulings in the fact pattern first. Underline them. Now you have a framework for reading the fact pattern.

Following are some common types of interrogatories:

(i) Were all of the items properly admitted in evidence?

(ii) What rights, if any, does S have to recover damages for breach of contract against P, and what damages, if any, including interest, are recoverable by S?

(iii) You are the attorney for Seller and have been asked by your client for an opinion letter evaluating the strengths and weaknesses of Seller's position. Prepare the opinion letter.

Consider each of the above interrogatories in turn:

(i) Were all of the items properly admitted in evidence?

In the July 1987 California Bar Examination, there was a typical bar examination essay question on evidence for which this was the interrogatory. The interrogatory alone tells the candidate that the question is an evidence question. Alerted to the fact that the question is an evidence question, the candidate will read the fact pattern with the basic checklist of the law of evidence in mind:

1. Relevance

2. Hearsay

3. Exceptions to Hearsay

4. Patient-Doctor and Other Privileges

35

On reading the fact pattern, the candidate finds that it concerns, among other things, the admission into evidence of statements that a passenger injured in an automobile accident had made to her physician. She told him that she and the driver of the car had been smoking marijuana at the time of the accident. The full and complete treatment of the admissibility of this item of evidence will include treatment of all four of the above matters. The successful candidate, alerted by the interrogatory to the relevant checklist, will discuss the relevance of the testimony, whether or not it is hearsay, whether it comes in as an exception to the hearsay rule, and whether it is privileged or otherwise excluded. Reading the interrogatory first is key.

Again, every bar examination interrogatory is really several questions. The question *Were all of the items properly admitted in evidence?* provides all of the following information: area of law, issues to be decided, legal framework to be used. It is crucial to start the reading process with careful and thoughtful reading of the interrogatory.

> (ii) What rights, if any, does S have to recover damages for breach of contract against P, and what damages, if any, including interest, are recoverable by S?

The New York State Board of Law Examiners distributes an information handbook to applicants for the bar, containing three sample essay questions with answers. The above interrogatory, attached to Question 1 (from the New York State Bar Examination) in this book, asks, first, whether S has a right to recover damages for breach of contract. It also asks what damages, if any, including interest, are recoverable by S. These are, in effect, two separate questions.

To answer the first question, whether S has a right to recover damages for breach of contract, we observe, again, that the framework for answering this question is the framework of the law of contracts. If it concerns the sale of goods, the framework is the Uniform Commercial Code, Art. 2.

Question 1, to which the above interrogatory applies, presents a fact pattern in which P and S do business on the telephone. P orders 200 men's suits of assorted sizes, at $75 each, with delivery on December 3, 1984, and payment due ten days after delivery. That same day, S mails P a form entitled "Acknowledgment of Order." The boilerplate contains an arbitration clause and provision for interest for late payment. There had been no prior discussion between P and S of any provision for interest or for arbitration. "P received the 'Acknowledgment of Order' form on November 13. There was no further communication between P and S until November 26, when P telephoned S and stated that, because he had overestimated his holiday season business, he was canceling his order. . . ."

Prior analysis of the interrogatory enables the candidate to answer the question. Following is the checklist the successful candidate will apply:

1. Law of contracts

2. Uniform Commercial Code

3. Elements of a contract

4. U.C.C. statute of frauds

5. Merchant's memo exception to the U.C.C. statute of frauds

6. Battle of the forms: requirements under the U.C.C. for additional terms to become part of the contract, where both parties are merchants

Notice that most parts of the above checklist come to mind on the basis of the interrogatory even before reading the fact pattern. For *every* interrogatory containing the word "contract," the first question is, *Is there a contract?* This, in turn, means "Is there offer, acceptance, and consideration?" For every question containing the word "contract," in a jurisdiction employing the Uniform Commercial Code, there is the additional question: *Does this contract fall under Article 2 of the Uniform Commercial Code?* For every contract under Article 2 of the U.C.C., in turn, there is the question, *Does the U.C.C. statute of frauds for the sale of goods apply?* If the contract is within the U.C.C. statute of frauds, the further question arises: *Does the contract fall within the merchant's memo exception to the statute of frauds?* And so on. Use of the word "contract" in the interrogatory gives the applicant a checklist of questions to answer as he reads through the fact pattern.

The New York examiners provide the following model answer. Clearly, the writer has proceeded straight down the checklist. The model answer is a model not only of knowledge of law but of logical clarity and skillful application of law to facts. We include here only the relevant parts of the answer. The entire question and answer appear in a later chapter.

A. Existence and Enforceability of Sales Contract Between P and S

"A contract for sale of goods may be made in any manner sufficient to show agreement, including conduct by both parties which recognizes the existence of such a contract" (U.C.C. 2-204[1]). "A definite and seasonable expression of acceptance or a written confirmation which is sent within a reasonable time operates as an acceptance. . ." (U.C.C. 2-207[1]).

S's "Acknowledgment of Order" form, which S sent to P on the same day that P placed his order, was accordingly sufficient to operate as an acceptance of P's order and to result in the formation of a contract for the sale of the 200 men's suits by S to P. The question then arises whether that contract was enforceable under U.C.C. 2-201, which is the statute of frauds applicable to any contract for the sale of goods for the price of $500 or more.

U.C.C. 2-201(1) first states, as the general rule, that in order for such a contract to be enforceable, there must be "some writing sufficient to indicate that a contract for sale has been made between the parties and signed by the party against whom enforcement is sought or by his authorized agent or broker." Here there was a writing sufficiently indicative of the formation of a sales contract, but it was not signed by P, the party sought to be charged, or his agent or broker. However, that was not a fatal omission since the statute creates an exception for dealings between merchants, and P and S were clearly merchants.

Thus, U.C.C. 2-201(2) provides that between merchants, if a written confirmation, sufficient against the party sending it, is received within a reasonable time and the recipient has reason to know its contents, the statute is satisfied as against the recipient if he fails to give written notice of objection to its contents within ten days after receipt thereof. In the present case, P received S's written confirmation on November 13, 1984, and he gave no written notice of objection thereto at all, either within ten days or otherwise. The contents of the confirmation were sufficient, and the mere fact that S's name was printed thereon rather than subscribed thereto was immaterial. *Pearberg v. Levisohn*, 112 Misc. 95. The requirements of the statute of frauds were therefore satisfied as against P.

The sufficiency of the written confirmation was not affected by the inclusion therein of additional terms. Thus, U.C.C. 2-207(1) states that the sufficiency of a written confirmation to serve as a valid acceptance is not affected by the inclusion of additional or different terms "unless acceptance is expressly made conditional on assent to the additional or different terms." No such situation is here presented.

> (iii) You are the attorney for Seller and have been asked by your client for an opinion letter evaluating the strengths and weaknesses of Seller's position. Prepare the opinion letter.

This interrogatory appears in the February 1988 New Jersey Bar Examination. In this case, the fact pattern contains several paragraphs of an Agreement of Sale by Seller to a firm called Starco, which agreed to buy substantially all of Seller's assets. The paragraphs at issue contain promises to indemnify the purchaser under certain conditions. The interrogatory thus refers back to those paragraphs. Reading the interrogatory first allows the applicant to search through the fact pattern for (a) "Seller's position" in respect of *what?* and (b) "strengths and weaknesses" in light of *what?*

2. Read every interrogatory involving a judicial ruling as at least two questions: (i) a procedural question and (ii) a question of substantive law.

> (i) Did the court correctly rule?

Bar examiners commonly ask for commentary on court rulings on motions or the introduction of evidence. They may also ask the candidate to write a legal opinion.

> (ii) State the proper ruling on each of Smith's arguments and explain your reasons for so ruling.

Let the student beware. You must read every interrogatory referring in any way to a judicial ruling as two interrogatories. One refers to procedure. The other refers to substance. Rare indeed is the bar candidate whose mind instinctively flashes that "Did the court correctly grant summary judgment" *really* means *both*:

> (i) Could the court find that "the pleadings, depositions, answers to interrogatories, and admissions on file, together with the affidavits, if any, show that there is no genuine issue as to any material fact and that the moving party is entitled to judgment as a matter of law?" Rule 56(c), F.R.Civ.P.

and

> (ii) Was the moving party correct as a matter of law?

When the bar examiners ask you: "Did the court correctly admit the evidence?" you have, again, both a procedural question:

> (i) Under which standard does a court correctly admit evidence of this type?

and a question under the rules of evidence:

> (ii) Is this question relevant? Hearsay? An exception to the hearsay rule? Privileged?

and so on.

3. Skim the fact pattern to decide the area(s) of law being tested and the legal relationships of the parties.

Look for the area of law on which the examiners intend to test you. Many a candidate has foundered on his blind preference for interpreting every legal question in the light of his own legal field of passionate interest. Is this torts or is it criminal law? Is it bankruptcy or is it secured transactions? Such questions can set the framework for a successful answer.

Having determined in a general way which areas the examiners intend to test you on, do not neglect to figure out the legal relationships of the parties. Such relationships as debtor–creditor, mortgagor–mortgagee, landlord–tenant, and bank–customer are not only important to the production of an essay that sounds lawyer-like, but also important to figuring out which questions you should be asking yourself.

For example, the fact pattern may describe an unincorporated business in which Sam Jones and his sister Eleanor Jones sell secondhand computers to schools, with Sam and Eleanor sharing equally in the profits of all the transactions of the business. One fine day, Eleanor Jones enters into a contract for office supplies for her and her brother's business. Ultimately, the office supply company must bring suit on the contract.

You will have to figure out whether the office supply company can reach Sam Jones's assets. That will be an easy question if you have taken the time to determine the relevant legal relationship of Sam Jones and Eleanor Jones. Because they share in the profits of all the transactions of the business, they are partner–partner. Every partner is an agent of the partnership. There you have the answer to the question.

4. Read the question quickly for sense, circling all names, transactions, and numbers (e.g., dates, times, dollar amounts, and quantities).

Rarely do bar examiners include gratuitous numbers. The occupations of the characters in the fact pattern may be gratuitous (cowboy, gas station owner), but the dates, times, dollar amounts, and quantities are usually significant. The same is true of the distinction between one transaction and another.

5. Where there are two or more of anything, distinguish one from the other.

The bar examiners rarely present a fact situation in which two characters become plaintiffs in identical actions with identical results. If there are two characters, look for ways in which they may bring different legal actions or in which legal actions they do bring will have different results. Always distinguish two of anything from one another.

This is especially important where the two things are procedural, not substantive. Bar candidates gloss over procedural distinctions at their peril.

The July 1989 Nebraska Bar Examination contained a contracts question that concluded as follows:

> Al brings suit against George for breach of contract. George defends alleging that he received no consideration, or in the event that the court found there was consideration, the consideration was not sufficiently adequate to support his promise to buy the inventory from Al.
>
> What result? Why? Discuss the issues fully.

It is crucial to observe that George is asserting more than one defense. In fact, George is asserting two defenses. Those defenses are different. George's *first* defense is that he received no consideration. That is, legally, *failure of consideration*. George's *second* defense is that the consideration George did receive, if any, was inadequate to support his promise. That is, legally, *inadequacy of consideration*.

Accordingly, a successful answer to this essay question will include two separate sections: one on failure of consideration and one on inadequacy of consideration. You will find a full outline and model answer to this question in a later chapter.

What is true for this question is true for all questions. Read extremely closely to distinguish two of anything. Read with particular care to distinguish two procedural issues.

6. Divide the question into sections, each one related to one topic of law.

We will be treating the outlining of your answer in great detail. At this point, it suffices to say that you can mark off the sections of the bar examination question as you read it. Only a few states present very short essay questions in which there is only one issue, and they are the exception to the rule. The questions in most states are quite complex. Where each question contains more than one issue, divide the essay into sections equal to the number of issues that that state's bar exam questions normally contain. The first step toward dividing the answer essay into sections is dividing the question into sections. Do not hesitate to mark up the question booklet wherever you find it helpful to do so.

Constructing A Model Paragraph

Clear reasoning is more important than getting the "correct answer." Form, grammar, and logic all count. Paragraph writing is the most important single skill you can develop. Each answer to each bar examination essay question will contain from one to six paragraphs. The single paragraph is the building block of a good essay.

Issue Spotting

You might (i) open each essay or even each paragraph with a statement such as: "The issue is . . .," or you might (ii) demonstrate by your answer as a whole that you have correctly identified the legal issues. We generally favor the second method. Time is short in writing essay answers on the bar examination, and good statements of the issue are very hard to write. In addition, it is usually obvious from the clear treatment of the legal issues that we stress exactly which issue the writer is dealing with. No separate issue statement is necessary.

Knowledge of Law

You must know the law to pass the bar examination. However, you need not know all the law. You will receive some credit for a clear and well-reasoned legal argument, even where you have made an incorrect or incomplete statement of the law. How much credit the bar examiners deduct for an incorrect statement of law will depend upon how fundamental the particular rule of law is. Bar examination graders typically receive an instruction urging them to consider each applicant's answers individually, taking into account both the applicant's knowledge of points of law and his demonstrated powers of reasoning and analysis. Such an instruction cautions the grader that on many legal questions there may be more than one correct answer. After all, many appellate courts publish both a majority view in a case and a minority view. All such instructions to graders emphasize that the point is not simply for the applicant to reach any particular conclusion.

Application of Law to Facts

You must choose which facts to discuss. Clearly, which rule you choose to apply and which facts you choose to discuss are two sides of the same coin. The bar examination grader will look not only at your choice of which facts to discuss but at how well you reason from your rule of law, through the facts, to your conclusions.

You must separate your statements of law, facts, and conclusions. There are many reasons for stressing this system. First, the bar graders are looking for all three, separately. If you provide the three elements separately, then the grader knows just by looking at your paper that you have satisfied the three categories for which he is looking. Second, if you write one sentence (or more) for law, a second sentence for facts, and a third for your conclusion, *you* will know that you have given the examiners the three categories they want to see.

It is unfortunately very common for bar examination candidates to skip straight from law to conclusion, without discussing the facts at all:

The Federal Rules of Civil Procedure require that the answer be served within 20 days, and therefore the answer here was not timely served.

Such an answer should read:

The answer was not timely served. Under the Federal Rules of Civil Procedure, the answer must be served within 20 days. Here, the summons and complaint were served on October 15, but the answer was not served until November 17, some 32 days later. Therefore, the answer was not served within 20 days, and was not timely.

Conclusion

Almost all bar examination questions call for a clear and definite conclusion, *e.g.,* "The court correctly ruled," or "The plaintiff can seek summary judgment." Likewise, for each point you discuss, you should give a clear and specific conclusion.

Model Paragraph

Every paragraph of your answer to a bar examination essay question must therefore be of the following form:

(Conclusion)

Rule

Application

Conclusion

When you start to write your answer, you may be unsure of your conclusion or unable to state it clearly and simply. Therefore, in actually writing your answer on the essay examination, leave space at the top of your page, and write the conclusion in that space after you have finished the rest of the paragraph.

Syllogism

Not suprisingly, this brief outline of a paragraph in a bar examination bears a strong resemblance to the outline of logical argument known in logic as a syllogism. In particular, the arguments we have been discussing take the form of a hypothetical syllogism:

(Rule)   If a creature is a man, he is mortal.

(Application) Socrates is a man.

(Conclusion) Therefore, Socrates is mortal.

The syllogistic form is clear in the following outline of a legal paragraph:

(Rule)   If an answer is served within 20 days, it is timely.

(Application) This answer was served within 20 days.

(Conclusion) Therefore, this answer is timely.

Diagramming the Argument

Students of logic will recognize this diagram, which visually represents the syllogism. Taking each of our syllogisms in turn:

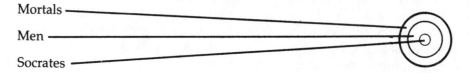

Mortals ——————————————————————

Men ——————————————————————————

Socrates ——————————————————————

Answers Timely Served ————————————

Answers Served Within 20 Days ———————

This Answer ———————————————————

How to Write the Paragraph

Leaving a blank space at the top of the page for your conclusion, start each of your following sentences with the appropriate key word:

(Rule)   Key word—UNDER (the common law rule) . . .

(Application) Key word—HERE, . . .

(Conclusion) Key word—THEREFORE, . . .

Beginning your sentences with the appropriate key words will help keep you within the framework of a good, clean, clear legal argument. You will be unlikely to stray from clear logical form.

(Rule)   <u>Under</u> the law of [New York State, or bankruptcy, or trusts or, . . .]

(Application) <u>Here</u>, . . .

(Conclusion) <u>Therefore</u>, . . .

This paragraph form should control your thinking and writing as you prepare for the bar examination. It will also serve you later on when you are drafting briefs and memoranda of law. Even when you are unable to sit with paper and pencil, you can still carry on with mental practice. Take different rules of law that you know well or that you have just learned in your bar review course, apply the rules to different fact situations, then draw the necessary conclusions. Do this in your spare time, while bathing, or running, or even when picking up your laundry. Practice so as to make the model paragraph your automatic approach to essay questions on the bar examination. If you use this logical form automatically and easily, and if you apply it to a competent knowledge of the law, you will pass the bar examination.

Examples

Here are some examples of paragraphs using this model form.

> Under the common law rule, burglary requires breaking and entering a building for the purpose of committing a felony therein. Here, defendants broke open the door of the Smith's house, intending to steal Doris Smith's computer. Therefore, as taking the computer would be a felony, they broke and entered for the purpose of committing a felony. Therefore, the charge of burglary properly lies.

> Under the common law rule, for a plaintiff to recover in negligence, he must demonstrate that the defendant owed him a duty of care and that the defendant breached that duty. Here, the plaintiff has demonstrated that the defendant owed him a duty of care but has not demonstrated that the defendant breached his duty of care. Therefore, the plaintiff cannot recover in negligence.

No matter how long or how dense an essay question fact pattern is, you can always reduce it to a small number of issues. You can handle each issue, individually, using this paragraph form. Thus, your paragraphs remain simple, clear, and logical. You handle every issue or part of an issue in the same way, using *Under*, *Here*, and *Therefore*.

Errors to Avoid

Wordiness

The following paragraph was written by a recent law school graduate. It wastes words. The extra words make reading difficult.

To determine whether the answer was timely served you would need to know the time limit as to when an answer must be served. Under the Federal Rules of Civil Procedure, the defendant in this action needs to serve his answer within 20 days of the date service of the complaint was considered complete upon him or herself. Thus, in this case, the applicable time of 20 days from when service was complete was twenty days from the third of November. Defendant H would have until November the twenty-third to serve his answer upon the plaintiff. Since the defendant served his answer on November the nineteenth, it was indeed timely.

Following is the same paragraph with the unnecessary words stricken, and a few connecting words (underlined) added:

~~To determine whether the answer was timely served you would need to know the time limit as to when an answer must be served~~. Under the Federal Rules of Civil Procedure, the defendant ~~in this action~~ <u>must</u> ~~needs to~~ serve his answer within 20 days <u>of</u> ~~from~~ the date of service of the complaint ~~was considered complete upon him or herself~~. ~~Thus, in this case,~~ <u>Here,</u> the ~~applicable~~ time ~~of 20 days from when service was complete was twenty~~ <u>ran</u> ~~days~~ from the third of November. Defendant H would have ~~until November~~ <u>to</u> the twenty-third to serve his answer ~~upon the plaintiff~~. ~~Since~~ /T/he defendant served his answer on November the nineteenth /./ <u>Therefore,</u> it was ~~indeed~~ timely.

The bar candidate's wordy unreadable paragraph is 111 words long. The edited paragraph is easier to read and is only 58 words long. Be brief.

Illogical Order

The following paragraph, also written by a recent law school graduate, places the *Application* of rule to facts before the *Rule*.

Defendant caused his answer to be duly served upon the plaintiff sixteen days after the plaintiff served process. The rule for an answer to be served is 20 days after the summons and complaint. Since the defendant served his answer within the time limit given by the rule, his answer was timely served.

You will notice that the writer must have sensed that his violation of the *Rule–Application* sequence was unnatural, and so he wrote the *Application* over again, before finishing with the *Conclusion*. The order of this paragraph, accordingly, is *Application–Rule–Application–Conclusion*. If you start with the rule of law and follow it with the application of law to facts, the conclusion will form a natural concluding sentence.

Conclusoriness

The following one-sentence paragraph contains only a conclusion and a rule, linked together with the word "because." There is no application of law to facts whatsoever. This type of writing, damned by law school professors under the rubric of "conclusoriness," is regrettably very common. It can be avoided by writing *rule, application,* and *conclusion* in separate sentences, and by avoiding use of subordinating connectives like "because" and "since."

> Defendant H did not have his answer timely served because the rule requires that the answer to a complaint be served within 20 days when service of process is made in personam in the state, and within 30 days under all other circumstances.

This paragraph also illustrates the tendency to use technical terms where they do not belong and where they can only lead to the appearance of incompetency. "In personam" does not mean the same thing as "in hand." The writer would have been better off using the homely, and correct, "in hand" rather than reaching for the Latin "in personam," which he did not understand and did not correctly employ.

To eliminate these errors the candidate should have written his first two clauses as two sentences:

> Defendant H did not timely serve his answer. The rule requires that the answer to a complaint be served within 20 days . . .

He should then have added the *Application*:

> Here, plaintiff served the summons and complaint on November 3, 1988. The time ran 20 days later, or November 23, 1988. Defendant did not serve his answer until December 13, 1988, some 20 days after the time period ran.

And then adding the *Conclusion*:

> Therefore, the answer was not timely served.

Wandering Away From the Topic

The candidate for the bar who wrote the following paragraphs showed an excellent sense of organization. He constructed a paragraph that contained *Conclusion*, *Rule*, *Application*, and *Conclusion*. However, not only does the paragraph suffer from repetitiousness and wordiness, but it also wanders away from the topic. The question is whether the answer was timely served. This candidate for the bar gratuitously offers the advice that the plaintiff "can seek declaratory judgment and other remedies available to her." In fact, where the answer is not forthcoming on time, the plaintiff may seek a *default* judgment. A *declaratory* judgment is something entirely different and not applicable here at all. The candidate thus gives the impression of understanding neither the limits of the question asked nor the meanings of the terms of art he volunteers to employ.

> The answer was not timely served.
>
> H did not timely serve his answer in response to W's complaint. Under the Federal Rules of Civil Procedure, an answer to a complaint, which has been duly served, shall be served within 20 days of the service. Under the facts, W duly served a complaint on H on November 3, 1988, and H's response or answer was served on November 19, 1989, wherein over one year has passed, or more than 20 days have passed. Therefore H's response or answer was not duly served upon W and, as a result, W can seek declaratory judgment and other remedies available to her.

Appropriately simplified, this response reads as follows:

> The answer was not timely served.
>
> Under the Federal Rules of Civil Procedure, an answer to a complaint shall be served within 20 days. Here, W served a complaint on November 3, 1988. H served his answer on November 19, 1989, more than one year later. Therefore, H's answer was not timely served.

Exercises

Each fact pattern below illustrates the application of the rule of law directly above it. Leaving space at the top for a restatement of your conclusion, write a paragraph in answer to each question, using the form *Rule–Application–Conclusion*.

1. Rule of Law:

Evidence that a person was or was not insured against liability is not admissible upon the issue whether he acted negligently or otherwise wrongfully. This rule does not require the exclusion of evidence of insurance against liability when offered for another purpose, such as proof of agency, ownership, or control, or bias or prejudice of a witness.

—Rule 411, Federal Rules of Evidence

Fact Pattern:

Peter Payne sued David Debit for his personal injuries, alleging that the floor outside Debit's shop, located in a suburban shopping mall, had been dangerously slippery. At trial, Payne's attorney, Charles Case, attempted to have introduced into evidence Debit's liability insurance, which included the area immediately outside the door of his shop. Overruling Debit's attorney's objection, the court permitted introduction of the insurance.

Question:

Did the court correctly rule?

2. Rule of Law:

"Hearsay" is a statement, other than one made by the declarant while testifying at the trial or hearing, offered in evidence to prove the truth of the matter asserted.

—Rule 801, Federal Rules of Evidence

Fact Pattern:

John Jacobs testified over objection at the negligence trial at which he was a defendant that his sister had told him that the plaintiff had been contributorily negligent.

Question:

Did the court err in admitting this testimony?

3. Rule of Law:

A person who is subject to service of process and whose joinder will not deprive the court of jurisdiction over the subject matter of the action shall be joined as a party in the action if (1) in his absence complete relief cannot be accorded among those already parties, or (2) he claims an interest relating to the subject of the action and is so situated that the disposition of the action in his absence may (i) as a practical matter impair or impede his ability to protect that interest or (ii) leave any of the persons already parties subject to a substantial risk of incurring double, multiple, or otherwise inconsistent obligations by reason of his claimed interest. If he has not been so joined, the court shall order that he be made a party. If he should join as a plaintiff but refuses to do so, he may be made a defendant, or, in a proper case, an involuntary plaintiff. If the joined party objects to venue and his joinder would render the venue of the action improper, he shall be dismissed from the action.

—Rule 19, Federal Rules of Civil Procedure

Fact Pattern:

In an action against a subordinate federal official, Richard Roe, it appeared that the agency itself, in the person of the Cabinet Secretary, John Janes, would have to be joined, so that the responsibility of the agency could be determined.

Question:

Richard Roe has moved to have John Janes added as a defendant in his official capacity. How should the court rule?

Stating Rules of Law

The paragraphs you write on the bar examination should all have the following form:

(Conclusion)

Rule

Application

Conclusion

Here, again, is a typical bar examination paragraph:

Conclusion: Tony may recover the amount paid for additional labor as consequential damages. *Rule*: Under Section 2-715(2)(a) of the U.C.C., consequential damages may include loss resulting from the buyer's needs of which seller at the time of contracting had reason to know. *Application*: Here, Specialty Ovens had reason to know that Tony would have to pay for additional labor if he had a new oven installed. *Conclusion*: Therefore, Tony may recover the amount paid for additional labor as consequential damages.

The statement of the rule of law is the most important single part of your bar examination essay paragraph. We begin here by teaching you to write a successful statement of each rule of law. You will write a still better paragraph by combining two or more rules of law, or rules of law and definitions, in the same paragraph. The chapter continues with instruction in building a pyramid of rules of law, emphasizing the importance of memorizing rules of law and of doing mental exercises on the clear and correct statement of rules of law.

Stating Rules of Law: How to Do it

Correctness

Everything in your bar examination essay answer hinges on the clarity and correctness of your statement of the rules of law. Note that it does not hinge exclusively on correctness; you can be wrong and still get some credit. You can be incomplete and still get some credit. You can be wrong quite often and still pass. You should aim, obviously, to get it right. While logical, analytical thinking and clear writing will gather points and bolster your score, the bar exam is still meant to be a measure of your legal knowledge. Memorize the basic rules of law so that you can readily restate them.

49

Clarity and Directness

Think through the rule of law mentally before writing it down. Substitute clear expressions for muddled ones. Substitute clear writing for muddled writing. Compare the following three statements of the New York rule of ("pure") comparative negligence, all taken from students' papers:

Clear: Plaintiff's negligence proportionately diminishes, but does not bar, recovery.

Muddled: The plaintiff who is negligent can still recover.

Very muddled: Plaintiff will not lose out if he is contributorily negligent.

The "very muddled" example is so confused that it mixes up comparative negligence, which is the rule to be stated, with contributory negligence, which is exactly the rule that does *not* apply in a comparative negligence jurisdiction.

Completeness

State each rule completely. Your statement of the rule of law is like, as it were, a set of pockets into which your statement of the application of law to fact will insert the relevant facts. Everything in your bar examination essay paragraph turns on the clarity and completeness of your statement of the rule of law.

Completeness means that if there are five elements in the tort of negligence then you will write down all five, not just one or two. To rush into writing the rule of law and put down only so much as is absolutely necessary to "answer" the question is to be unrestrained and not lawyer-like.

Complete: Negligence requires a legal duty, breach of that duty, actual cause, legal cause, and harm.

Not complete: In negligence one party breaches his legal duty and that causes someone else harm.

The latter definition is incomplete, and within a bar examination essay, it is self-defeating. The bar examination grader may have each one of the elements of negligence on his checklist for grading the essay.

The following statement of the rule of comparative negligence is incomplete:

| The plaintiff's negligence diminishes, but does not bar, recovery.

It leaves out the fact that the diminution is proportional. Correctly and completely stated:

| The plaintiff's negligence *proportionately* diminishes, but does not bar, recovery.

The bar candidate should not feel that just because his first efforts to be clear, complete, and accurate make him feel awkward he should give up. These skills, like all other skills, require practice.

Distinctness in the Parts of the Rule: Order Among the Parts of the Rule

While a bilateral contract may be defined as "a promise for a promise," very few legal rules are so simple. Usually there is more than one element. When you state the legal rule on the bar examination, it is crucially important to put down as many of the elements as possible. In addition, it is important to keep the parts of the rule separate from each other and in chronological or other logical order.

> *Parts of Rule Distinct*:   The elements of adverse possession are possession that is actual, exclusive, under claim of right, notorious and open, uninterrupted, and hostile.
>
> *Parts of Rule Muddled*:   The elements of adverse possession are possession that is known to be exclusive, openly actual, claiming no interruption, and hostile.
>
> *Parts of Rule Distinct*:   Under the majority rule in *Palsgraf*, a defendant will not be liable in negligence, unless what he did created an unreasonable and foreseeable risk of harm to the plaintiff.
>
> *Parts of Rule Muddled*:   Under the majority rule in *Palsgraf*, defendants are only liable where harm is foreseeable.
>
> *Parts of Rule in Order*:   The following are the elements of felony murder: intent to commit a felony; death resulting from attempt to commit the felony or from commission of the felony; the felony is the proximate cause of the death.
>
> *Parts of Rule Not in Order*:   Felony murder is where there is a death that results from a felony, or from an attempt to commit a felony, that the defendant intended to commit.

Spend some time every day working to simplify and clarify the statement of rules of law. You may take the rules from the Federal Rules of Civil Procedure or the Federal Rules of Evidence. You may take them from the notes for your bar review course. You may even take them from the newspaper. Read the rule, state its meaning to yourself, then restate it in simpler terms and fewer words. That is the kind of tight and accurate writing you will need on the bar examination. It is also the kind of writing you will aim for in your legal practice.

How to Build a Pyramid of Rules of Law

Often, your paragraph will contain two or more rules of law together:

Conclusion: Smith and Jones did have a contract for the sale of 400 widgets. *Rules:* Under [state] law, a contract requires offer, acceptance, and consideration. Consideration may be any benefit to the promisor or detriment to the promisee. *Application*: Here, the letter from Smith to Jones recited the offer and acceptance and the consideration, which was Jones's promise to pay for the widgets in three equal installment payments. *Conclusion*: Therefore, there was a contract.

In this case, the second rule is in fact a definition of one of the terms ("consideration") in the first rule. In other cases, the second rule may be a state law following from a constitutional principle. The first rule may be a general rule, and the second may be an exception to the first rule. The second rule may be a corollary to the first rule or it may simply be a less general rule.

Rule: Under Rule 408 of the Federal Rules of Evidence, admissions made in the conduct of settlement negotiations are inadmissible to prove liability. *Corollary*: Admissions made in the course of offering to pay medical bills, however, are admissible.

Rule: Under article III, sec. 2, of the Constitution, Congress has the power to create inferior federal courts and can determine the jurisdiction of those courts. *Corollary*: Congress cannot, however, change or expand the jurisdiction of federal courts beyond that permitted by article III.

Rule: Under the common law, a privilege protects confidential communications between client and attorney. *Exception*: This privilege does not apply, however, where the client consulted the attorney for assistance in committing a crime or fraud.

Every time the rule contains a term of art, the bar candidate should define that term.

Rule: The plaintiff may recover both compensatory and punitive damages. *Definition*: Compensatory damages compensate the victim for actual loss, such as loss of earnings and permanent disability. *Definition*: Punitive damages, also known as exemplary damages, punish the defendant.

Likewise, where full explication of the rule of law requires the making of a technical distinction, the candidate with sufficient time may spell out that distinction.

Writing the Rules of Law

In writing your outline for each bar examination essay question, remember to write the rule or rules of law that "answer" the question. Remember to leave space for related rules of law. Likewise, in writing your essay in your bluebook, remember to leave ample white space above each paragraph.

The truth is that it is usually the rule that immediately answers the question that springs to mind first. For example:

Admissions made in the course of offering to pay medical bills are admissible.

The more general rule, "admissions made in the conduct of settlement negotiations are inadmissible to prove liability" comes to mind only *after* the rather narrow rule about offering to pay medical bills has already been written down. That is why this book suggests that you leave so much white space *above* what you write.

As you look at your essay outline, perhaps with five rules of law, examine each one. See which higher or more general rules of law you can add above it. See which definitions of terms of art, or less general rules, you should add below it.

It is by building these pyramids of rules of law that you will obtain the maximum number of points for each essay. Remember, the constitutional principle comes before the relevant state rule of procedure; the general rule comes before the specific; the rule comes before the exception.

Memorizing the Rules of Law

It goes without saying that in order to state the law, you must know the law. And the way to know the rules of law is to memorize them. To score high on the essay part of the bar examination, you must memorize the basic rules of law in each of the six major areas of law (contracts, torts, constitutional law, criminal law and procedure, evidence, and property) that are tested on the Multistate Bar Examination. That does not mean that you have to memorize everything in the *Restatement*. It does mean that you must memorize the *basic* rules of law in each area. You must also memorize the *basic* rules of law in each of the major areas in your state bar examination. Typically, these include domestic relations, wills and trusts, and corporations.

In order to memorize, you must overcome your prejudices. Law school professors tend to oppose memorization. Perhaps this is because the common law is genuinely flexible, and every apparent rule is bound to the facts of the case in which it is announced. Perhaps this prejudice is related to the theory that legal education is like scientific education in that the student studies the legal cases as though they were scientific experiments, deducing principles from them. This viewpoint stresses reasoning and excludes memorization. However, it also ignores the fact that students of science must memorize constantly in order to be able to interpret what they discover in performing experiments or what they see before them on the dissecting table.

Another possible explanation for the prejudice against memorization comes from the hierarchy of law schools, those that aim to follow the scientific model, on the one hand, and those, on the other hand, that aim to prepare students for the state bar examination and, presumably, local practice. Whatever the source of the opposition to memorization, law school professors impose it unfairly on their students.

It pays to memorize. It pays in law school and it pays off on the bar examination—handsomely.

Memorization is your friend. Make flash cards. Test yourself daily, going over and over the same basic material on your flash cards. Do not try to penetrate deeply into every subject when you study it. Make sure that you simply repeat the same flash cards, over and over, every single day. You will memorize, and you will have the material available in your memory when you need it for the bar examination.

Using the Key Outline for a Successful Bar Examination Essay

We have been teaching you a unique method for constructing successful bar examination essays. The basic building block of this simple and effective method is the paragraph. Another effective tool is the builder's plan, or the Key Outline.

As you know well by now, every paragraph has the form of *(Conclusion)–Rule–Application–Conclusion*. The key words are the first word of the *Rule*: UNDER; the first word of the *Application*: HERE; and the first word of the *Conclusion*: THEREFORE.

You will construct your essay on scratch paper, out of the building blocks of these paragraphs. This will hold true regardless of the number of principal rules of law in your state's typical bar examination essay question. If there are two principal rules of law, your essay will contain two paragraphs. If there are five principal rules of law, your essay will contain five paragraphs.

What is the Outline?

A second unique feature of our method of writing bar examination essays is *the outline, which is simply a list of principal rules of law.*

Using our method, your outline will contain no conclusions, no issues, and no facts. It will consist solely of a list of the rules of law that will follow the word UNDER in the paragraphs of the essay you will write. (See pages 56 and 67 for examples of Key Outlines.)

Why shouldn't your outline of the bar examination essay contain conclusions (e.g., "Jones will prevail in his case against Dr. Smith")? First, as a practical matter, you are under such severe time pressure in reading the interrogatory and fact pattern and writing your outline that you do not have time to reach conclusions. Your outline cannot contain conclusions for the simple reason that you often do not know your conclusions or should not until you identify the rules of law and apply the facts to them.

Second, if you do begin an outline with a conclusion, you will find yourself automatically filling the outline with the facts that support the conclusion. Before you know it, your hand has taken on a life of its own, and you are writing the entire essay on your scratch paper. Time is passing. You do not have time to write the essay itself.

Why shouldn't your outline contain statements of the legal issues? (e.g., "The issue is whether Dr. Smith's act was negligent")? First, since there is rarely a need to write a statement of the issue in the essay, it is a waste of time to write it in the outline. Second, when a student writes "issue statements" in his outline, he rarely has any idea at all of what to write next. Anyone who has grasped our method of paragraph writing, however, knows that what follows the rule (UNDER) is the application (HERE), and that what follows the application is the conclusion (THERE-FORE). An outline consisting wholly of a list of rules (UNDER-statements) easily converts itself into an essay in which each of those rules is the lead sentence of a logically compelling paragraph.

Outlining your essay by listing the rules of law applies equally to short-essay and to long-essay exams. The two examples that follow show you the method in action—question, outline, and model essay answer.

Two-Rule Example

The Nebraska Bar Examination has very short essay questions that require, at most, two principal rules of law. That is, you write at most two main paragraphs to answer each of these questions.

As you sit down to read the first essay on the Nebraska Bar Examination, you will write down two numbers on your scratch paper, representing the two parts of your outline:

1.

2.

When you have followed each number with a rule of law, your outline is finished.

George and Al, residents of Nebraska, were close friends. They owned auto parts stores. George owned three stores in Omaha, and Al owned one store in Lincoln. Al was new to the business, and George told him that he wanted to help Al progress faster.

In November of 1987, the two entered into a written contract wherein Al agreed to allow George to stock and maintain an auto parts inventory for Al's store. George told Al that he (George) could buy parts from wholesale suppliers at greater discounts than could Al and that the additional purchases that Al made might even increase the discounts that George could get for Al and himself. The contract provided that George would be reimbursed for any travel expense he actually incurred in traveling to and from Omaha but that he would not receive any compensation for his services to Al. The contract also provided that, at Al's option, George would buy from Al, at Al's original cost, any unsold inventory on hand one year after the signing of the contract.

In November of 1988, Al decided to quit business because of poor sales and requested that George buy the inventory as provided in the contract. George refused.

Al brings suit against George for breach of contract. George defends alleging that he received no consideration, or in the event that the court found there was consideration, that the consideration was not sufficiently adequate to support his promise to buy the inventory from Al.

What result? Why? Discuss the issues fully.

The paragraph immediately above the call of the question shows that George has not one but two defenses: "George defends alleging that he received no consideration, or in the event that the court found there was consideration, that the consideration was not sufficiently adequate to support his promise to buy the inventory from Al."

This sentence provides the framework for the outline: (i) failure of consideration and (ii) inadequacy of consideration. The applicable rules follow:

1. Under the common law of contracts, a contract requires offer, acceptance, and consideration. Any detriment to the promisee or benefit to the promisor is consideration.

2. Under the common law of contracts, any consideration, no matter how slight, is sufficient to support a contract.

The following model answer for the question uses these sentences as the base for its two paragraphs. In addition to the two main paragraphs, there is a summary at the beginning and end of the essay. The words *Rule, Application,* and *Conclusion* would *not* appear in the bar examination essay you submit. They appear here to show you how the paragraphs conform to the model. The paragraph headings (*First defense: failure of consideration* and *Second defense: inadequacy of consideration*) *should* appear in the final essay. These headings draw the grader's attention to the points you are discussing.

Bar Examination Essay

Conclusion. Al will prevail in his suit against George for breach of contract.

First defense: failure of consideration. Rule: Under the common law of contracts, a contract requires offer, acceptance, and consideration. Any detriment to the promisee or benefit to the promisor is consideration. *Application:* Here, Al and George had agreed on all terms. Al's promise to buy his auto parts inventory through George was a detriment to Al, and a benefit to George. *Conclusion:* Therefore, George's first defense must fail.

The first rule in the outline is the basis of the first paragraph.

Second defense: inadequacy of consideration. Rule: Under the common law of contracts, any consideration, no matter how slight, is sufficient to support a contract. *Application:* Here, George expected to be able to obtain increased discounts on his purchases for his own auto parts stores as a result of the volume of purchases he made for Al's stores. In addition, as noted above, Al promised to buy his inventory through George. Even if this benefit to George and detriment to Al constituted slight consideration, they would be adequate to support a contract. *Conclusion:* Therefore, George's second defense also fails.

The second rule in the outline is the basis of the second paragraph.

Accordingly, since both of George's defenses fail, all other things being equal, Al will prevail in his suit against George for breach of contract.

Multi-Rule Example

Each essay in the Utah State Bar Examination requires from four to six principal rules of law. That is, the candidate will write between four and six major paragraphs. Following are a typical question, a Key Outline showing the five sections the candidate would have in his own outline, and a model answer using the format of Rule–Application–Conclusion.

Utah State Bar Examination, February 1990

In December, 1985, Ned LeGence enrolled in a basic scuba diving instruction course at Utah Diving Instruction and Professional Supply (DIPS). The dive instructor for Ned's class was Mike Nelson, an employee of DIPS. Ned rented his equipment from DIPS. Included in the rental equipment was a Deep Quest 2000 air tank manufactured in 1982 by the Deep Quest Corporation, and a depth gauge made locally by DIPS.

After completing the six-week course, Ned went on a final open water checkout dive in the ocean with his class, with Mr. Nelson as the leader. While on this open-water checkout dive, Ned decided to separate himself from his underwater group and swim deeper to look for shells along the ocean bottom. Mr. Nelson saw Ned move away from the group, but decided to stay with the rest of the group and not follow him.

Ned knew, from reading the books supplied to him in his diving course, that below 180 feet there was a danger of becoming disoriented and "light-headed" because of a phenomenon known as nitrogen narcosis, or "rapture of the deep." When Ned in fact started to become light-headed, he looked at his depth gauge which registered his depth at only 150 feet. He therefore continued to stay on the bottom, becoming progressively more disoriented and "light-headed" until he lost consciousness. He later was found by his instructor who rushed him to the surface. As a result of his ordeal, Ned was seriously injured.

A later examination of the incident by an independent diving expert revealed the following additional facts:

(a) The Deep Quest 2000 dive tank had been lined on the inside with a material which, when subjected to air and moisture over a period of time, gave off toxic fumes, causing a condition similar to nitrogen narcosis. Although this phenomenon was well known to the Deep Quest Corporation, no recall letter had been sent.

(b) The depth gauge being utilized by Ned was worn out and had become inaccurate. Ned was actually at 190 feet when he thought he was at 150 feet. This inaccuracy was known by the dive shop, but shop employees thought that the depth reading was "close enough."

(c) DIPS' own company policy required that there be two instructors present during basic open water checkout dives. However, in recent months, because of declining revenues, DIPS had only used one instructor, even with large classes such as Ned's.

In February, 1990, Ned has asked you to advise him as to the causes of action, if any, which he may have for his injuries, to consider the potential defendants in the case and the potential cross-claims, counterclaims and/or defenses which may be raised by defendants.

Key Outline of Bar Examination Answer:
LeGence v. Deep Quest, et al.

I. Ned's Causes of Action

   A. Against Deep Quest Corporation

      1. *Negligence.* The elements of negligence are duty of care, breach of duty, cause-in-fact, proximate cause, and injury.

      2. *Strict Products Liability.* The seller is liable in strict products liability where (i) he is in the business of selling goods of that type, (ii) it is expected to and does reach the consumer in substantially the condition in which it was sold, and (iii) the defect proximately caused the injury.

      3. *Warranty.* Under the Uniform Commercial Code, where the seller is a merchant in goods of that kind, a warranty that the goods be merchantable is implied in a contract for their sale. The warranty is that the goods will at least be such as are fit for the ordinary purposes for which such goods are used.

   B. Against DIPS Supply

      1. *Negligence.* See above.

      2. *Strict Products Liability and Warranty.* See above.

   C. Against Mike Nelson

      1. *Negligence.* See above.

II. Cross-Claims and Defenses

   A. Cross-Claims

      Proximate cause or legal cause requires that "but for" the conduct of the defendant, the injury to the plaintiff would not have occurred.

   B. Defenses

      1. *Deep Quest.* Proximate cause. See above.

      2. *DIPS.* Strict products liability: See chain of distribution. Negligence: Proximate cause. See above. Contributory or comparative negligence.

      3. *Mike Nelson.* As for DIPS, above. Contributory or comparative negligence.

   C. Other defenses

      1. *Statutes of Limitations.*

      2. *Notice under the Uniform Commercial Code.*

Model Bar Examination Answer:
LeGence v. Deep Quest, et al.

I. Ned's Causes of Action

   A. Against Deep Quest Corporation

      1. *Negligence.* Under tort law, the elements of negligence are duty of care, breach of duty, cause-in-fact, proximate cause, and injury. Here, Deep Quest had a duty to users of its products to exert care not to harm them. It apparently breached that duty in lining the dive tank Ned used with a substance that gave off toxic fumes when exposed to air and moisture over a period of time. (Whether Deep Quest knowingly breached its duty will be a matter for discovery.) The fumes were apparently the cause in fact of Ned's losing consciousness and of his injuries. "But for" the fumes, Ned may argue, he would not have suffered his injuries. There were, in fact, serious injuries. Therefore, Ned may be able to prove a case in negligence.

2. *Strict Products Liability*. Under tort law (or under the Restatement [Second] of Torts), someone who sells a product in a defective condition that is unreasonably dangerous to the user or consumer is subject to liability for any physical harm caused thereby if (i) the seller is engaged in the business of selling that type of product, (ii) it is expected to and does reach the consumer without substantial change in the condition in which it was sold, and (iii) the defect proximately caused the injury. The defect in the product may be (i) a design defect, (ii) a manufacturing defect, or (iii) a defect in the warnings given to the user. Here, Deep Quest is engaged in the business of selling dive tanks. The lining of the tank was expected to and did reach Ned in the condition in which it was sold. Apparently the defect proximately caused the injury. If Ned argues that use of the lining was a design defect, he will have to prove lack of ordinary care. If he argues that it was a manufacturing defect, he does not need to prove negligence. Therefore, Ned can argue that Deep Quest is liable to him in strict products liability.

3. *Warranty*. Under the Uniform Commercial Code as adopted in.[state], where the seller is a merchant in goods of that kind, a warranty that the goods be merchantable is implied in a contract for their sale. The warranty is that the goods will at least be such as are fit for the ordinary purposes for which such goods are used. Here, Deep Quest is a merchant in dive tanks. It therefore warrants that the tanks are at least such as are fit for the ordinary purposes, here, deep sea diving, for which such goods are used. It must also give such warnings as are required by the product's risks. Therefore, [subject to state law on the privity required for suits in warranty] Ned can assert a case in warranty against Deep Quest.

B. Against DIPS Supply

1. *Negligence*. Under the tort law of [state], the elements of negligence are duty of care, breach of duty, cause-in-fact, proximate cause, and injury. Here, DIPS owed a duty to Ned of reasonable care. It arguably breached that duty in two ways, first, by not following its policy of requiring two instructors for deep water checkout dives and, second, on a theory of *respondeat superior*, by Mike Nelson's allowing Ned to separate himself from his group. If Ned argues that DIPS's breach of duty was the cause-in-fact of his injuries, he will be subject to the defenses discussed below. Likewise, with regard to DIPS's breach of its duty to him being the proximate cause of his injuries. As to his having suffered injuries, the last element, the fact pattern does not permit dispute. In addition to asserting the liability of DIPS in negligence for the breaches of duty just discussed, Ned may assert that DIPS breached its duty in not removing the defective depth gauge from its inventory of rental equipment and having the gauge either replaced or repaired.

2. *Strict Products Liability and Warranty*. DIPS was in the distribution chain to Ned, and he should therefore include DIPS as a defendant in the strict products liability and warranty actions.

C. Against Mike Nelson

1. *Negligence*. Under the law of this jurisdiction, the elements of negligence are as stated above. Ned may assert that Nelson breached his duty of care in several ways. First, he failed to go after Ned and return him to the group. Second, he failed to comply with DIPS's "two instructors" policy. Third, if he was implicated in the decision to use the faulty depth gauge, he would be personally liable, along with the dive shop.

II. Cross-Claims and Defenses

A. Cross-Claims
Each of the defendants could claim that the conduct of one or more of the others was in fact the proximate cause of the harm that Ned suffered. Each one, therefore, could cross-claim against each of the others. For strategic reasons, however, they might decide not to do so.

B. Defenses
All of the defendants will argue that they were not negligent and that their conduct was not a proximate cause of Ned's injuries.

1. *Deep Quest.* Deep Quest will argue that the coating on its product was not the proximate cause of Ned's injuries. Instead, he suffered from nitrogen narcosis as a result of (i) the improper reading on his depth gauge and (ii) his own negligence.

2. *DIPS.* As to the action in strict products liability, DIPS will argue that it was only in the chain of distribution and that it was not responsible for design or manufacturing defects. As to the action in negligence, DIPS will argue that nothing it or its employees did or failed to do was the proximate cause for Ned's injuries. DIPS will attempt to show that Ned's condition resulted from the eroding liner inside the tank and not from excessive depth. It will argue that Mike's allowing Ned to separate from the group was not the proximate cause of Ned's injuries, since the toxic effect would have occurred wherever Ned was, regardless of how many instructors were present, and at any depth.

In response, Ned will argue that these arguments cut the other way, against Mike Nelson and DIPS for not preventing Ned from leaving the group.

3. *Mike Nelson.* Mike Nelson will raise the same defenses as DIPS. He will claim, in addition, that Ned was negligent in leaving the group, and that Ned's own negligence was the proximate cause of his injuries.

C. Other defenses

1. *Statutes of Limitations.* [State statutes of limitations on negligence, breach of warranty under the Uniform Commercial Code, and strict products liability differ. It may well be, however, that the statutes of limitations on all of Ned's causes of action have already run.]

2. *Notice under the Uniform Commercial Code.* Under the U.C.C., where tender has been accepted, the buyer must notify the seller of breach of warranty within a reasonable time or be barred from any remedy. Where the buyer is not a merchant, the "reasonable time" may be longer than where he is. Defendants will in any event assert that Ned did not give sufficiently prompt notice and that recovery in breach of warranty is therefore barred.

Why Your Outline Must Contain Only Rules of Law

- Most bar examination essay questions are relatively straightforward. If they were not relatively straightforward, it would be impossible for the bar examiners to grade so many of them in a short period of time. The outline containing only rules of law reflects the simplicity of the examination.

- The bar examiners are looking for legal reasoning that applies black-letter law to a statement of facts. That is why the outline must contain only rules of law. Every section of the essay must set out a rule of law and then apply it to the facts.

- You must write an outline that contains only rules of law because that way you will simplify the task of taking the examination. Once you have set out the required number of rules of law on your outline, you know that you can write the essay. All you have to do is add the *Application* and *Conclusion*.

- Isolating the rules of law on your outline will make it clear to you whether or not you have enough rules of law to write a passing essay.

- Writing a simple outline containing only rules of law helps you to plan your time. If your state bar examination has essays with four main points of law, and you have, by some chance, only ten minutes left in which to write, you will be able to write a complete, successful essay. All you have to do is to put more than one rule of law (that is, more than one statement beginning with UNDER) into each paragraph.

- Perhaps most compelling is the observation that if your outline shows a list of rules of law, it will look as much as possible like the grader's scoresheet. Your essay becomes a means of transmission from your outline to the grader's checklist. If your outline mirrors the grader's checklist, you will assuredly succeed on the essay part of the bar examination.

Errors to avoid

Avoid writing facts in your outline, instead of just rules of law:

Wrong: It is negligence if Jones tripped Smith.

Right: The elements of negligence are duty of care, breach of that duty, actual cause, proximate cause, and harm.

Avoid writing conclusions in your outline, instead of just rules of law:

Wrong: Jones will be liable in negligence.

Right: The elements of negligence are duty of care, breach of that duty, actual cause, proximate cause, and harm.

Avoid writing questions or issues in your outline, instead of just rules of law:

Wrong: The issue is whether Jones was negligent.

Right: The elements of negligence are duty of care, breach of that duty, actual cause, proximate cause, and harm.

Putting It All Together

This chapter traces the essay-writing process for one question (a New York question) from start to finish, from interpretation of the interrogatory, through outlining, to writing. It includes commentary on bar candidates' answers to the question.

Each essay in the New York State Bar Examination includes five or six principal rules of law. That is, the candidate must write five or six major paragraphs. The question we study in this chapter is the one analyzed in part in an earlier chapter. This time, we take it from analysis of the call of the question to the finished product.

Essay Question

S is a manufacturer of men's suits, and P is a retailer of men's clothing. On November 12, 1984, P telephoned S and placed an order for 200 men's suits of assorted sizes, at a price of $75 per suit, to be delivered by S to P on December 3, 1984, payment being due 10 days after delivery. P had not previously dealt with S.

Later that same day, S mailed to P a form entitled "Acknowledgement of Order", which was not signed by S but had S's name printed thereon and which read as follows:

> "P's order of November 12, 1984 accepted for 200 men's suits, assorted sizes, $75 each, delivery on December 3, 1984, payment due 10 days after delivery, interest of 1-1/4% per month charged on payments made after 10 days. Any dispute arising hereunder shall be submitted to arbitration, pursuant to the rules of the American Arbitration Association, and such arbitration shall be the exclusive remedy to resolve any such dispute."

There had been no prior discussion between P and S of any provision for interest or for arbitration.

P received S's "Acknowledgement of Order" form on November 13. There was no further communication between P and S until November 26, when P telephoned S and stated that, because he had overestimated his holiday season business, he was canceling his order. S thereupon told P that the 200 suits which P had ordered were ready for delivery to P, and that if P canceled his order, P would be liable for damages for breach of contract. P's response was that there was no contract between P and S and therefore no breach of contract by P, and P thereupon terminated the telephone conversation.

Later that same day, S notified P in writing that because P had canceled his order, S intended to resell the 200 suits for P's account and hold P liable for any damages that S might suffer. Despite due diligence, S was unable to find another purchaser for the 200 suits until January 15, 1985. On that day, acting in good faith, S resold the suits to a department store for $50 per suit, the highest price which S could reasonably obtain. Prior to the sale to the department store, S had incurred warehouse charges for storing the suits.

S claims that he has the right to recover damages against P for breach of contract, including interest at the rate of 1-1/4% per month, and to proceed by arbitration to recover such damages. P denies that S has any such rights.

(a) What rights, if any, does S have to recover damages for breach of contract against P, and what damages, if any, including interest, are recoverable by S?

(b) What rights, if any, does S have to proceed by arbitration to enforce his claims against P, and what procedural remedies, if any, are available to P if S proceeds by arbitration?

Step 1. Use the interrogatory to structure the outline.

Following is the interrogatory of this bar examination question:

(a) What rights, if any, does S have to recover damages for breach of contract against P, and what damages, if any, including interest, are recoverable by S?

(b) What rights, if any, does S have to proceed by arbitration to enforce his claims against P, and what procedural remedies, if any, are available to P if S proceeds by arbitration?

You should write six numbers, equally and widely spaced, along the left-hand margin rule of the scrap paper you are using for your outline:

1.
2.
3.
4.
5.
6.

First Interrogatory. To the *left* of the numbers on the outline, write the "issues," the topics of the principal rules of law you will put into the outline. The first part of the first interrogatory here asks *what rights S has to recover damages for breach of contract against P*. Since "rights" is plural, it is safe to assume that the first several numbers of the outline will deal with the basis of S's right to recover for breach of contract.

The second part of the first interrogatory asks *what damages, if any, including interest, are recoverable by S*. Treatment of damages will probably require one paragraph. Since interest is one element of damages, and usually a relatively minor point, it will probably be part of that same paragraph, rather than taking its own paragraph. Accordingly, it is probably safe to assume that the "damages" issue will take up only one principal paragraph.

At this point, the outline will look like this:

(S's rts. breach/K)   1.

2.

3.

(S's dmgs. › int.)   4.

5.

6.

(Since the outline is strictly for your own use, you should feel free to abbreviate and code it in any way that is meaningful to you. In the essay itself, you must formally spell out all words except those conventionally abbreviated in legal writing.)

Second Interrogatory. The first part of the second interrogatory asks *what rights S has to proceed by arbitration to enforce his claims against P*. Again, "rights" is plural. However, experience has shown that the last interrogatory in a series of bar examination essay question interrogatories is usually a mop-up interrogatory, with fewer principal paragraphs than earlier interrogatories. Accordingly, place "rights to arb" to the left of one number on your outline.

The second part of the second interrogatory asks *what procedural remedies, if any, are available to P if S proceeds by arbitration*. Although "remedies" is plural, suggesting that you should search for two or more remedies, this is clearly a "mop-up" question, requiring no more than one principal paragraph.

The outline now looks like this:

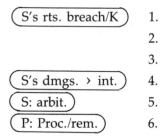

(If you discover, in the course of expanding and filling out your outline, that you have misjudged the number of paragraphs required by a part of the interrogatory, just scratch out the numbers and renumber the paragraphs appropriately.)

At this point you still have not read the fact pattern. Even without reading the fact pattern, however, the question is now intelligible. The bar examination essay question is no longer a monster coming around the corner with its guns blazing. It is, at the most, six separate short-answer paragraphs. It is six separate parts. You know that you can handle the question if you can come up with five or six principal rules of law that fit the parts of the question.

Step 2. Outline the bar examination essay question.

As you read the bar examination fact pattern, you decide which area or areas of law the examiners are testing and draw on your bank of mental subject outlines for the basic questions in that area, or areas, of law.

Here, the question is clearly a contracts–U.C.C. question. The basic outline, by points to be answered, is roughly as follows:

1. Is there a contract?

2. Is it under the U.C.C.?

3. Is it enforceable? (Does it fall, for example, under the statute of frauds?)

4. Is it taken out of the statute of frauds?

5. Does the Battle of the Forms section of the U.C.C. apply?

6. What remedies are available for breach?

Contract formation is the first topic. The candidate must *always* make sure that there is an offer, acceptance, and consideration. Here, as is normally true, you must state for the examiners that S and P formed a contract. Spell out, in your answer, that the December 3, 1984, telephone conversation was an offer, which P accepted on his

"Acknowledgment of Order" form. The first item in the outline, accordingly, is *Formation of Contract.*

Reading the fact pattern in this New York State Bar Examination essay question, next note that the contract that S and P formed on the telephone ("P telephoned S and placed an order. . . .") was for the sale of goods of $500 or more. In fact, it was for $1,500 ("200 men's suits . . . at a price of $75 per suit"). The U.C.C. statute of frauds requires that a contract for the sale of goods of $500 or more be in writing, and signed by the party to be charged, in order to be enforceable. Under the U.C.C., however, the requirements of the statute of frauds can be satisfied in any of several ways, including a written confirmation of a telephone conversation. Between merchants, if the party who receives the confirmation has reason to know its contents, the written confirmation satisfies the requirements of the statute of frauds unless written notice of objection is given by the recipient within ten days of receipt.

These rules will form the basis of the second paragraph, or the first two paragraphs, of the essay answer. The outline for the answer, with all of the rules written out in full, should look approximately like the following example. (Time is at a premium on the bar examination. You should therefore abbreviate the rules on your outline. You should, of course, write them out in full on your answer.)

(S's rts. breach/K)   2. Under the Uniform Commercial Code as adopted in [state] a contract for the sale of goods is governed by Article 2. Under the UCC statute of frauds, a contract for the sale of goods of $500 or more must be in writing, signed by the party to be charged, in order to be enforceable. The requirements of the statute of frauds may, however, be satisfied by a written confirmation of a telephone conversation which, between merchants, satisfies the statute of frauds if not objected to within 10 days.

    3.

(S's dmgs./int.)   4.

(S: arbit.)   5.

(P: Proc./rem.)   6.

The next question is whether the written confirmation is in accordance with the contract. Here, it is not. The candidate is not told whether "payment due 10 days after delivery" is in accordance with the custom of the trade. In any event, it appears to be of minor importance. However, two other terms are presumably additional to or different from the original agreement:

[I]nterest of 1¼% per month charged on payments made after 10 days. Any dispute arising hereunder shall be submitted to *arbitration*, pursuant to the rules of the American Arbitration Association, and such arbitration shall be the exclusive remedy to resolve any such dispute. (Italics added.)

While the inclusion of interest is minor under the U.C.C., the inclusion of an arbitration clause is a material alteration in the contract. Following is the applicable law, which you would note as the third main point on your outline:

    3. Under the U.C.C. as adopted in [state], between merchants additional terms which are included in the contract become part of the contract if there is no objection within a reasonable time, unless they materially

alter the contract, or the offer expressly limits acceptance to the terms of the offer.

The next point on the outline is what damages, if any, including interest, S is entitled to ("S's dmgs./int.").

You, as a bar candidate, may know and be able to list all of the seller's remedies under the Uniform Commercial Code. You will in any event recognize that in this situation the seller, S, is entitled to resell the suits in a commercially reasonable manner and to recover as damages the difference between the contract price and the resale price. Where the resale is by private sale, the seller must give the buyer "reasonable notification of his intention to resell."

These points will accordingly appear on the outline. They are written out in full below, for illustration. Under the pressure of time of examination conditions, you will usually write in the outline only one or two words to indicate each rule, not the entire rule, as here:

4. Under the Uniform Commercial Code, the seller's remedies include, under appropriate circumstances, stopping the goods in transit, suing for the price, asking for further assurances, retrieving the goods, retaining the deposit or 20%, whichever is less, suing for lost profits, and exercising the right to reclaim goods from an insolvent buyer. Where the seller resells the goods, he may do so in a commercially reasonable manner, at public or private sale, and recover as damages the difference between the contract price and the resale price, together with incidental damages. Where the resale is made by private sale, the seller must give "reasonable notification of his intention to resell." The seller need not show that the resale was made at the market price where he makes the resale in good faith and in a "commercially reasonable" manner.

If you are thoroughly familiar with these rules, and as a bar candidate you should be, you will simply list the names of the rules or make notes to yourself to remind yourself of the applicable rules as you prepare your outline, Your outline, then, might contain the following as item number four:

4. Seller's remedies. Resale of goods: measure of damages. Notification of private sale. Need not show resale was market price where commercially reasonable manner.

The next item on the outline is S's right, if any, to proceed by arbitration. This has in fact already been covered by the discussion of the applicability of the rules governing the "Battle of the Forms." You have a choice. You may write an additional paragraph, restating the conclusion regarding arbitration so as to conform to the order of the questions in the bar examination interrogatory. More economically, you will include reference to your conclusions regarding S's not having a right to arbitration in the paragraph in which you treat P's procedural remedies. That part of the outline will appear approximately as follows:

5. Under [state] law, the party opposing arbitration may move for a stay of arbitration. Alternatively, he may oppose the other party's application for an order compelling arbitration.

Outline with Notations of Rules

(K form.)

1. Formation of contract. Evidence of agreement. U.C.C.

(S's rts. breach/K)

2. Statute of Frauds. Merchants memo exception.

3. U.C.C. Battle of the Forms.

(S's dmg./int.)

4. Seller's remedies. Resale of goods; measure of damages. Notification of private sale. Need not show resale was market price where commercially reasonable manner.

(S: arbit.)
(P: Proc./rem.)

5. Opposition to arbitration: move for stay; oppose application for order.

Notice, again, that this outline contains *no* conclusions, and *no* applications of rules to facts. It should be clear at this point that a good, strong notation of the applicable rules of law provides the best possible framework for writing the essay answers.

Step 3. Write the essay.

Go ahead and try writing this essay right now. Do not expect a perfect product. A first effort is just that—a first effort. As you proceed through this book, writing more and more bar essay answers, you will find your skill and fluency improving.

The following are essays bar candidates wrote in class in response to this same New York State essay question. The students were instructed to use the method you have just learned. It was the first full essay they wrote employing this method. Accordingly, their application of the method is imperfect, just as yours will be. Read these essays *after* writing yours. Comments appear in the right-hand margin; you can learn from them.

Sample Essay I

An Enforceable Contract Was Formed Between S and P

To be an enforceable contract under New York law, there must be an offer, an acceptance, and consideration. Moreover, there must be compliance with the statute of frauds. Here, P's telephone conversation with S on December 3, 1984, was an offer, which P accepted that same day by P's "Acknowledgment of Order" form. Moreover, this form recited consideration of $75 per suit. Therefore, if it complied with the statute of frauds, there is an enforceable contract between P and S.

To be enforceable under the U.C.C., contracts for the sale of goods valued at over $500 must be in writing and signed by the party to be charged with breach of that contract. Here, the contract between P and S called for the delivery of goods valued at over $500. Although the contract was in writing, it was not signed by P, the party to be charged with its breach. However, the contract satisfied the U.C.C.'s statute of frauds because it falls within the Merchant's Memorandum Rule.

The essay starts with the basic question in the Contract/UCC field: Is there a contract?

The use of the Model Paragraph format is excellent: *Under—Here—Therefore.*

However, the "Acknowledgment" was enough to constitute "acceptance" under contract law, but not enough to satisfy the statute of frauds.

Here, the writer correctly states the statute of frauds provision that is applicable.

The writer correctly applies the statute of frauds to the fact pattern.

The writer is correct that the contract satisfies the statute of frauds because of the Merchant's Memo Rule.

Under the Merchant's Memorandum Rule, a contract satisfies the statute of frauds if an oral agreement for the sale of goods occurs and the terms of that agreement are incorporated into a writing by a merchant to that agreement, and sent to the other party. If that other party fails to object to that writing within 10 days, the merchant's memorandum satisfies the statute of frauds. Here, S reduced the terms of the oral agreement to a writing and sent it to P on an "Acknowledgment of Order" form. P did not object to this writing within 10 days of receiving it. Therefore, the statute of frauds was satisfied and there was a binding contract.

Under New York law, as between merchants, additional terms contained in the memorandum become part of the contract unless:
  A. The offeror expressly objects to those additional terms within a reasonable time after receiving the acceptance,
  B. The offer expressly conditions acceptance of the offer on these terms,
  or
  C. The acceptance materially *alters* the terms of the offer.

The Acceptance of the Offer Did Not Materially Alter the Terms of the Offer

Under New York law, including the U.C.C., an acceptance materially alters the terms of an offer if it includes:
  A. A clause requiring a party to submit to jurisdiction in a particular court.
  B. A change in the statute of limitations.
  C. Alteration in the normal risk of loss.
  D. Arbitration as the exclusive method for resolving disputes, where that is not the standard method in the industry.
  E. Alteration in express or implied warranties.

Here, the acceptance called for disputes to be submitted to arbitration. Because it can be inferred that arbitration is the standard for settling disputes in the garment industry, the provision for arbitration is not a material alteration of the offer, and it will become part of the contract. Likewise, because the provision for interest did not materially alter the terms of the offer it became part of the contract.

S May Receive Both Incidental Damages and Loss of Bargain Damages

Under the U.C.C., the non-breaching party can seek damages for the loss of the bargain and incidental damages caused by the breach. Here, S can seek damages for P's breach. Those damages will include the costs incurred to store the goods in the warehouse. Also recoverable by S will be the difference

---

The essay correctly states and applies the Merchant's Memo *Rule*. The paragraph is an excellent example of the Model Paragraph form.

Excellent, thorough, point-for-point *Application* of the rule of law to the facts in the fact pattern.

Clear and satisfying *Conclusion*.

The essay provides an excellent statement of the Battle of the Forms provisions that apply between merchants.

Note that the list is in a vertical column. This is the correct way to set out a list, so that the grader can see how many items appear.

This conclusion is set out clearly, and underlined. That is good. Unfortunately, the conclusion is wrong. Clarity, however, will help the writer to achieve a good grade.

The *Rule* is correctly stated. It is, again, a list (illustrative, in this case, not exhaustive) of types of contract provisions that constitute material alteration of the original agreement. It is right to set out such a list vertically.

Correct *Application*.

The writer introduces here a rule, described as an inference, for which there is no basis in the fact pattern. Do not draw the inference that because something occurs in the fact pattern it must be (i) standard procedure or (ii) self-explanatory. Do not assume anything. If you do assume something say that you are *assuming* it. The writer here assumed that arbitration must be standard. He had no basis for that assumption. It made him come to a conclusion that was simply wrong.

Good, clear statement of *Conclusion*.

The essay sets out a clear statement of the *Rule* for S's damages. The writer could have included a list of the alternative remedies available to the seller under the U.C.C.

between the price P agreed to pay, to wit, $75 per suit, and the lesser amount P was able to sell the suits for, to wit, $50 per suit. Moreover, S will be able to recover interest at 1-¼% per month.

The essay clearly *applies* the Rule to the fact pattern, using the numbers.

In fact, S may recover only the statutory rate of interest.

S May Proceed by Arbitration to Enforce His Rights

Under New York law parties to a contract containing an arbitration clause will be compelled to arbitrate disputes covered by that clause, provided the clause is *explicit*. Here, the contract between S and P clearly called for the arbitration of disputes arising from the contract. This arbitration clause was clear and explicit. Therefore, S may proceed by arbitration to enforce his claim against P.

This is a clear statement of the *Conclusion*. Because of the candidate's unjustified assumption that arbitration was the custom of the garment industry, this conclusion is wrong.

Simple and plain statement of procedure.

As throughout this essay, this is a fine application of the Model Paragraph format.

P May Petition the Supreme Court to Stay the Arbitration Proceeding

Under New York, law, a party may petition the Supreme Court to stay arbitration if the contract did not clearly call for arbitration or the dispute is not within the arbitration clause.

Note: In New York State, the Supreme Court is a court of original jurisdiction. The highest court is the Court of Appeals.

Sample Essay II

Conclusions

(a) S can recover for breach of contract and can recover $5000 plus incidental costs (including warehousing and resale costs).

(b) (1) S will not be able to enforce the arbitration provision; (2) P can move for a stay of arbitration and the court should sustain the motion.

(a)(1) Valid Contract

Under the U.C.C., Article II, a valid offer and acceptance as well as consideration are conditions precedent to a valid contract. In addition, the party to be charged must sign the agreement.

Here, there was a valid offer by P to S and a valid acceptance by S, who confirmed the order with an "Acknowledgement of Order" form. Although the party to be charged did not sign in this circumstance, it is not a material deficiency that will defeat the contract.

Therefore, there exists a valid contract between P and S that is enforceable at law.

Essay begins with responses to the examiners' interrogatories. This is what should appear on the first page of the test answer booklet.

Answer to (a) ought to state that there is an enforceable sales contract. That to (b)(1) should state that S has no right to arbitration.

Essay properly opens with the *basic* issue: Is there a contract? "Conditions precedent" is used for "elements."

The writer has stated part of the statute of frauds, as though it were an issue of contract formation.

The writer has not laid down the basic rules, including the rule for operation of buyer's failure to respond to the "Acknowledgment" as adequate *acceptance*. The writer has also not stated the applicable *statute of frauds*. Nor has the writer stated the *merchant's memo exception*, satisfying the statute of frauds. Instead, the writer skips straight from the existence of the contract to a conclusion that it is enforceable.

(2) Breach of Contract

Under U.C.C. Article II, a breach of contract by the purchaser of goods is measured by the difference between the contract price and the proceeds upon resale plus any incidental resale costs or warehousing costs. In addition, the party in breach must be contacted when the seller of those goods resells at a private sale.

Here, the damages would be calculated as follows: The contract price ($15,000) minus the resale price ($10,000), which is $5,000, plus the warehousing costs and any other selling costs of the seller. Although the purchaser in breach was not contacted before the sale, it is not material here, due to the good faith on the part of the seller.

Therefore, the seller, S, will receive $5,000 + incidental costs, including warehousing.

(b)(1) Arbitration

Under U.C.C., an arbitration clause is a material contract term and is not enforceable unless agreed upon by the offeree. (Or the merchants had previously done business and an arbitration clause was an industry standard.)

Here, the parties had never done business together, and there was no assent on the part of P to accept the arbitration provision.

Therefore, the arbitration clause will not be enforceable and the provision will be discarded by the court.

(b)(2)(A) S's Procedure to Enforce ARB

Under the rules of civil procedure, S can make a motion to compell arbitration. The Court will review the contract and decide whether the arbitration provision is enforceable.

Here, based upon the additional material term "arbitration" being added without agreement by the party to be charged, the Ct will find the clause unenforceable.

Therefore, the motion by S will be dismissed.

(b)(2)(B) P's Motion to Stay ARB

Under the rules of civil procedure, P can make a motion to the court to stay arbitration based upon the invalidity of the clause.

Here, because the arbitration clause was a material change, not agreed upon by the party to be charged, the arbitration clause is invalid.

Therefore, the court will sustain P's motion.

This section of the essay is much better. It correctly states the rule for damages upon resale, and it correctly states the rule requiring notification of a private sale. The answer would have been fuller had the writer summarized the U.C.C. seller's remedies.

Essay correctly applies the rule for damages, doing the arithmetic, which is correct, and the right way to write such an essay.

Essay is simply wrong that no notification was given to the buyer: S need only give notice of intention to resell, which he did.

There is no treatment at all of the interest provision in the "Acknowledgment."

This essay has delayed discussion of the additional terms in the "Acknowledgement" form until explicitly required by the examination interrogatory. Unfortunately, the writer does not place his rule regarding the arbitration clause, correctly described as a "material term," where it belongs, namely in the context of the more general rule of the "Battle of the Forms" in U.C.C. sec. 2-207. Furthermore, to have an arbitration clause as an industry standard is not the same as the merchants' having previously done business.

The word "compel" is misspelled.

Motions are not dismissed, they are denied. It is important to use legal terms correctly.
This essay has done an excellent job, throughout, of treating each issue in Model Paragraphs. The usefulness of the technique is especially clear here, where there is relatively little to say about P's procedural remedies. Using the form *Under—Here—Therefore* produces a lawyer-like paragraph.

Sample Essay III

a)

Under contract law, a valid contract requires an offer, acceptance, and consideration.

The Uniform Commercial Code (U.C.C.) governs any contract for the sale of goods involving 1 or more merchants. The Statute of Frauds requires that contracts for the sale of goods for $500 or more be in writing and be signed by the party to be charged.

Here, where P telephoned S and placed an order and S mailed P an acknowledgment form, a valid contract was formed. Since the contract was for an amount exceeding $500, it must be and was in writing. The U.C.C. holds that as between merchants a printed acknowledgment form is a sufficient writing. P & S were clearly merchants.

Under the U.C.C., when a buyer breaches a contract, the seller has certain available remedies. The seller can:
1) stop delivery and reject the goods;
2) sue on the price;
3) demand assurances;
4) resell the goods;
5) keep part of the buyer's deposit;
6) sue for lost profits;
7) exercise the right to reclaim goods from an insolvent buyer.

Here, S has opted to resell the suits on the open market. Under the U.C.C., when a party learns of the other party's breach, the nonbreaching party must attempt to mitigate damages.

The seller may "cover" and the remedy would be the difference between the contract price and the resale price, plus the consequential damages.

Here, 200 men's suits at $75 is $14,100. S resold the suits for $50 each, making only a $10,500 profit. From the $10,200 the additional costs for storage are subtracted. Therefore, buyer is liable for the difference between 14,100 and 10,200, which is 3,900, plus the storage costs and any other incidental or consequential damages.

The writer clearly intended to label the parts of the essay, but did not go back, perhaps because of lack of time, to insert the labels. This is a significant omission.

Essay starts with good laying out of basic rules of law, contract formation, applicability of the U.C.C., statute of frauds applying to the sale of goods.

Essay does a good job of *Application:* tying facts to law.

Courts "hold;" the U.C.C. "provides." In fact, P and S *were* clearly merchants, but it would have been better to have quoted the U.C.C. definition of a "merchant," and applied it to them.

Essay skips straight from formation of the contract to seller's remedies for breach, delaying handling the Battle of the Forms issues. Excellent job of setting out in full the basics: the list of seller's remedies under the U.C.C.

Good, clear *Application* of the general rule for available seller's remedies. Note, however, that "open market" is an ambiguous term. It suggests that the writer might not have absorbed the fact that the seller resold the suits at a private sale, after giving notice of his intention to resell. Essay correctly states the applicable rule for the measure of damages.

Unfortunately, the writer made an elementary mistake in computation. It is not true that "200 men's suits at $75 is $14,100." It is $15,000. Furthermore, the difference between the contract price and the resale price is simply not the seller's *profit.* In addition, what starts out as $10,500 inexplicably becomes $10,200. The writer is also confused in saying that storage costs are *subtracted.* Although the paragraph is chaotic, the writer will receive some credit for effort to do the arithmetic.

b)

Under the U.C.C., a merchant cannot unilaterally arrange to arbitrate any disagreement regarding the contract. Under the U.C.C. merchant memo rule, additional or different terms will alter the contract except if:

(1) both parties are merchants and the party did not object within a reasonable time;
(2) the contract was conditioned on full adherence to the original contract terms;
(3) an arbitration clause is present.

Here, since an arbitration clause will alter a contract, the unilateral incorporation of the arbitration term by S will enable P to refuse to conform to the addition of the clause.

Under the U.C.C., when 1 party unilaterally adds an additional or different term, the other party has the procedural remedy of moving to set aside this term.

Here, since S has already included the arbitration term without P's consent, P can go to the court and ask that the arbitration term be set aside, thus, not rescinding the contract in its entirety.

This is in fact not the merchant's memo rule, but rather the Battle of the Forms rule, sec. 2-207. The essay presents a garbled version of the rule, with the essentials present, but in peculiar relations to one another.

There is no treatment of the interest provision in the "Acknowledgment."

One does not "conform to the addition of a clause."

The writer appears to have made up a procedural rule to provide a route to the conclusion he wishes to reach. As a makeshift, this rule, while overbroad by several orders of magnitude, is at least serviceable.

While this essay starts out very well, its grip on the U.C.C. loosens, and the final sections are not lawyer-like.

Sample Essay IV

I. Rights of S to Recover Damages

A valid contract requires offer, acceptance and consideration. Any detriment to the promisee or benefit to the promisor is consideration. A contract which is made between one or more merchants for the sale of goods is governed by Article 2 of the U.C.C. A Contract for the sale of gds. of $500 or more, must be in writing and signed by the pty. to be charged in order to comply with the statute of frauds.

In a K between 2 merchants an exchange of memos will be an enforceable K. Any additional terms become part of the contract if not objected to within 10 days or if not a material alteration.

Here, P and S had an enforceable sales contract. There was a valid offer, acceptance and consideration. P is in breach of the contract for the 200 suits as between S and himself.

Label at top of first section reflects wording of interrogatory, so accomplishes purpose of labels: helpful to the grader.

Essays begins with the basic question in the contracts/U.C.C. area: Is there a contract? That is the correct first question to ask. Note, however, that while there is a definition for "consideration," there is no definition provided for "acceptance." However, the existence of an effective "acceptance" under the U.C.C. is in fact an issue. P's nonresponse to the "Acknowledgment of Order" constitutes an "acceptance." Otherwise, this essay treats the applicable *Rules* in the correct order: Applicability of the U.C.C.; statute of frauds; merchant's memo exception to the statute of frauds. It does not, however, state that the rule regarding merchant's memoranda is in fact a way of satisfying the statute of frauds. It thus misses the opportunity to list all of the ways a contract under the U.C.C. may satisfy the statute of frauds.

The *Application* is hurried and conclusory.

II. Damages which are recoverable by S

In a breach of contract the Seller may recover the K price *plus* the costs incurred for storage provided he has "covered" by selling the gds. and mitigating damages.

Here, S, acting in good faith, mitigated dam. by reselling the gods. at a lower price to a dept. store. S resold the goods at below the K price and received an additional $5,000.

Therefore, S is entitled to recover the K price minus the resale price, or $5,000 plus the costs incurred for storage of the suits.

III. S's rights to proceed by arbitration

An additional term in a contract which would force the other party to submit to arbitration is an additional term which is a material alteration of the contract. The parties need not submit to arbitration.

Here, S's additional term which states that disputes will be submitted to arbitration is therefore unenforceable.

P may move for a stay.

Again, the essay labels the sections appropriately, using the wording of the interrogatory.

The statement of the rule providing for the seller's damages is garbled. It does not make sense. It would make sense if it read: "may recover the contract price *minus the resale price* plus the costs incurred . . .," etc.

This essay employs abbreviations. *Do not abbreviate on the bar examination*.

The writer is stumbling around looking for how to describe the measure of damages, and the application to the facts. The *Application* would be simple, however, had the *Rule* been stated correctly.

The *Conclusion* is entirely correct. Finally, a safe landing.

The essay never states the Battle of the Forms rules of the U.C.C., sec. 2-207. Thus, the *Rule* in this section, which is in fact a subordinate provision in the Battle of the Forms rules, is stated out of context. The essay accordingly skips over *Application* of the Rule, and jumps to "The parties need not submit to arbitration." The sentence beginning with *Here*, is thus just a repeated *Conclusion*. This section of the essay is conclusory because it does not observe Model Paragraph form.

Summary

Here is how you put it all together in writing the bar examination.

First, on your scrap paper, write the numbers, from 1 to 2, or from 1 to 4, or from 1 to 6, corresponding to the number of principal points of law normally found in the essays on your state's bar examination.

Next, read the interrogatory of the question. Break it down into as many parts as there are numbers on your outline, and make a note to the *left* of each number on your outline indicating the topic it will deal with.

Outline

Negl.	1.
Summary J/ment	2.
Warranty	3.
M/Dismiss	4.
Damages	5.

Read and reread the fact pattern. Make sure you understand it.

Write the rule of law that will decide the issue to the right of each number on your outline. Do not write facts. Do not write conclusions. Do not write a statement of the issues. Write the main rule of law you will need. Read the question, again.

When you have a rule of law for each number on your outline, go back and add higher-level rules of law (constitutional principles, more general rules, mnemonics), for each number on your outline.

Schematically, your outline will look like this:

		(Higher level rule)
Topic	1.	MAIN RULE OF LAW
		(Definitions, exceptions, corollaries)
		(Higher level rule)
Topic	2.	MAIN RULE OF LAW
		(Definitions, exceptions, corollaries)
		(Higher level rule)
Topic	3.	MAIN RULE OF LAW
		(Definitions, exceptions, corollaries)

Now turn your attention to your bluebook. Your time should be about halfway up. You should have a full outline of rules of law for your essay. Now all you have to do is fill in the application of that law to the facts, and spell out the conclusions.

Leave the first page of the bluebook blank. You will come back to it at the end, and add your short-form conclusions to the simple interrogatories on the essay question

(e.g., "1. A may recover from B in negligence; 2. The court will grant A summary judgment," etc.)

When completed, page 1 of your bluebook will look like this:

1. Short Response to First Interrogatory.

2. Short Response to Second Interrogatory.

3. Short Response to Third Interrogatory.

Go to the next page of the bluebook. Halfway down, write the word "Under," and write out the rules of law you have next to the number 1 on your outline. Start your next sentence "Here," and carefully apply the law to the facts. Start your last sentence "Therefore," and draw your conclusion.

Go to the next page of the bluebook. Halfway down, write the word "Under," and write out the rules of law you have next to the number 2 on your outline. Complete this page in the same way as the first page.

And so on, for each number on your outline.

Now go back to the first page of the bluebook, and write in the short responses to the interrogatories on the examination paper.

Insert labels where needed, e.g., "*Negligence*," or "*A v. B*."

Each subsequent page of your bluebook should look like this:

Label

UNDER . . . . Main Rule of Law
HERE, ...
THEREFORE, ...

When the maximum suggested time is up, STOP—no matter what. You have written one successful bar examination essay. Congratulate yourself and go on to the next one.

Good work! Good luck!

Part III

Bar Exam Questions and Essay Answers

Introduction

Part III contains a number of sample bar exam essay questions. These questions offer you the opportunity to practice and perfect your techniques for bar exam essay outlining and writing. Take one question at a time; analyze, outline, apply the Model Paragraph technique, and write a well-organized essay. As you practice, you will find yourself becoming proficient at analyzing and outlining questions in any field of law. With sufficient practice, you may be able to outline without having to write out the whole essay.

The questions have been taken from the bar examinations of eight states, from New York to California. Many of the questions have been chosen from fields such as contracts and real property, where there is a substantial area of agreement among the states. As you write your own answers, consider the laws of the state in which you will be taking your bar exam. Insert the name of your state, and conform your answer to the law and practice of that state.

The bar exam essay questions are followed by a full set of bar exam essay answers. Complete your own outline or essay answer to each question before turning to the answer provided. Keep in mind that the rules of evidence applied in the answers are the Federal Rules of Evidence. Except where otherwise noted, the rules of civil procedure are the Federal Rules of Civil Procedure. In other areas, the answers have usually been based on uniform laws or model codes, the Uniform Probate Code, for example. In several questions in the state section, however, the question itself indicates that New York or California law applies.

All of the answers here are written in Key Outline and Model Paragraph format. The basic structure of each answer is the principal rules of law (the Key Outline). Every paragraph or group of paragraphs is written in the format *(Conclusion)—Rule—Application—Conclusion* (the Model Paragraph).

The answers are sample answers, not model answers. Some are student-written; not all are perfect answers. You can look at any answer, however, and see how many main topics you could have had in your outline, how many rules of law you could have stated, and how you should have applied the law to the facts. In short, you will see how you might have written a better essay. Do not simply glance at an answer and say, "But I didn't know the law," or "I knew that." Take the time to analyze each answer against the question and against your own answer. See how each one is put together. Learn. You may find it helpful to write an answer more than once.

Many answers contain citations to statutes, cases, or reference books. These are strictly for your convenience. The bar examiners do not expect you to include citations (except, perhaps, for mention of a pivotal case like *Miranda*).

Use these essays to master the techniques of legal writing that you will use on the bar examination. Supplement these essays with the essays, if any, that your own bar examiners publish. Once you are admitted, you will use many of the same techniques in your legal practice.

Bar Exam Questions

Question One

Ted Typical entered into a one-year lease with the Building Realty Company, on July 1, 1987, for a two-room apartment at 431 East 48th Street, rent of $1400, payable monthly on the first of the month. When the lease expired, Building said nothing, and neither did Ted. On July 1, 1988, however, Ted paid $1400 to Building Realty Co., as usual. Ted continued to pay his rent monthly on the first of the month, and Building Realty Co. continued to accept it. On August 15, 1989, however, Ted called the Building Co. office and announced that he was moving out on August 25, in order to move to Chicago and enter the University of Chicago Law School, and so he would not pay rent on September 1, 1989, or thereafter.

Your client, Building Realty Co., asks you for a letter explaining whether it can hold Ted liable for the rent for a full one-year period, through June 31, 1990. If that is not possible, it would like to know whether it is at least entitled to the rent for September, 1989.

Question Two

Jacques Henault, a 19-year-old French-Canadian, was wanted for questioning about the murder of a man in Brattleboro, Vermont. In late June, Henault was arrested and arraigned on a charge of breaking and entering in New York. A week later he pleaded guilty to the charge and was sentenced to 90 days in jail. He was represented by a Public Defender at the arraignment, change of plea, and sentencing.

In mid-July, a team of Vermont investigators questioned Henault in the New York jail where he was serving his sentence. At the beginning of the questioning, the investigators informed Henault that he was under suspicion for murder and read him his *Miranda* rights. When asked if he understood his rights, Henault indicated that he did and agreed to waive them. At a break in the questioning, Henault was again informed of his *Miranda* rights and again agreed to waive them. He then confessed to the murder.

Henault later waived extradition and returned to Vermont to stand trial for the murder. His new counsel in Vermont has moved to suppress the confession.

What legal arguments can be made both for and against suppressing the confession, and what are the policy bases for those arguments? Include in your discussion the facts (whether or not set out in the fact pattern) that are crucial to your analysis and explain why.

Question Three

In December, Andy told his Uncle Ed that he had just been accepted to Acme Law School, the same law school Uncle Ed graduated from years ago. He also told Uncle Ed that he planned to start Acme in the fall. One week later, Uncle Ed wrote to Andy:

> I was excited to learn that you have decided to go to law school and that you have chosen Acme. I would like to make things a little easier for you. Since you will attend Acme, I will pay your tuition while you are there.

Andy promptly replied, "Thank you for your generous offer. I had planned on applying for a scholarship or a loan to cover the cost of tuition, but now I won't have to."

Uncle Ed paid the tuition for the first semester, but then had an argument with school officials and told Andy just before the start of the second semester that he would not pay any more money to Acme. It's too late for Andy to apply for financial aid or obtain a loan for the money needed for the second semester's tuition. Andy will ultimately be eligible for aid or a loan to enable him to continue his legal education. However, his applications can't be processed in time to get him the money before the second semester of his first year. Andy does not want to have to sit out that semester.

Question: Discuss whether Andy has an enforceable contract with Uncle Ed.

Question Four

Joe's Bar and Grille was destroyed one night after hours by an explosion. The owner, Mrs. Joe, was accused of criminal arson. At Mrs. Joe's trial the Assistant District Attorney asked the following question, and was provided the following answer:

> "Q: And then what did she say?
> A: She said she left the gas stove on."

With regard to this exchange, briefly discuss *all pertinent* evidentiary issues regarding the admissibility or inadmissibility of the answer in each of the following situations:

1. One of Mrs. Joe's employees, Ed Willard, testified that Mrs. Joe made this statement to him the morning after the fire.
2. Mrs. Joe's six-year-old niece, Nancy, testified that she overheard her aunt say this when Mrs. Joe was talking to someone on the telephone a few days after the fire. (*Do not discuss* any of the issues raised in Part 1.)
3. A fire marshal, Fred Marsh, testified as an expert witness that during his investigation of the fire Mrs. Joe's six-year-old niece told him that Mrs. Joe said this while she was talking to someone on the telephone a few days after the fire. (*Do not discuss* any of the issues raised in 1 or 2.)

4. If in any of the above scenarios Mrs. Joe's counsel does not timely object or move to strike, what would be the consequences if this question and answer are reviewed on appeal? If her counsel timely states "Objection" without stating a specific ground for the objection, what is the effect of such an objection on appeal?

Question Five

Irma Pace was walking along a busy downtown city sidewalk when a wasp landed on her shoulder. Tom Dant, walking behind Irma and a stranger to her, saw that the wasp was about to sting Irma and slapped it with a firm blow. The blow crushed the wasp but startled Irma, causing her to trip and dash her head against a fire hydrant. Her scalp was gashed open, and blood poured from the wound.

Irma Pace brought an action in two counts against Tom Dant. Count One alleged negligence and Count Two alleged battery. After a trial in which evidence was introduced to prove the foregoing facts, Tom Dant moved for a directed verdict. How should the court rule? Write a memorandum decision.

Question Six

Fred Feeder owned a large cattle-feeding operation in Keith County, Nebraska. His feeding operation took place on 1,000 acres of land that he owned. A first mortgage with Keith National Bank covered this property. Fred Feeder also had second and third mortgages on the property as well as various financing arrangements covering the feeding operation with another bank. Fred Feeder encountered financial problems, filed a petition in bankruptcy, and was adjudged a bankrupt by the Bankruptcy Court for the District of Nebraska.

Phil Prior, the attorney for Keith National Bank, filed a complaint to foreclose the first mortgage in the United States District Court for the District of Nebraska and asked that it be transferred to the bankruptcy court, which was handling all of the related financial matters. Sam Second, the attorney representing the bank holding the second and third mortgages, filed a motion to dismiss in the United States district court. Sam argued that a federal bankruptcy court does not have jurisdiction to consider a foreclosure action on land situated in Keith County, Nebraska.

Can the United States district court confer upon the bankruptcy court the ability to consider a real estate foreclosure action? Discuss.

Question Seven

Perelman, a Nebraska resident, brought an action in a Nebraska court to quiet title to certain bottom land situated on the Missouri River. The river forms the boundary between the states of Missouri and Nebraska.

Bryan, a Missouri resident, appeared in the action challenging the jurisdiction of the Nebraska court and also challenging the right of Perelman to have title quieted in his name.

The Nebraska court found that it had jurisdiction because the land was situated in Nebraska. The court quieted title in Perelman. Bryan appealed, but the Supreme Court of Nebraska affirmed the decision of the lower court.

Two months later, Bryan filed suit in a Missouri state court asking the court to take jurisdiction because the land was located in Missouri and to quiet title in the land in him.

The Missouri case was removed to the federal district court, with jurisdiction based on diversity of citizenship. The federal court found that the land was in Missouri.

May the federal district court overturn the ruling of the Nebraska court? State the reasons for your answer.

Question Eight

Lightning from a thunderstorm set fire to a building on the movie set owned and operated by the Cheapo Movie Production Company (Cheapo). The building, a mock castle, was surrounded by a moat filled with water. The cast and filming crew used a bridge as the regular means of traveling across the moat.

A group of five actors from a touring theater company was visiting the castle set. They were not affiliated with Cheapo in any manner and had made a special request to be permitted to visit, which Cheapo had granted, though reluctantly. Several employees of contracting companies constructing the castle under contract with Cheapo were also on the set.

Fire broke out and an alarm sounded.

The five visiting actors and four of the non-Cheapo workers rushed across the bridge to escape the fire. The bridge, though it looked sturdy, was built for temporary use, and it could not support so many people at once. The bridge fell and Hard Worker, an electrician employed by a contractor to work on the set, and Ann Actor, one of the visiting thespians, were badly hurt.

Actor and Worker both sue Cheapo for negligence. Cheapo denies liability and raises appropriate defenses. Before trial, Cheapo moves for summary judgment in each action. All of the foregoing facts are proved by affidavits and admissions.

You are the trial judge. Write a brief memorandum in each action granting or denying each motion, explaining your reasons with care. If you deny a motion, indicate which issues require trial.

Question Nine

One afternoon Alice decided to go shopping at Thrifty's. It was an extremely windy day, and Alice had trouble opening the doors to Thrifty's due to the force of the wind. Nonetheless, Alice finally did get in and eventually bought herself a dress. When she approached the exit door, Alice remembered that the wind was strong that day. She gave the following statement to her attorney regarding her exit:

Q. When you got to that door, what did you do?

A. Well, I pushed the door and just got my foot out. I expected the door to go open and come back like regular doors. I thought, well, I can go out. I pushed the door, and here come a big gust of wind and brought the door back.

Q. At the time the gust of wind came up, were you holding the door open for yourself?

A. Yes.

Q. And did you feel the pressure of the wind against the door?

A. Yes.

Q. Now is the action of the door slowed by any mechanism that you could feel?

A. No. That was what I expected. When the door flew open, like, I expected it to go back like regular doors do.

Q. You expected it to go back slowly?

A. Yes.

Q. What happened to you?

A. It caught my foot.

As a result of the accident, Alice's ankle was broken. She filed suit against Thrifty's alleging the following specific acts of negligence:

1. Permitting the door, which opened into an unprotected and very windy area, to remain for many months without any effective retarder to sudden closing.

2. Failing to repair or replace the retarder thereon, when the defendant knew it was inoperative and had ample opportunity to repair.

3. Failing to warn plaintiff of the danger.

It was further alleged in the plaintiff's petition that the specific acts of negligence of the defendant were the proximate cause of the damages suffered by the plaintiff and that the defendant is liable to the plaintiff under the doctrine of *res ipsa loquitur*.

Question: Are the foregoing pleadings proper for the plaintiff's attorney to proceed with the case under the theory of *res ipsa loquitur*? Discuss.

Question Ten

About six months ago, John Smith was convicted, after a jury trial, of engaging in a racketeering conspiracy. Smith did not testify at trial. Smith managed millions of dollars in assets of the benefit plans of two large union locals. The jury found that he had skimmed $1.8 million in concealed commissions, claiming half of that for his own benefit and paying about half in payoffs to certain union officials. The union officials were not named defendants in the same trial. Smith has been sentenced, and his appeal is pending before a federal court of appeals. In his appeal, he seeks a new trial.

Smith has been subpoenaed to testify before a federal grand jury (not the grand jury that indicted him) investigating the actions of the union officials. Ron Jones, the prosecutor who represented the government at Smith's trial and who would most likely represent the government at Smith's retrial if he should win his appeal, is the prosecutor seeking to examine Smith before the grand jury. Jones has obtained an order granting Smith "use" immunity in connection with his testimony.

Smith has moved to quash the grand jury subpoena on two grounds:

1. That "use" immunity is not sufficient to protect his fifth amendment privilege against self-incrimination in a case where he may be subject to a retrial if his pending appeal is successful; and

2. That his sixth amendment right to counsel will be violated because Jones has informed Smith that while his attorney may wait outside the grand jury room, he may not be present during Smith's testimony.

State the proper ruling on each of Smith's arguments and explain your reasons for so ruling.

Question Eleven

Seller and Buyer discussed for months the possibility of Seller's selling Buyer his farm known as Greenacre. Finally, on Wednesday morning, May 3, Buyer received the following telegram from Seller: "Will sell Greenacre for $250,000. Offer is irrevocable. Reply by wire at once." In response Buyer sent a letter to Seller stating: "I accept your offer to sell Greenacre for $250,000. Let's close the deal next week." Buyer's letter was mailed Wednesday afternoon, May 3. On Thursday, May 4, before Buyer's letter arrived, Seller sent the following telegram to Buyer: "My offer is revoked. Greenacre is no longer for sale." Buyer received the second telegram on Thursday, May 4. Seller received Buyer's letter Friday morning May 5.

Question: Buyer retains you to advise him whether he has an enforceable contract to purchase Greenacre from Seller. State your advice and the reasons for it.

Question Twelve

Following the stock market crash in 1987, John sued his stock broker, Slick, for fraud under the state Uniform Securities Act. John claimed that Slick had made unauthorized trades in stocks just prior to the crash that resulted in John's losing a large sum of money. Prices of stocks that Slick traded for John were related to the Dow Jones Industrial Average. John's lawyer, Justice, hired Stanley, an old high school classmate, as an expert to testify at the trial. Stanley is the manager of a large stock brokerage firm. Stanley still works part-time as a stock broker, but his customers in fact buy only municipal bonds. The last time Stanley actively traded stocks was ten years ago.

Stanley has been called to the stand by Justice. Stanley has prepared a large chart that shows the allegedly unauthorized trades and the Dow Jones Industrial Average for each day over a two-month period.

Stanley testifies that the information on the chart regarding the Dow Jones Industrial Average was obtained by him from the *Wall Street Journal* and that he has the newspapers available. He testifies that the information regarding the stock trading on the chart was obtained from the monthly statements Slick sent to John following the crash.

Justice attempts to question Stanley regarding his expert opinion on the fraudulence of the trading. Can Stanley testify as an expert regarding the trading? Discuss. Can Justice introduce as evidence the charts that Stanley prepared? Discuss.

Question Thirteen

Sara, owner of Blackacre, was interested in selling it. She listed the property for sale with Broker. Broker interested Perch in buying Blackacre, and Perch signed an offer addressed to Sara to buy Blackacre (describing it fully) for "$100,000.00, $10,000.00 tendered now." Sara was out of town so Broker phoned, described the offer, and asked if she wished to accept it. Sara said, "It sounds okay. Please send me a copy." Broker agreed, hung up, and then signed the acceptance "Sara, by Broker." $10,000.00 was paid by Perch and was held by Broker in his trust account.

Two days later, Sara received a cash offer of $130,000.00 for Blackacre. She told Perch that her supposed contract with him was cancelled and offered to return the $10,000.00. Perch refused the money and sued for specific performance.

Discuss and decide.

Question Fourteen

Plaintiff Packaging Equipment Corporation is an Illinois corporation with its principal place of business in Illinois. At its plant in Illinois it manufactures packaging equipment that is sold throughout the United States. Defendant Electrical Components Company is a Delaware corporation with its principal place of business in Salt Lake County, Utah. Defendant's products are manufactured at its Utah facility and are sold only in the western United States.

In 1987, defendant was contacted by plaintiff's sales representative regarding buying a component packaging machine manufactured by plaintiff. During the course of the sales presentation, many representations concerning the quality, efficiency, and appropriateness of the component packaging machine were made to defendant. Relying on the sales presentation, defendant purchased the packaging equipment for $75,000 and made a down payment of $7,500. The equipment was shipped from plaintiff's plant in Illinois to Utah. After the packaging equipment was received and put into operation by defendant, the equipment failed to perform in the manner represented. Defendant told plaintiff that the equipment was totally unacceptable and that it would not pay the $67,500 balance due under the sales contract; defendant also demanded the return of its

$7,500 down payment, stating that the equipment would be returned to plaintiff when arrangements for the refund of the down payment were made.

After defendant arranged to purchase the packaging equipment, it was contacted by Box Company regarding the purchase of containers to be used with the new packaging equipment. Box Company is a Nebraska corporation totally independent of plaintiff. Box's representative stated that its containers were totally compatible with plaintiff's packaging equipment. Based upon those representations, defendant ordered $20,000 in containers from Box. When defendant attempted to use the containers, it discovered the containers were not compatible with the packaging equipment. As a consequence, $5,000 worth of containers were effectively destroyed when defendant attempted to use them with the packaging equipment. Defendant now has an inventory of $15,000 of these unusable containers.

Assume you are the attorney for defendant Electronic Components Company and address the civil procedure issues involved in each of the two following scenarios.

Scenario I

Plaintiff Packaging Equipment files an action in the United States District Court for the District of Illinois seeking to recover from defendant Electronic Components the $67,500 balance due under the contract for the sale of the packaging equipment. An appropriate summons and an artfully drawn complaint in that action were properly served upon defendant two days ago. Defendant's president advises you that the only contact defendant had with plaintiff was with plaintiff's sales representative in Utah and mail and telephone communications with plaintiff's Illinois plant. Defendant's president also indicates that all witnesses to the failure of the equipment to perform reside in Utah, as does plaintiff's sales representative. Finally, he advises you that defendant would like to attempt to recover from plaintiff the $7,500 down payment.

1. Does the United States district court in Illinois have jurisdiction of the claims and parties?

2. What motions under Rule 12(b), Fed.R.Civ.P., should be filed in the pending action and why?

3. What, if any, additional preliminary motions should be filed in the pending action and why?

Scenario II

Assume the same facts as Scenario I except the action filed by plaintiff against defendant is filed in the United States District Court for the District of Utah.

1. Does the United States district court in Utah have jurisdiction of the claims and parties? Why or why not?

2. What, if any, motions should be made pursuant to Rule 12, Fed.R.Civ.P.? Why?

3. What other responsive pleading(s) to plaintiff's complaint should be filed and what should those pleadings contain? Who is required to sign such pleadings and what is the significance of doing so?

4. May defendant litigate his claims with Box in the pending litigation with plaintiff? Why or why not? If so, what initial pleadings should be filed on behalf of defendant to join Box in the action?

Question Fifteen

There is already a direct tax on distillers. Assume that Congress, in its quest to balance the budget, has passed a special tax on income from the sale of wine, beer, and distilled spirits, payable by any entity receiving such income.

Some states, including South Carolina, Montana, and Iowa, as part of their exercise of the police power, have established state liquor stores as the only establishments in those states where liquor may be purchased by the bottle.

The legislatures and governors of those states believe that the states' legitimate interest in liquor control justifies state-owned liquor stores and regulation of liquor sales through state-controlled distribution. They believe that the income derived from state liquor store sales should be immune from federal taxation.

As the Attorney General of Ames, you are asked by the attorneys general of the states affected to join with them as *amicus curiae* in their suit arguing that federal taxation is improper.

What would your response be to the merits of their case? What is the basis for your response?

Question Sixteen

Ted Savage, a 20-year-old carpenter, decided to unwind after a long week of work. Although Ted's driver's license had been suspended (he had recently been convicted of driving while intoxicated), Ted drove from his home to the city for a few drinks. On his way home, Ted stopped his car at a red light. Although his car was on the right side of the road, it sat about four feet beyond the white line denoting the point at which vehicles must stop while waiting for the traffic light to change. Before the light turned, Vince Leonard drove his brand new Chevrolet (which he had purchased that day from "Honest Frank's," a local car dealer) into the same intersection. Vince approached the intersection from Ted's right. Vince attempted to make a left turn around Ted's stopped car, but failed. Vince's car collided head on with Ted's.

Vince told the police that, although he may have made the turn a trifle fast, he lost control of the car because the steering mechanism completely failed.

Ted, who had not been wearing a seat belt, was badly injured and was rushed to Forest Hospital. The only physician on duty was Dr. Mark Stanley, a young resident. Dr. Stanley concluded that Ted needed immediate surgery, but would be unable to tolerate anesthesia because he was intoxicated. Accordingly, he did not arrange for the surgery for several hours. When the surgery was finally performed, Ted's legs could not be saved and were amputated. The surgeon who operated on Ted chastised Dr. Stanley because the surgeon believed that Ted's intoxication would not have precluded surgery at an earlier time, when Ted's legs could have been saved.

Describe and analyze the claims that the parties will make against each other, the defenses that will be raised, the damages that will be claimed, and each party's prospects for success.

Question Seventeen

Undercover narcotics agent Fred Mertz was attempting to buy cocaine. An informant put him in contact with Ricky Ricardo, who told him he had some cocaine stored, but that it would take two or three weeks more to get the amount Mertz was seeking. Besides, Ricardo said, he wanted to get Mertz checked out and would have him killed if he was a cop. He said that he employed people to do just that.

Mertz completed an affidavit recounting his ten years experience as an undercover narcotics agent and the fact that Ricardo was a "known" drug dealer. A valid arrest warrant was issued and executed by local officers Cramden and Berle, who were both experienced police officers.

Cramden and Berle knocked on Ricardo's door and he opened it. They drew their guns, advised Ricardo that he was under arrest and handcuffed him in the doorway. Once Ricardo was in custody, they entered the apartment and made what they termed a routine "protective sweep." Officer Berle stated that he "wanted to see if anyone else was there."

The officers entered the living room and saw two doors leading to other rooms. On entering the first room, they saw packages appearing to be cocaine lying in plain view on top of a box. When they lifted the packages, they discovered several fully loaded firearms and $100,000 in small bills. Testing confirmed that the packages contained cocaine.

The second room was locked. They asked Ricardo for permission to search. The officers told Ricardo that they would attempt to get a search warrant if he did not consent. Ricardo said "Okay," but later refused to sign a waiver form. Cramden forced the door and found books and records which appeared to record Ricardo's illegal business dealings.

Ricardo has moved to suppress the cocaine, firearms, money, and books and records. Discuss and decide which evidence, if any, should be admitted.

Question Eighteen

S owns the Great Marathon Sub Shop, a sandwich shop directly across the street from the Great Marathon Amusement Park. Most of S's business has come from people going into or leaving the amusement park.

On January 15, B contracted with S to buy the Great Marathon Sub Shop. The written sales contract provided in part: "S warrants that she is the owner of the real and personal property which is the subject matter of this sale. S makes no other representations or warranties whatsoever."

A week later, the Great Marathon Amusement Park announced that it was going out of business and would not reopen. Neither B nor S had had prior indication that the Great Marathon Amusement Park planned to close. B wants to cancel his contract to buy the sandwich shop from S. Identify and evaluate the issues.

Question Nineteen

While on a "leaf-peeping" tour of Vermont during the month of October of 1988, Cary Collector, a collector of oil paintings, stopped to dine at a quaint tavern. Cary noticed on the wall an oil painting that he identified as an original painting by Honus Hamlin, a famous colonial painter.

Believing the painting to be worth about $50,000.00, Cary asked if he could speak to the owner, Paul Pigeon. When his waitress introduced the owner of the inn to Cary, Cary said that he was very interested in the painting "because of the unique blend of the colors." He did not mention the fact that he believed that the painting was done by Mr. Hamlin. Cary offered to purchase the painting for $500.00. Mr. Pigeon, thinking that this was an extremely good deal, agreed. The two signed a simple agreement which called for Cary to pay $500.00 in cash within thirty days and to pick up the painting when he paid.

Ten days later Cary returned to Vermont to pay and to pick up the painting. While having dinner, he mentioned to his waitress (who had also been his waitress on his previous visit) that he had come for his painting and that he would be in the next morning to pay Mr. Pigeon and pick it up. The waitress, who was in the middle of a feud with Mr. Pigeon, told Cary that after he had made his deal with Mr. Pigeon, a noted art collector, Sally Sotheby, had been in the tavern and had told Mr. Pigeon that the painting was in fact by Hamlin. It was the only painting of a local landscape known to have been done by Hamlin and, because it was unique, it was worth $350,000.00. Sally had offered to purchase the painting from Mr. Pigeon at that price, and Mr. Pigeon had agreed. Sally was expected in town in two days with the $350,000.00 in cash.

Cary arrives in your office early the following morning. He wants you to do whatever you can to stop the sale to Sally and to force Mr. Pigeon to sell the painting to him for the agreed-upon $500.00 price.

What steps will you advise Cary to take? What defenses should be raised? What is the likelihood of success for Cary?

Question Twenty

A new client, Jane Developer, comes to you. Jane wants to sue the Herman Edwards Construction Corporation ("HECC"). In April of 1988, Jane met with Herman Edwards, the President of the corporation, and with the corporation's lawyer. Jane agreed to hire HECC to build a small office building. HECC's lawyer prepared a single written contract that both Jane and Herman signed at the meeting. Jane believes the contract provided that HECC would be paid $50,000.00, plus the actual cost of materials and labor. HECC's lawyer took the original; no copies were ever made. Jane has only some handwritten notes that she made at the meeting.

HECC completed the building in September of 1988, and was paid in full by Jane Developer. During the first major rain storm, however, the roof leaked, causing substantial damage to the interior of the building. Jane had the roof inspected by Alice Jones, a high school dropout who has built the most successful construction firm in town. She has installed and repaired dozens of roofs. Ms. Jones has told Jane that shoddy construction caused the leaks and that HECC had the same problem on three other jobs. While inspecting the roof, Ms. Jones found some empty whiskey bottles that she suspects were left there by HECC employees. Jane has pictures, taken by her secretary, showing the water leaking inside from the roof. Her secretary has since left town and cannot be located.

Jane arranged a meeting with Herman Edwards and HECC's lawyer to settle the dispute between Jane and HECC. At the meeting, Jane learned that the contract had been lost in a fire at the office of HECC's lawyer. Herman argued at the meeting that the roof materials, which Jane had selected, caused the leak. Herman also admitted during the meeting that some of his roofers like to have a couple of drinks with lunch. HECC's lawyer then asked for a break and he and Herman stepped into the hall. They left the door to the conference room open, however, and Jane could hear everything they said. Herman told the lawyer: "I know the boys got drunk and botched the job, but she can't prove it. Besides, I'll deny that the roof was part of the job—she has nothing in writing." They then returned to the conference room. No settlement was reached.

You will institute a lawsuit by Jane against HECC. Describe: (1) all the evidence that you will attempt to present on Jane's behalf; (2) the objections that will be raised; and (3) the likely rulings on the admission of the evidence.

Question Twenty-one

Owen owned Blackacre, a farm on the outskirts of town, in Ames, a race-notice jurisdiction. His daughter Sara lived in the city and attended the university, but for years had put in half-time or more helping Owen run the farm. In gratitude, Owen, in January 1989, gave Sara a duly executed quitclaim deed conveying Blackacre to her as a gift. She continued to live in town and did not record the deed.

A couple of weeks later, Owen was visited by Rich, who offered a certified check for $500,000 if Owen would sign a duly prepared deed conveying Blackacre to Rich. Owen, thinking Sara would be delighted, signed the deed and accepted the check. He then phoned Sara, who was not delighted. She asked, "When did he leave?" When Owen said, "Just now," she hung up, dashed to the recording office, and recorded her deed. Rich, who had had no idea of Sara's interest, recorded his deed from Owen the following day. He then had the pleasure of giving a deed of Blackacre to his son Devo, a land developer, as a gift.

Within days, Sara sued Devo to quiet title to Blackacre in herself. Devo counterclaimed to quiet title in himself. Discuss and decide.

Question Twenty-two

The senior partner of your law firm gives you the following facts and asks you to write a brief memo setting out the federal constitutional law issues:

Doug and Debbie were married two years ago, and your client, Doug, was just served a Summons and Complaint for divorce and a Motion for Custody and Support. Doug did not live with Debbie before their marriage.

One child lives in the home—a fourteen-year-old girl. While Doug does not deny that he could be the father of the girl, neither of them disputes that there were many other possible fathers. Blood tests are inconclusive and no action was ever filed to resolve paternity. Both Doug and Debbie are equally fit to have custody of the girl, who has never lived outside the home.

It happens that both Debbie and the girl are pregnant and in their first trimester. Debbie's pleadings seek assurance that both she and the girl can get abortions. Debbie wants her daughter to have an abortion. The girl does not want an abortion. Doug agrees with the girl. The natural father of the girl's child has waived all rights.

State law provides for the following:

1. That paternity is conclusively presumed by a husband and wife living in the same home as to children also living there;

2. That a paternity action must be brought within eight years of the birth of the child in question;

3. That a determination of paternity allows the imposition of an obligation to pay for child support;

4. That a husband may veto his wife's decision to have an abortion;

5. That custody shall be determined by what is in the "best interests of the child."

Doug wants to know answers to the following questions:

1. Can he be required to pay child support for the girl?

2. Can he prevent his wife from having an abortion?

3. Can Doug or Debbie prevent or cause the girl to have an abortion?

4. Assuming Doug is the girl's father and that he seeks custody of the girl, can the parents' and girl's positions on the girl's abortion be considered by the court in determining custody?

Note: This question does not require any knowledge or application of the 1989 ruling by the U.S. Supreme Court upholding various provisions of a Missouri law regulating abortion.

Question Twenty-three

Diane, a citizen of the District of Columbia, was driving in Ohio. In her car were her brothers, Dave and Richard, citizens of Florida and New York, respectively. While in Ohio, she was involved in a traffic accident with a stalled band bus. The bus was being towed by a tow truck owned and operated by a citizen of Pennsylvania. Diane's husband, Bruce, who is a citizen of and lives in Ohio, owns the car Diane is driving. The bus was unlicensed, and its ownership was unknown at the time of filing of Diane's and Bruce's lawsuit against the tow truck operator in the federal district court of appropriate venue. Counsel for Bruce and Diane made no independent inquiry about the ownership of the band bus.

In their complaint, Diane and Bruce name the tow truck driver and "John Doe," the owner of the band bus, as defendants. They allege that "John Doe" is not a citizen of Ohio. "John Doe" was never served with process and never appeared in the action. Their claim is for property damage to the car and loss of consortium.

In response, the defendant tow truck driver answered by generally denying liability. In addition, he filed a third party complaint against the bus driver, Bill, alleged to be a citizen of Ohio.

Questions: 1. May Diane and Bruce maintain this case in federal court? 2. What effect will citizenship of the persons named in this question have in this case? 3. Did Diane and Bruce's counsel comply with Fed.R.Civ.P. 11 in attempting to find the citizenship and current address of the band bus owner?

Question Twenty-four

Connie Customer and her husband, Herbert, stopped at the local Ray-Mart to do some Christmas shopping. It was 5:00 PM in December and starting to darken. None of the exterior lights on the building or parking lot lights was on. Herbert let Connie off at the front entrance and parked next to the building, approximately 150 feet to the right of the front entrance. By 6:30 PM their shopping was done. Darkness had fallen, and it had started to sleet. Herbert took the packages to the car. Connie told Herbert just to turn on the headlights when he got to the car, and she would follow them to the car.

Connie saw the headlights go on and decided to walk next to the building to protect herself from the sleet. There was no sidewalk along the side of the building. Out on the surface of the parking lot, the illumination was sufficient to see clearly. It was very dark along the side of the building, however, and Connie could see nothing ahead of her except the glow of the headlights. She kept moving and bumped her head against an electrical meter mounted on the side of the building. Connie suffered serious cuts and scarring to her face. You are the attorney for Ray-Mart. Evaluate Connie Customer's claim.

Is Ray-Mart under a duty to light the side of the building where there is no walkway when all other parts of the parking lot surface are lighted? Discuss.

Question Twenty-five

Defendant, a nursery school teacher, was accused by the parents of three-year-old Pureheart of engaging in improper sexual contact with their child. The parents filed a municipal court complaint charging defendant with the disorderly persons offense of "simple assault," which is statutorily defined as "attempting to cause or knowingly causing bodily injury to another." Defendant pleaded guilty and was given the maximum sentence of six months in jail.

Following the tremendous publicity generated by the case, the county prosecutor obtained defendant's indictment for the second degree crime of "sexual assault," which is statutorily defined as "committing an act of sexual contact with a victim who is less than 13 years old." Defendant pleaded not guilty.

Prior to trial, Pureheart was permitted to testify in chambers with only the judge, prosecutor, and defense counsel present. Cross-examination was limited to written questions prepared by defense counsel and then asked by the judge. This procedure was allowed over defendant's objection because of unrebutted testimony by a psychiatrist at a pretrial hearing that Pureheart would suffer irreparable psychological damage if compelled to testify in open court with defendant present.

At trial the court admitted into evidence the videotape of Pureheart's testimony in chambers and proof of defendant's plea of guilty to the simple assault charge. The court rejected the proffer of expert testimony by defendant's long-time psychiatrist that defendant was psychologically incapable of committing a sexual assault on Pureheart. The judge ruled that such testimony would be inadmissible because "it embraced the ultimate issue to be decided by the jury." Defendant did not take the stand and rested without offering any evidence.

During closing argument the prosecutor told the jury: "I believe every word of Pureheart's testimony and find defendant to be a depraved and vicious beast whose conduct is more vile than the lowest form of animal life." Defendant was found guilty by the jury and sentenced to 15 years in jail to commence immediately after the simple assault sentence is served.

Discuss and evaluate the issues that defendant should raise on appeal. Assume defendant's trial counsel made all proper objections in a timely manner.

Question Twenty-six

Alpha Foods, Inc., wanted to replace its computerized cash registers with a newer, faster model. The National Computer Machinery Corp. ("NCM") informed Alpha that it was about to introduce a "revolutionary" new machine that would suit Alpha's needs "perfectly." To reinforce this claim, NCM installed a prototype system at one of Alpha's stores. It worked perfectly. Alpha ordered 50 such devices, for a total purchase price of $60,000.00. The sales contract, which NCM drafted, and which was signed by both parties, contained no performance specifications. It stated conspicuously that "[t]his sale is made by Seller without any implied warranty of merchantability or fitness."

The goods were delivered on March 1. Now—some time after acceptance and installation—Alpha has discovered that the new machines, although workable, are significantly less efficient than hoped and not up to the standard of the prototype. Alpha wants to reject the machines and have the purchase price returned. Alpha maintains that had it known that the machines would perform at this level, it would never have purchased them. NCM responds that these machines were sold without warranties or specifications. It has refused Alpha's demands. NCM says that it will work with Alpha to iron out "the few bugs" in the machines.

Based solely on this set of facts, what is Alpha's best argument in support of its claims of (1) breach of warranty and (2) right to reject?

Question Twenty-seven

Peter, an employee of Big D Corp. ("Big D"), was severely injured in an accident at Big D's plant. Peter sued Big D, alleging, among other things, that Big D's equipment was antiquated and that its safety practices were inadequate. Big D denied Peter's allegations, claiming that Peter's carelessness was the cause of the accident. Assume for purposes of answering this question that an employee may bring an action for negligence against his employer and that it is not barred by the Workers Compensation Statutes. At trial, the following occurred:

A. Dan, who was Big D's vice-president in charge of plant operations at the time of the accident, could not remember the circumstances that led to the purchase of the equipment that Peter was operating. Another vice-president, who was in charge of acquisitions and who did not testify, had prepared detailed written summaries of all purchases every month. Dan was allowed to review the summary for the month in question and then testify.

B. On direct examination, Dan testified that nothing more could have been done before the accident to make the work area safer. On cross-examination, Peter's attorney asked, "Isn't it true that just one month after the accident your company commissioned a safety analysis of the area where the accident occurred and then corrected problems noted in the analysis?" The trial court sustained an objection to this question and did not compel Dan to answer.

C. Frank, Big D's foreman, did not see the accident. However, seconds before the accident, Frank saw Peter operating the forklift on which he was injured. Frank was allowed to testify as to his opinion of the speed at which Peter was driving the forklift.

D. Big D called Wendy as a witness. Wendy did not work at the plant and did not see the accident. However, she received a letter from a friend who had witnessed the accident. The letter was written a week after the accident and described the accident in detail. The friend was a worker at the plant and was not a party in the action. Because of his relationship with Peter, the friend did not want to testify. Big D's attorney asked Wendy to describe the accident from the letter. Testimony was permitted.

E. At the conclusion of testimony, the trial judge believed that both sides had neglected to call a key witness who was not a party in the case and who could, in the trial judge's opinion, offer significant evidence concerning the accident. The trial judge himself called the witness to testify.

Assuming that proper objections were timely made, were the trial court's rulings correct? Discuss your reasoning in each situation in one to three paragraphs. Your discussion of situation E should include explanation of the procedure that should be employed in the questioning of the witness if the witness is allowed to testify.

Question Twenty-eight

John, while unmarried, on March 9, 1988, properly executed and acknowledged a deed conveying his farm to his only sister, Mary. He placed the deed in a safe-deposit box that he had previously rented in his and his sister's names. He sent a key to his sister, Mary. Mary received the key. There was a note attached to the deed which stated, "to be delivered to my sister, Mary, after my death." Mary never opened the safe-deposit box.

John married Judy on July 24, 1989. Shortly thereafter, a will was prepared and properly executed which left all of John's property to his wife, Judy. John placed the will in his safe-deposit box.

John continued to manage his farm, receive the income, and pay all taxes. John did not change the lease of the safe-deposit box. On January 15, 1990, John died. Shortly thereafter, Mary, Judy, and Judy's attorney opened the safe-deposit box. They discovered the deed with the note attached and the will.

Who is entitled to the farm? Discuss, giving reasons for your answer.

Question Twenty-nine

Your client, Adolphus Longstaff, owns 500 acres of beautiful, rolling country-side on which he is building expensive single-family homes on two-acre lots.

The project is licensed to be a subdivision of the county. It is to be called "The Horns," in honor of Mr. Longstaff's maternal grandparents, Thomas and Sarah Horn. You have done a fine job in title and recording work, platting, obtaining necessary permits, setting up corporate ownership, and negotiating favorable contractor arrangements.

The houses in The Horns are being designed by an architect from Omaha who is fascinated by the prosperity of the rural Michigan economy and who wishes to honor it and her own home community in the design of the houses. She calls the style "Cornbelt Gothic." It involves distinctive exterior features, such as rough-hewn shingles, wagon-wheel or split-rail fencing, front porches, and a decorative windmill in each yard.

Your client wants to preserve this architecture on all houses in The Horns. He does not want any homeowner to have the power to change profile, roofing, exterior detail, or any of the twenty-three other distinctive exterior features of the Cornbelt Gothic style.

The question is how best to do this. Please give your client at least two alterna-tives for implementing his plan. Indicate briefly the advantages and disadvan-tages of each.

Question Thirty

AAA Corporation owed money to Creditor on a promissory note. AAA with-held payments on the note because of a dispute arising from subsequent busi-ness dealings between the parties. Creditor, wanting to be paid, filed suit in federal district court upon the note. The summons and complaint were served personally by a U.S. marshal on Mary, who is a part-time receptionist for AAA. Mary, not understanding what a summons and complaint are, threw them into the wastebasket, and never informed anyone at AAA.

AAA had no knowledge of the above facts until two months later, when AAA received a letter from Creditor. The letter stated that a default judgment had been entered thirty days earlier against AAA for $51,000 and that Creditor intended to pursue his post-judgment remedies.

Question: What relief might be available to AAA concerning the default judgment?

Question Thirty-one

Ewin Racing Association, Inc., is a private corporation licensed by the Neuter State Racing Commission to conduct harness racing and engage in harness racing in the state of Neuter. Ewin rents its facilities, the Ewin Harness Racetrack, from the state for one dollar per annum. It pays substantial taxes on its wagering income to the state. In order to obtain and keep a license to operate a racetrack in the state of Neuter, private racing associations like Ewin must have all officers and stockholders and all internal rules and policies approved by a majority vote of the Racing Commission members. All persons engaged in racing, *e.g.*, owners, trainers, drivers, and grooms, must be licensed by the State Racing Commission. Private associations must also allow racing judges, who are licensed and employed by the Neuter Racing Commission, to oversee the conduct of races and enforce the Racing Commission rules and regulations.

David Driver, a licensed harness driver, races at the Ewin racetrack. On two separate occasions during the spring of 1989, David's license was suspended, without hearing, for two weeks by a state racing judge, for violations of the same Racing Commission regulation. In the second suspension order, the racing judge noted that David seemed to be consistently violating the regulation requiring all drivers to use their best efforts to win each race they participate in. The judge recommended further action on the grounds that David's driving was potentially detrimental to competitive racing.

In July 1989, pursuant to an internal rule that allows the management of Ewin to revoke the racing privileges of any driver sustaining two or more suspensions during a calendar year, the management revoked David's racing privileges and had him removed from the racetrack. No hearing was held and no reason was stated for the exclusion.

David brought suit in federal court claiming that Ewin's revocation of his racing privileges violated the U.S. Constitution. He does not challenge the two state-imposed two-week suspensions. The district court dismissed David's complaint for failure to state a claim upon which relief could be granted.

Discuss the issues on appeal. Assume all state remedies have been exhausted.

Question Thirty-two

A state statute requires farmers to fence pastures abutting railroad tracks to prevent the risk of train wrecks and the loss of livestock. On January 1, 1989, the Short Peninsular Railroad Company (SPR) negligently loaded a rail car. As a result, a crate fell off and broke a hole in Farmer Plow's pasture fence along the railroad's right of way. State Road 47 abutted the opposite boundary of the railroad's right of way, 30 feet from the broken fence.

Plow saw the crate smash the fence and immediately called the SPR office. An SPR agent promised "to send a repair crew as quickly as we can round one up," but warned "this is New Year's Day and we may be delayed." Plow retorted, "I, too, am celebrating New Year's Day and ain't going to do a damn thing to fix that fence. I'm holding SPR responsible!" That ended the conversation. Plow left the farm on a visit to his parents-in-law for the day.

On the morning of January 2, 1989, Tex, one of Plow's bulls, wandered through the broken fence and began grazing on the railroad right of way. An approaching train blew its whistle, and the bull bolted onto State Road 47. Just at that moment, Don Duts approached driving his pickup truck on State Road 47. He had been looking down and fumbling in his clothes to locate a lighted cigarette that he had dropped and looked up just as the bull dashed in front of him. Duts' vehicle hit the bull before Duts could step on the brake. The truck overturned.

Another motorist, Paul Pail, stopped to give assistance. Just as Pail emerged from his vehicle, the bull suddenly sprang to his feet, lunged into Pail, and then dropped dead. The bull's horn pierced Pail's heart, killing Pail within minutes.

Pail's personal representative consults you about an action against SPR. Discuss the legal arguments for and against an action against SPR and decide whether to take the case. Discuss only the action against SPR.

Question Thirty-three

At 9:00 PM on December 15, 1984, the Goldfield police received a call from a resident reporting that his home was being burglarized. Patrolman Palmer was dispatched to the scene and encountered Dan Denton walking in the direction of a car parked in front of the residence. He conducted a pat-down search of Denton, which disclosed a glass-cutting tool and car keys in his jacket pocket. Palmer used these keys to unlock the car and discovered jewelry and silverware hidden under the front seat. The resident identified these items as having been taken from his home.

Palmer told Denton he was under arrest for burglary. He fully advised Denton of his *Miranda* rights and asked Denton if he wished to make a statement. Denton replied, "I'm not saying anything until I talk to a lawyer."

Denton was immediately brought before the municipal court judge, who advised Denton again of his *Miranda* rights. The judge accepted Denton's application for a Public Defender to represent him. Reasonable bail was set, and Denton was placed in the county jail because he was unable to post bail.

The next morning two county detectives visited Denton at the jail. They told Denton they were investigating a homicide that had occurred in September of 1984 during the burglary of a Silvertown residence. The detectives fully advised Denton of his *Miranda* rights, which Denton stated he understood. They asked Denton if he would answer some questions regarding the Silvertown murder. Denton replied: "I'll tell you all I know about that job because I only drove the getaway car. I didn't have anything to do with killing the old lady. But I'm not talking about the Goldfield job until I get to see my lawyer."

The Grand Jury indicted Denton for burglary of the Goldfield residence and for felony murder of the Silvertown woman. His attorney has filed a motion to suppress (a) the glasscutter, the jewelry, and the silverware seized at the time of arrest, and (b) the statement Denton gave to the county detectives regarding the Silvertown murder.

Discuss and evaluate the admissibility of this evidence.

Question Thirty-four

Paula planned to take the February 1990 bar examination. She wanted to take a trip following the exam. On January 5, 1990, Paula sent a postcard to Agency asking it to send information to her about February tours to the Carnival in Rio de Janeiro, Brazil.

On January 15, Agency sent Paula a brochure about its four-day "Carnival" tour. It listed the following terms and conditions:

EXPENSES: The total package including airfare, hotels and provided meals, will cost only $500 per person. Once your participation is confirmed, Agency guarantees that this price is fixed and will not be withdrawn or increased.

RESERVATIONS AND DEPOSITS: Reservations should be made as early as possible to guarantee participation. In order to receive a confirmed reservation, a nonrefundable deposit of $200 per person is required.

MISCELLANEOUS: Agency reserves the absolute right to refuse or discontinue service to anyone if Agency determines that it would be in the best interests of the tour.

(The above provisions constitute the entire "terms and conditions" regarding expenses, reservations, and deposits.)

On January 23, Paula sent Agency a letter by certified mail: "Please reserve one seat at $500 for your February Carnival tour." She enclosed a check for $200.

On January 25, Agency called Paula and told her that the price listed in the brochure was a mistake and that the tour cost $5,000. When Paula protested, Agency told her that she sounded like a "troublemaker" and that it wouldn't allow her on the tour in any event. Paula told Agency that it was now too late for her to sign up for other tours and that she would sue Agency if it did not allow her to join the February Carnival tour.

Paula's certified letter to Agency arrived at Agency on January 27.

Discuss whether an enforceable contract exists and, if so, at what price. Your discussion should include all relevant formation-of-contract and contract defense issues.

Question Thirty-five

On November 27, 1988, Lewis went to the Mervyn's store on East Canyon Boulevard and presented Penny, a clerk at Mervyn's, with a $600 men's coat. The coat was a size-40 leather coat with a Mervyn's tag. Lewis told Penny that the coat was not the style he wanted and requested the return of the $600 paid for the coat. He told Penny that he had received the coat as a gift and that he therefore had no receipt. Penny gave Lewis $600.

Upon returning the coat to the coat rack, Penny noticed an empty hanger on the rack with the notation "Size 40" imprinted. A tag normally removed by clerks at Mervyn's was still attached to the coat returned by Lewis. Penny called the police.

Sgt. Smart, an expert in fingerprint analysis, obtained a fingerprint from the empty hanger. She compared the fingerprint from the hanger with fingerprint records for Lewis received from the California Bureau of Investigation. (California is a neighboring state.) The fingerprints were an exact match.

Dennis, a clerk at Mervyn's on Lake Street, had observed Lewis at the Lake Street store on November 19, 1988. Lewis had approached him about returning a woman's overcoat valued at $300. When Dennis asked Lewis to wait so that he could go back to check the price, Lewis had sprinted out the door.

Lewis is charged with theft arising from the November 27 incident at East Canyon Boulevard. During trial, the prosecution seeks to introduce the testimony of Dennis regarding the November 19 incident. Is Dennis's testimony admissible? Discuss.

The prosecution calls Sgt. Smart to the stand. Sgt. Smart produces the California fingerprint records, which the prosecution seeks to introduce. Are these admissible? Must the California fingerprint records be admitted in order for Sgt. Smart to testify about her findings?

Question Thirty-six

You are a new member of the Bar and have decided to pursue a practice in real property. As luck would have it, your first clients are a young couple in the process of purchasing their first home. They hand you a copy of their earnest money sales agreement, dated January 3, 1990, executed by them as buyers and bearing the signatures of the sellers. They also give you a copy of a preliminary title report furnished by the sellers and issued by a local title insurance company, dated January 10, 1989. They have been approved for an FHA loan by a local mortgage company. Your clients understand little of the contents of these documents and ask you to examine them, answer questions, and provide legal assistance in their purchase and the closing of the sale.

Your examination of the title report shows that title is vested in the sellers' daughter. The report lists the following exceptions (objections to insuring marketable title):

1. Unpaid county property taxes for the year 1984, and each additional year to the date of the report

2. A judgment against the sellers for $1,150, docketed December 15, 1981

3. A judgment against the sellers for $500, docketed October 9, 1982

4. A deed of trust executed by the sellers, recorded February 5, 1983, securing a promissory note of $20,000 to a local lender

5. A judgment against the sellers for $2,000 docketed July 20, 1988

6. A notice of mechanics lien for $3,500, recorded November 17, 1988

7. Unpaid sewer assessments of $350, certified to the county for the year 1987

Your clients return two or three days later and hand you a set of unsigned closing statements prepared by the mortgage company. They inform you that the sellers recorded a deed to their daughter in February 1983, in case of their untimely deaths, but the daughter, now seventeen years of age, is willing to sign a deed of conveyance. Also, the sellers object to paying some of the closing charges that the mortgage company claims they should pay. The sellers threaten to call off the sale if the charges are not resolved to their satisfaction. The parties are in a hurry to close, and the matter requires your immediate attention.

The charges to which the sellers object are as follows:

A. A document preparation fee for the buyers' loan of $250;

B. A tax service fee of $100 to check on the payment of property taxes during the life of the buyers' loan;

C. Loan discount points of $2,500. HUD regulations do not permit the buyers to pay them and the earnest money sales agreement made no provision for loan discount points.

Your clients want to know if they can acquire good (marketable) title as matters stand and, if not, what must be done to clear the exceptions stated in the title report. Also, whether the sellers have to pay the charges to which they object, and whether the sellers can call off the sale.

Please write your response and provide your legal analysis item by item.

Question Thirty-seven

M.D. Parker (M.D.), a 28-year-old Senior Resident physician in obstetrics at the College of Medicine, was driving his new 1985 Chrysler LeBaron home through the mountains for Thanksgiving in November 1985. As he neared Soldier Summit, the temperature had dropped, snow began to fall and, due to thick fog, visibility was near zero.

Upon reaching the summit, his car stalled and the engine died as if out of gas—even though the gas gauge read 3/4 full. (Evidence later showed that the car was, indeed, out of gas, that the gas gauge was defective, and that the general defect was known by Chrysler Corporation. Chrysler had failed to order a recall because of the expense and the fact that, according to an interoffice memo, "the defect would probably not cause any serious damage—only inconvenience to the owner.")

Juan Martinez (Trucker Juan), an independent owner-operator of an 18-wheel rig, had contracted with D.P. Tile to haul roofing tile over Soldier Summit, beginning December 1, 1985. However, two days before Thanksgiving, D.P. had received an order for a load of tile that needed to be in Denver immediately. Trucker Juan agreed to deliver the load. However, due to mechanical problems with his own truck, Trucker Juan drove a truck owned by D.P., which was loaded with roof tile far in excess of the gross weight permitted by law. Both Trucker Juan and D.P.'s dock superintendent knew of the violation.

Trucker Juan was traveling in the right lane, slower than the posted speed limit due to the heavy load, the falling snow, and the sudden foggy condition. Knowing the pass was not extensively traveled late at night, and knowing the route well, he had turned off his headlights (leaving only his parking lights on) in order to aid his night vision in the fog.

Meanwhile, several miles behind Trucker Juan, Melvin Tew (Trucker Tew), a long-haul driver for Fast Freight, Inc., was completing the last leg of his overnight route. Trucker Tew was late for supper and traveling 80 miles per hour in order to make up the time.

As Trucker Juan approached the summit he did not see M.D.'s stalled and unlighted vehicle until he was approximately 50 yards away. Trucker Juan tried to swerve to miss the vehicle but in doing so ran into Trucker Tew, who was passing at very high speed. The impact of the two trucks forced Juan's truck into M.D.'s stalled vehicle with a glancing blow, with M.D. still at the wheel. Although the car was only moderately damaged, M.D., who did not have his seatbelt fastened (he *never* did), was thrown from the car and suffered serious physical injuries.

Today M.D. Parker walked into your office and asked you to evaluate the case. Please identify and *analyze* the potential causes of action M.D. has against Trucker Juan and Chrysler. In addition, identify and briefly analyze any significant defenses and cross-claims Trucker Juan and Chrysler may raise.

Question Thirty-eight

In June 1989, Bob Buyer became interested in purchasing a popular club and restaurant known as the Stratosphere, which had nightly live music played by popular local rock-and-roll bands. Buyer and Sam Seller, the owner of the Stratosphere, met together once or twice a week for several weeks to negotiate the purchase and sale.

Buyer told Seller that his biggest concern was that, although Buyer had substantial restaurant experience, he had no experience in operating a club or hiring bands. Seller assured Buyer that Buyer's lack of experience in operating a club would be no problem because the Stratosphere had developed good relations with local bands, and Seller promised to assist Buyer in getting bands to play at the Stratosphere if Buyer bought the club.

In early July 1989, Buyer finally agreed to purchase the Stratosphere for a total purchase price of $400,000. For tax reasons, Buyer and Seller agreed that Buyer would pay a portion of the purchase price to Seller in the form of consulting fees in exchange for Seller's assistance in getting bands to play at the Stratosphere.

The written purchase agreement, prepared by Buyer's lawyer, provided for a total purchase price of $300,000, to be paid with $100,000 at closing, and $50,000 each year thereafter until paid in full. The contract contained a standard integration clause.

During the meeting on July 14, at which the parties executed the purchase agreement, Buyer also typed up another document for Seller to sign:

Consulting Agreement

1. Sam Seller hereby agrees to provide consulting services to, and at direction of, Bob Buyer for 2 years from date hereof, $50,000 per year, payable at end of each year.

2. Sam Seller agrees not to compete.

   Dated: July 14, 1990

   /s/ Sam Seller
   /s/ Bob Buyer

Seller reviewed and signed both of these agreements. Buyer gave Seller a check for $100,000. Seller provided Buyer with a list of local bands, with the names of the band managers and their phone numbers.

Over the first few months of operation, Buyer had trouble getting bands to play at the Stratosphere. He never asked Seller to help him. Seller never volunteered his assistance. After one year of operation, the Stratosphere went out of business. Buyer made no payments to Seller beyond the initial $100,000 paid at closing.

Seller commenced an action against Buyer seeking to recover $200,000 as the remainder of the purchase price owed under the purchase agreement. Seller also seeks to recover $100,000 owed under the consulting agreement.

Buyer comes to you for advice and provides you with a copy of the summons and complaint and the two written agreements. Your informal investigation reveals that several months after the agreements were executed, Seller opened another club and restaurant in a town located approximately 75 miles away from the Stratosphere and that many of the bands listed on the list of bands provided by Seller to Buyer were playing regularly at Seller's new club.

Does Seller have an enforceable claim against Buyer for the remaining $200,000 owed under the purchase agreement? Does Seller have an enforceable claim against Buyer for payment of the $100,000 under the consulting agreement? Discuss the issues, claims, and defenses.

Question Thirty-nine

On July 1, 1985, Les Orr entered into a written agreement with Lisa Lott to rent his one-family dwelling to Lott for three years at a monthly rental of $500, payable in advance on the first day of each month. Failure to pay rent by the 10th day of the month constituted a "default" by the tenant. The agreement contained the following clause:

> Tenant shall have the option to renew the within lease under the same terms and conditions. Tenant shall have the further option during the lease term to purchase the subject premises at fair market value.

Lott made timely rental payments for three years. On July 1, 1988, she paid $500 to Orr but said nothing about the option to renew. On August 12, 1988, Lott tendered an additional $500 to Orr with a short note which said:

> I hereby exercise my option to renew the lease, but only for an additional two years.
>
> /s/ Lisa Lott

Orr scrawled the word "NO" over Lott's handwriting and promptly returned the note to her along with a Notice to Quit the premises on September 15, 1988. Lott replied with another note to Orr as follows:

> I hereby exercise my option to purchase the property for $75,000, which is more than it is presently worth.
>
> /s/ Lisa Lott

Orr does not want either to rent or to sell the property to Lott. He has retained your legal services.

Prepare a memorandum to Orr advising him of his potential rights and liabilities.

Question Forty

You have been appointed to file an appeal for Mr. Ralph Malph, who has been convicted of sexually abusing a neighborhood child. The child, Betty Small, age six, was taken to Dr. N.O. Itall, a clinical social worker, after her parents noticed she had been having nightmares and that she seemed to want to be alone more often. They had started to notice the changes in their daughter shortly after Malph moved into the neighborhood. Betty had been to Malph's house by herself on a few occasions, and Malph had purchased small gifts for the child. After a couple of sessions with the child, which were unrecorded, Dr. Itall concluded that Betty had been sexually abused by Malph. The authorities were notified and an investigation ensued. Although physical examination by a physician revealed no physical signs of abuse, charges were filed and a trial was held.

At trial, the following occurred. Dr. Itall was allowed to stay at the prosecution table when other witnesses were excluded from the courtroom. When Itall was asked to leave, the prosecutor stated, "He's our expert." After some other witnesses had testified, Itall was called as a witness for the prosecution. Itall testified that he had graduated from Reputable University with a Ph.D. in Social Work. He had become interested in the field of child sexual abuse some years before and had written and published approximately a half-dozen papers on the subject. Itall had been consulted on a few cases by the police. He had had suspected abuse victims referred to him by the police. As Itall began to recite the titles of his many papers, Malph's retained defense attorney rose to stipulate that Dr. Itall was qualified as an expert in the field of child sexual abuse.

When questioned about the methods he employs, Itall told of a new method he had developed that he alone had used to decide whether children are the victims of sexual abuse. Itall conceded that he had not published the results of his work or the procedures of his method, but claimed that a paper detailing the method had been submitted to a journal for publication and that as soon as other social workers saw the paper, the method would revolutionize the diagnosis of child sexual abuse. Itall then briefly described the method and testified that application of the method to the facts reported to him by Betty Small, and to information he heard at trial, allowed him to determine that Small had been sexually abused. Finally, near the end of Itall's direct testimony, Itall was asked his opinion concerning the alleged abuse of Small. Itall stated, "In my professional opinion she was sexually abused." He then pointed to the defendant and said, "That man, Ralph Malph, molested Betty Small." Largely as a result of the testimony of Dr. Itall, all of which was admitted, Mr. Malph was convicted.

Assuming that proper and timely objections, all of which were overruled, were interposed during Itall's testimony, what evidentiary issues do you raise on appeal concerning Itall's testimony and what arguments do you make?

Question Forty-one

Amanda sued Ben in federal district court on a dispute over money owed. Ben answered the complaint, denying the material allegations set forth in the complaint and raising numerous affirmative defenses, including claims of setoff, breach of contract, failure of consideration, and bar by accord and satisfaction.

Amanda served Ben with interrogatories and requests for production of documents, all pertaining to not only Amanda's claims but also Ben's asserted defenses. Amanda's discovery requests were very broad, were somewhat unclear, and requested information and documents that may not be admissible as evidence at trial. Ben failed to respond to these discovery requests within the permitted time, and after repeated demands from Amanda, has still not filed responses, nor has he filed any objection or request to limit the discovery.

Amanda wishes to use whatever remedies she may have available for Ben's failure to respond to her discovery requests.

Question: Discuss fully the remedies available to Amanda for Ben's failure to respond to her discovery requests, including the arguments upon which Amanda would rely in requesting relief from the court. State the objections Ben might raise to Amanda's requests for discovery.

Question Forty-two

Attorney Smith, a Native American admitted to practice law in the State of Arizona, had been serving as tribal attorney for his tribe. He had received an award from the Arizona Bar for his work with the tribe. Smith applied for admission to the Utah State Bar. Utah Bar reciprocity rules allow oral examination of applicants licensed to practice elsewhere. Smith took the Utah test along with 17 other applicants who had applied under the same reciprocity rule as Smith. The other 17 were Caucasian.

At the time of his examination, Smith felt the questions asked were biased and incomplete. A day after his examination, he received a letter from the bar office notifying him that his application was incomplete and requiring an additional $100 processing fee. Inquiry showed the other 17 applicants had made the same error without being assessed a similar processing fee. One week later the Utah Bar notified Smith that he had failed the examination. Two weeks later Smith learned that one of his application references had been contacted by a bar staff member questioning his referring a Native American. The other 17 applicants passed their oral examinations and were admitted to the Utah Bar.

Smith requested from the bar a copy of the questions asked him, his responses, the model answers and his exam score. He asked for the same information as to the other 17 applicants for purposes of comparison. The bar notified him that (1) the questions wouldn't be disclosed in order to preserve secrecy of the examination content, (2) no record was made of the oral answers, and (3) the standard used to judge the answers was subjective, and thus model answers were not available.

Smith was notified by the bar that his complaints would be reviewed by a bar grievance committee at a hearing held at his convenience, at which time the bar would determine what relief, if any, should be granted.

Smith has come to you seeking your assistance in analyzing legal theories available to him in challenging the decision that he had failed the examination. In lawyer-like fashion, review the basic constitutional law principles relevant to his case. Use the facts to support your conclusions regarding his chances of success.

Question Forty-three

At 1:00 AM on June 15, 1989, Patrolman observed a vehicle driven by defendant leaving the Long Branch Saloon in Dodge City. Patrolman proceeded to follow the vehicle.

About a mile from the Long Branch, defendant stopped to pick up a hitchhiker who was carrying a large backpack. The backpack was placed in the trunk of defendant's vehicle and the trunk was locked. Patrolman continued to follow the vehicle for several miles through the downtown section of Dodge, and Patrolman finally stopped the car solely because he had a "gut feeling" that there was criminal activity taking place that required further investigation.

Patrolman asked the driver for his driver's license and registration. Because he appeared "very nervous and shaky," Patrolman instructed him to exit the vehicle. Patrolman began to frisk the driver and he felt a bulge in his front pocket. Driver said it was chewing tobacco; Patrolman directed him to remove it. A small round canister fell to the ground. Patrolman opened it and found a brownish leafy substance that he believed to be marijuana. Patrolman did not smell the suspected marijuana prior to examining the contents of the canister.

Patrolman called for backup and then commenced to question the passenger whom he described as a "throwback to the 60's, a long-haired, hippie type." Passenger readily consented to a search of the vehicle, including his backpack, stating that "he had nothing to hide." Over strenuous objection by Driver, passenger gave Patrolman the keys from the ignition.

Patrolman searched the trunk, including all of the contents of the backpack. He found nothing suspicious in the backpack. Next to the backpack he did locate approximately 100 baggies containing a white powdery substance that he believed to be cocaine. He then conducted an inventory search of the vehicle and located a set of scales skillfully hidden under the back seat of the vehicle. He placed the driver under arrest for various drug offenses and took him into custody. (The State Crime Lab certified that the canister contained marijuana and that all baggies tested positive for cocaine.)

The driver was formally charged with the following offenses under the laws of this state:

1. Unlawful Possession of Drug Paraphernalia, a Class B misdemeanor

2. Possession of a Controlled Substance, a Class B misdemeanor (marijuana, a Schedule I Controlled Substance)

3. Possession of a Controlled Substance with Intent to Distribute, a Second Degree Felony (cocaine, a Schedule II Controlled Substance)

You have been retained by the defendant to prepare a memorandum in support of a suppression motion. You are advised by your senior partner that the county attorney is notorious for raising a "good faith exception to the exclusionary rule" argument in search and seizure cases. Thoroughly discuss all arguments that ought to be raised in your memorandum in support of the motion.

Question Forty-four

During the summer of 1985, Shirley Barton and her husband, William, purchased a house perched on the side of a hill in Anytown, Ames. They used the house only in July and August for vacations. The adjacent property, located below the Bartons' on the hill, is a private school, the Raymond Military Academy. The Academy has been in operation and located on the adjacent property for more than 100 years. Two hundred students attend grades seven through twelve at the Academy. Twenty of the students are residents of Anytown, which does not have a school. The Academy allows Anytown residents to attend school at reduced tuition, which Anytown pays. The remaining students are from out-of-state families.

The Bartons knew about the school before they bought the house. The Bartons did not notice the school's activities during their summer visits because it was closed.

In September of 1986, the Bartons retired to their Anytown home. Soon, they discovered serious troubles. Every school day, the academy students march on the school's parade grounds. The noise from the students' marching drills is deafening. The students constantly chant during their one-hour drill sessions. In November, an even more serious problem emerged. The school is heated by a thirty-year-old furnace. The furnace spews thick black smoke that usually drifts directly up the hill to the Bartons' property. Shirley is able to tolerate the smoke, but the smoke causes William trouble breathing, as he has emphysema resulting from a forty-year cigarette habit.

On December 1, 1986, the Bartons complained to the Academy's headmaster about the noise and smoke. The headmaster was sympathetic, but offered little help, explaining that the Academy had financial difficulties. There was no money available to replace the furnace, and consultants had reported to the school that it could not be modified to eliminate the smoke. The Academy's principal financial donor is an eccentric retired colonel, who conditions his annual gifts upon the requirement that students march for one hour each day while loudly chanting drill refrains.

On December 2, 1986, the Bartons come to you for help.

1. Describe the forms of relief that are available to the Bartons
2. Describe the action that must be taken to secure each form of relief
3. Analyze the defenses that will be presented and the prospects for securing relief

Question Forty-five

Dodd's twenty-five-year-old insolvent son seriously injured Parks in an assault. Dodd wrote to Parks, "I know I have no legal liability, but if you agree not to sue my boy, I will reimburse you for all medical bills you incur as a result of this incident." Parks immediately replied, "I accept your offer."

Two months later, Parks wrote to Dodd, stating truthfully, "I am in need of funds. My medical expenses to date are $1,200 and my treatment is not yet finished." Dodd replied, "Your expenses are higher than I thought they would be. I cannot afford to pay all of your expenses, but if you will accept it as payment in full for my agreement to pay all of your bills, I will send you $800 on the first of next month." Parks then wrote, "Although it is not what you owe me, I have urgent need for the money and so I will accept $800 as payment in full." On the first of the following month Dodd notified Parks that she would pay nothing to her. Thereafter, Parks finished her treatment. Her total medical expenses were $1,500. To date, Dodd has paid nothing to Parks.

Question: Identify and discuss the legal claims and remedies Parks has, if any, against Dodd for her promise to pay for medical treatment.

Question Forty-six

Oaner owned a four-acre, square-shaped parcel fronting on Forest Avenue in Green Pines. In 1978, Oaner agreed to sell to Byer a two-acre portion of the property that included the entire frontage on Forest Avenue. At that time, Oaner and Byer discussed the reservation of an easement from Forest Avenue to Oaner's remaining landlocked parcel. During the discussion the parties agreed that Oaner would have the right in the future to designate the location of an easement up to 50 feet in width on the Byer property. There was then no permitted use under the local zoning ordinance that required a right of way greater than 50 feet in width. The deed from Oaner to Byer contained the following provision:

> Grantor reserves to himself, his heirs, successors and assigns, a right of way over the lands conveyed hereby to Grantee for vehicular and pedestrian traffic between Forest Avenue and the remaining lands of Grantor.

In 1982, Byer contracted to sell his parcel to Uzer. Byer approached Oaner and requested Oaner to designate the location of his easement. Oaner refused to do so and demanded instead that Byer purchase his remaining property at a price that was twice its then fair market value. Byer would not do so and conveyed his parcel to Uzer by bargain and sale deed with convenants against grantor's acts.

Uzer built a plant on the property in 1983 and, for the security of his operations, fenced in the entire perimeter of the property.

Oaner has decided to develop his property as an office building site. This use is permitted by the Green Pines zoning ordinance, but a 60-foot-wide right of way is now required by the ordinance for construction of an office building. The zoning ordinance also permits residential use with a minimum 20-foot-wide right of way to the land-locked parcel.

Oaner has instituted litigation seeking equitable relief designating a 60-foot-wide easement over the property of Uzer, which would include Uzer's present 40-foot-wide driveway. Uzer is willing to permit a 20-foot right of way along his boundary line, which would not include the driveway.

A) Discuss the rights and liabilities of Uzer; and

B) Draft the easement that you would have requested on behalf of Oaner if you had represented him at the time of his conveyance to Byer.

Question Forty-seven

In 1988 Peter began using Homebrew Shampoo, manufactured and sold by Derrick. After only a few days, he developed a scaly rash and his hair started falling out. Although he immediately stopped usage, he was completely bald in two months. Peter sued Derrick for making and selling a defective product that caused baldness and rash. He sought not only compensatory damages, but punitive damages, claiming that Derrick knew the product was defective when he sold it.

Peter intends to call Victor at trial, to testify that Victor noticed some hair loss within a few weeks of starting to use Homebrew Shampoo back in 1984. Victor continued to use the product nonetheless, and within two years he lost most of his hair and complained to Derrick about the shampoo. He had no rash. All that now remains of Victor's hair is a thin strip around his ears and on the back of his head.

Question: Analyze the admissibility of Victor's testimony according to the Federal Rules of Evidence, indicating any potential problems suggested by these facts.

Question Forty-eight

In 1983, following hearings on the pollution dangers of high-sulphur-content fuels and the problems of assuring adequate fuel supplies for the nation, Congress enacted the Federal Energy and Pollution Control Act (FEPCA). FEPCA provides standards for the use by public and private utilities of various major fuels. It sets maximum permissible pollution levels. FEPCA imposes a ban on the use by such utilities of all fuels having over a designated level of sulphur content, regardless of pollution levels actually produced by emissions. The congressional hearings included substantial testimony on the difficulty of measuring hazards to health from the use of high-sulphur-content fuels.

The state of Neuter has large supplies of fuels with high sulphur content. The state allows the use of high-sulphur fuels even though emissions exceed the normal pollution standards otherwise mandated by state law. Utility companies in Neuter have installed equipment designed to use these high-sulphur-content fuels. Contracts have been entered into based on the availability of this cheap, plentiful source of fuel. Consumers in Neuter enjoy lower energy costs as a result.

Conformity to FEPCA requirements will prevent use of Neuter's high-sulphur fuels. Costs of alternative fuels would be much higher. In addition, some Neuter utility companies might even be forced to go out of business.

Discuss the constitutionality of FEPCA. Do not discuss any due process, equal protection, or contract clause issues.

Question Forty-nine

On June 1, 1986, Owens contracted to sell his residence to Byer for $100,000 cash with a deposit of $10,000. The contract provided that the seller would convey "good and marketable title, free and clear of all liens and encumbrances." A closing of title was to take place "on or before September 1, 1986," at the office of Byer's attorney.

On August 20, 1986, Byer told Owens that he would need about two weeks additional time to raise the necessary funds. Owens replied that he had to close title on September 1, 1986, in accordance with the contract, because he needed the proceeds to purchase another home that same day. To make sure the closing was not delayed, Owens sent a certified letter to Byer on August 25, 1986, setting the closing date for September 1, 1986, at 10:00 AM at the office of Owens's attorney. Time was specifically made "of the essence."

The next day Owens realized that September 1 was a legal holiday (Labor Day). He immediately sent a telegram to Byer stating: "Disregard letter of 8/25/86. Change closing date to 9/2/86. Time still OF THE ESSENCE." Byer received both the certified letter and the telegram on August 27, 1986. He then called Owens and requested an extension of seven days. By letter dated August 29, 1986, Owens replied: "Without waiving any of my rights, I will close title on September 5, 1986, but no later."

On August 30, 1986, Byer for the first time examined a copy of Owens' recorded deed. Title was derived from Sam Sellalot on February 1, 1952. Byer noted that the third course of the metes and bounds description recited "From the edge of Main Street North 30° West 200 feet to Babbling Brook." Byer's survey showed it was 220 feet from Main Street to Babbling Brook. At the end of the deed description were the following clauses:

A. Reserving unto the Grantor herein a right of way from Main Street to the rear of the property for public access to Babbling Brook for fishing and other recreational purposes.

B. Subject to rights of Powerful Electric Company to install, maintain, repair and replace electric lines over the premises to any dwelling erected thereon.

Sellalot's signature on the deed was witnessed by and acknowledged before Owens, who happened to be a Notary Public. A notary's stamp and raised seal were duly affixed to the deed.

Byer promptly notified Owens on September 2, 1986, that the deed raised certain questions in his mind. Owens replied by merely renewing his demand that Byer close title no later than September 5, 1986, or risk forfeiture of his deposit.

Because the house has increased greatly in value, Byer wants to consummate the purchase. However, he cannot raise the necessary funds until September 8, 1986, at the earliest. Byer has consulted you to represent his interests. Draft a letter to Owens' attorney fully setting forth Byer's legal position.

Question Fifty

Cotton Basics ("CB") manufactures plain white cotton tee shirts, which are frequently used for silk screening. On April 1, CB received a call from Toto's Tees, a local company with which CB had not previously done business. The parties discussed the availability and price of CB's white tee shirts. Immediately thereafter, Toto's sent CB the following letter:

> Cotton Basics Order Department:
>
> Please send 20 dozen white cotton tee shirts by April 21. We understand that the price is $8.00 per dozen, seller to pay delivery costs.
>
> Very truly yours,
> Toto's Tees

Three days later, Toto's received a letter from CB that read: "This is to confirm your order of 20 dozen white cotton tee shirts, to be delivered by April 21, $8/dozen, seller to pay delivery costs. Your attention is further drawn to the terms and conditions on the bottom of this confirmation."

A statement at the bottom of the confirmation, written in boldface red, stated: "Cotton Basics makes no warranties, express or implied, with respect to tee shirts sold. There are no implied warranties of merchantability or fitness for a particular purpose."

The tee shirts arrived on April 21 and Toto's prewashed them to prepare them for silk screening. The tee shirts had a shrinkage rate of 15 percent. The customary shrinkage rate for white cotton tee shirts in the industry is 8–10 percent.

Toto's telephoned CB about the shrinkage problem. CB stated that there were no warranties of the shrinkage rate of the shirts, and that they would not take them back. CB demanded that Toto's pay for the shirts.

Toto's has come to see you. Toto's would like to send the shirts back and not pay. What are the arguments for and against returning the product?

Question Fifty-one

Lawfirm leased a third-floor suite in a new office building designed for lawyers. The building was well known for its state-of-the-art centralized electronic support facilities. Those centralized facilities included word processing, computerized research terminals, and electronic mail and telephone systems. Soon after Lawfirm moved in, a defective water pipe burst and caused flooding in the basement. Pipeco had manufactured and installed the defective pipe. The pipe was replaced the next day, but the water damage rendered the central facilities inoperative for several weeks. Lawfirm's suite was undamaged.

As a result of this incident, Lawfirm's employees were unable to perform and bill for some of their usual work; several contracts could not be drafted and produced for Lawfirm's clients, who lost valuable deals as a result; and one major client discharged Lawfirm as retained counsel.

There is no factual dispute as to the cause of the interrupted service or its effect on Lawfirm's operations. Lawfirm has filed suit against Pipeco to recover for its economic loss.

The complaint contains three separate counts: (1) negligence, (2) strict liability, and (3) breach of implied warranties. Pipeco has moved for judgment on the pleadings, or in the alternative for summary judgment, on all three counts. You are the judge's law clerk.

Write a draft opinion deciding the motion.

Question Fifty-two

Denise was walking through a park one evening when a man jumped out of the bushes with a knife and threatened to rape her. Denise fled. As the man pursued her, Denise picked up a very large rock, turned, and threw it at him. The rock missed him and, instead, struck the head of a jogger who happened by. The jogger died shortly thereafter from the injuries suffered. The would-be rapist fled the scene and was never identified.

Question: Denise is prosecuted for murder of the jogger. Discuss the elements the prosecution would have to prove to convict her of murder and any defenses that these facts reasonably suggest might be available to her. Do not discuss her liability for any other crimes. Apply common law principles.

Question Fifty-three

While Mary was walking along a downtown street, she saw her husband, Jack, running out of a bank carrying a bag. At home that night Mary asked Jack what he was doing in the bank that day, and he told her that he robbed it. Because of this disclosure, and Jack's subsequent indictment for bank robbery, Mary divorced Jack. At Jack's federal bank robbery trial, held after the divorce, the prosecutor wants to call Mary as her first witness to testify that Jack admitted the bank robbery and to testify that Jack has a bad reputation in the community as to his truthfulness and honesty.

Question: Discuss whether the prosecutor can expect, over all appropriate objections, to have Mary so testify.

Question Fifty-four

Following an unsuccessful eight years of national campaigning, presidential candidate George Washington planned to return to his home state of East Virginia. Supporters wanted to welcome Washington home at the Mt. Vernon International Airport where he would arrive. The Airport is a large airport, serves several major airlines, and has four concourses and many gates. The planned welcome-home gathering would involve about 500 enthusiastic supporters and a 15-minute speech by Washington to the crowd.

The Airport is owned and operated by the State of East Virginia Department of Transportation. One of the Airport's regulations forbids any gathering of more than 200 people in the common areas. This regulation is designed to avoid congestion and to promote the smooth operation of the Airport. The Washington supporters have requested permission to hold their welcome-home gathering in the Airport, but the Airport has denied this request, citing the regulation against gatherings.

Question: The Washington supporters ask you to file a lawsuit seeking to obtain access to the Airport gate for the welcome-home gathering. Discuss your arguments and evaluate the Washington supporters' chances for success.

Question Fifty-five

Otto Owens is the owner of the Cycle City Bicycle Shop ("Cycle City"). On April 1, Cycle City entered into a written contract with Timbertrack, a newly formed company that manufactures and sells folding mountain bikes. Timbertrack agreed to supply Cycle City with five folding mountain bikes every other month for the next year. Timbertrack agreed to deliver five bikes on the first day of each of the months of May, July, September, November, January, and March. The price to Cycle City was $250 per bike. Cycle City's retail customers would pay $400.

Timbertrack made its deliveries on May 1 and July 1. Owens paid promptly.

On July 15, Mark Marsden, the owner of a bicycle shop in the next county, told Owens that Timbertrack was in financial difficulty and was several months behind in shipments to his shop.

On July 16, Owens comes to your office. He explains that the next shipment of bikes is due on September 1. He is concerned that they will not be delivered in time for his annual Labor Day sale.

Owens also tells you that he can order a virtually identical bike from Fast Freddie's for $225 apiece. Owens is certain he can sell Fast Freddie's model for the same $400 retail price.

Owens asks you whether he can cancel his contract with Timbertrack and order the bikes from Fast Freddie's. Please advise.

Question Fifty-six

Mr. and Mrs. Homeowner and their two children reside in the rural Borough of Meadow View. Their home is located in a zone that permits only one-family dwellings. About a year ago they decided to build an addition to their home so that Mrs. Homeowner's widowed mother could live with them. They submitted plans to the Meadow View building inspector that showed an additional bedroom on the ground floor with a small efficiency kitchen and a bathroom. The addition contained no separate entrance of its own; it was connected to the remainder of the house by a hallway off the living room.

The zoning ordinance of the Borough of Meadow View prohibited multi-family dwellings in all zones. A multi-family dwelling was defined in the ordinance as "a building designed for or occupied by more than one family." A one-family dwelling was defined as "a separate building designed for or occupied exclusively by one family." The term "family" was defined as "one or more persons living and cooking together as a single housekeeping unit, exclusive of household servants."

Mrs. Homeowner told the building inspector that the addition was intended to create a mother-daughter type facility, but this was not stated in the application. The building inspector issued a building permit and construction was commenced shortly thereafter. The work was nearly half completed when Watchful, a neighboring property owner, became aware of the proposed use and complained that it would violate the zoning provision restricting all dwellings to one-family use. He immediately commenced an action against Homeowner and the Borough of Meadow View seeking to enjoin further construction and to revoke the building permit.

While the litigation was pending, Meadow View amended its zoning ordinance to provide: "Mother-daughter dwelling units shall be permitted in all residential zones." No other changes were made to the zoning ordinance, which previously made no reference to mother-daughter type uses.

Both Homeowner and Watchful have filed motions for summary judgment contending that the above facts, which are not in dispute, entitle them to judgment as a matter of law.

You are the law clerk assigned to research the matter and to prepare a memorandum for the court's guidance in deciding the motions.

Write the memorandum.

Question Fifty-seven

For Bart's fifth birthday, his mother invited several children for cake and ice cream, including Jason, her neighbor's son of the same age. He arrived with a package, which he gave to Bart, saying, "My mommy picked this out just for you."

Bart eagerly unwrapped the package and was delighted to find a toy called "Violent Volcano." It contained a model of a volcano for assembly and two vials of liquid. The liquids, when poured together into the opening at the top, would create a chemical reaction simulating the smoke and noise of a volcanic eruption. The legend on the side of the box said, "CAUTION: NOT FOR CHILDREN UNDER 5 YEARS OF AGE." The instructions warned against shaking the vials prior to pouring because the agitation could cause the liquid substances to explode upon mixing.

While his mother talked on the phone, Bart and his friends began to assemble the volcano. However, when it was time for their favorite program, they went to the T.V. room, leaving the various parts and the two vials on the table. Some ten minutes later, as his mother continued her conversation, Bart's 18-month-old brother entered the room and spotted the toy. He picked up each of the vials and shook them. However, when they failed to do anything interesting, he replaced them on the table and left the room.

Shortly thereafter, the older boys returned to the volcano, and poured the contents of the vials into it. The ensuing explosion caused Bart to suffer facial burns and Jason to incur an eye injury.

Suit was commenced on behalf of Bart and Jason against a number of parties, including the mothers of both boys. All parties except the mothers settled prior to trial, and the matter proceeded to trial without a jury. The judge found the facts as set forth above. As the law clerk, in order to assist the judge in rendering an opinion, you have been requested to prepare a memorandum discussing the liabilities and any legal defenses of the mothers.

Question Fifty-eight

Sally Smith was married to Joe "Rambo" Smith, a well-known karate expert. Throughout the course of the marriage, Joe frequently physically abused Sally. One day, Joe beat Sally because he did not like the dinner she prepared. He then left the house. On his way out of the house, he turned around and shouted, "I'm going to come back and kill you."

Sally, fed up with the beatings and also nervous that Joe would indeed come back and kill her, called up Frankie, an old friend of hers. She told Frankie, "I've had it. Joe has beaten me up one too many times, and I'm sick of it. I'll give you $10,000 if you kill Joe. I think he's down at the karate club working out." Frankie agreed to kill Joe and said he would leave right away to do it.

About an hour later, Sally had second thoughts. She called Frankie's house and left the following message on his answering machine: "I've changed my mind; I think it would be a mistake to do what we decided to do. It would be better if we sought counseling." Frankie had already left the house, and about half an hour later, he found Joe at the karate club and shot and killed him.

Question: Discuss the possible charges against Sally and Frankie, and their potential defenses, using common law.

Question Fifty-nine

On February 10, 1988, Dan Divot, a struggling car salesman in Cleveland, Ohio, received a telephone call from his old college classmate, Bob Backswing, the golf pro at Rolling Hills Country Club in Fairway, Ames, an isolated town in northeastern Ames. Bob and Dan had been on the same college golf team in the late 70's, and Bob called Dan to ask him if he would be willing to work as his assistant pro at Rolling Hills. (Bob was to be Dan's employer.) Bob offered to pay Dan $25,000 a year and told Dan that he would have this job "as long as I'm head pro here at Rolling Hills." Dan indicated that he wanted to be paid $30,000 a year, but Bob said that $25,000 was all that he could afford. Dan indicated that he really needed $30,000 a year, but that he thought that he and Bob could work out the final salary after Dan arrived on the scene. One of the conditions of Dan's employment would be that, upon termination, Dan would not be able to be a teaching professional at any club within 25 miles of Rolling Hills Country Club for a period of 15 years.

Dan did some preliminary investigation into the country club situation in northeastern Ames and made some inquiries about other golf courses. He was advised that there were only two golf courses within 75 miles of Rolling Hills Country Club and that they were both about 30 miles from Rolling Hills. Dan called Bob back three days later and told him that he would accept his offer, but that he still wanted $30,000 a year. Bob said that the best he could offer "for now" was $25,000, but they could talk about the matter later. Dan arrived in Fairway, Ames, on April 1, 1988, and started working for Bob at that time.

Ten days after Dan started work, Bob Backswing called Dan into his office and told Dan he had taken a job as head pro at Lakeview Country Club (one of the other two courses in the area). Bob said, "I will unfortunately have to terminate your employment with me at Rolling Hills effective three weeks from today."

Dan has relocated his entire family to Ames. He wishes to remain here. He has been offered a job as head pro at Eagle's Nest Country Club, but has now determined to his chagrin that Eagle's Nest Country Club is in fact only 24 miles from Rolling Hills, and not 30 miles as he had heard. Bob has told Dan that he must enforce the restrictive covenant and that he will seek an injunction if Dan takes the position at Eagle's Nest.

Dan asks your assistance. If Bob seeks an injunction, what legal defenses will you present? What is the likelihood of success in avoiding the injunction? Discuss any claims Dan may have against Bob beyond a claim for compensation for services rendered until his termination date. At what *rate* is Dan entitled to be paid?

Question Sixty

Harriet was Vicki and David's next-door neighbor. One night she heard violent noises followed by Vicki's yelling, "My God, darlin', you're killing me." When the paramedics and police arrived, Vicki was found alone, bleeding profusely from an obvious stab wound in her chest. She said weakly, "If I don't make it, don't let David get away with this." At the hospital, Vicki told the treating physician that David had stabbed her during a domestic dispute. While recovering, she gave a signed and notarized statement to the police, telling them the same thing.

At the time of David's trial for assault, Vicki and David are together again, and when she is called to testify by the prosecution, Vicki denies that David was the one who stabbed her or that she ever said he was.

Question: Using the Federal Rules of Evidence, discuss the admissibility of Vicki's statements, indicating whether and to what extent they would be admissible.

Question Sixty-one

For ten years, Mr. and Mrs. Jones (Seller) owned a modest house on 20 acres in northern Vermont. In the fall of 1987, they decided to sell their property. The Joneses engaged the services of a real estate broker (Broker) to sell the property for $70,000.00. Unknown to either the Broker or Seller, the property contained underground marble deposits worth close to $1,000,000.00. Through confidential, though lawful, means, presence of the marble deposits was known to Slick Snively (Slick), a businessman of sharp practices specializing in undervalued situations and quick profit.

Slick submitted a written offer to purchase the property for $70,000.00. His offer stipulated that the $50.00 deposit accompanying the offer was to be applied to the purchase price or returned to Slick if the offer was not accepted by the Seller. On January 10, Seller endorsed acceptance on the offer of purchase and had it delivered to Slick's attorney. The contract gave Slick the right to survey the property prior to closing.

On January 29, on a visit to the property, Mrs. Charles Dion, wife of an elderly former farm worker, went onto the property and had a conversation with Slick's surveyor. Mrs. Dion disclosed that her husband, who had been born and raised at the house, had that morning entered into a contract directly with Seller to purchase the property. The purchase price was to be $75,000.00 and, as called for by the contract, a deposit of $7,000 had been delivered to the Joneses.

The agent informed Mrs. Dion that Slick had already entered into a contract much earlier in the month. He suggested that Mrs. Dion see the attorney for Slick. The next evening, Mr. Dion went to the attorney's office to inquire about the property and informed Slick's attorney that he had made a deposit of $7,000.00 toward its purchase and had entered into a contract. The attorney for Slick told Mr. Dion that he had been hired to abstract the title. He also stated that he was "working for another party, therefore I can't talk to you and suggest you best see your lawyer." With this Mr. Dion left.

Seller executed and delivered a deed to convey title to Mr. Dion on February 11, 1988. The deed recited a consideration of $75,000.00. Mr. Dion took possession of the property after receiving and recording the deed.

Discuss the respective interests of Slick and Mr. Dion in the property. If the question of ownership were to be taken to court, what would be the arguments and counter-arguments of Slick and Mr. Dion? What remedies are available to the parties? What do you believe the decision of the court should be and upon what grounds?

Question Sixty-two

Congress adopted a federal statute comprehensively regulating the transportation of spent nuclear fuel which, among other things, provides that no such material may be transported within ten miles of any municipality with a population of 10,000 or more. The statute provides, "Any restriction of a state or political subdivision thereof which is inconsistent with any part of this statute is unenforceable."

The legislature of the State of Northwest subsequently passed a law "intended to complement and be consistent with" the federal law. The Northwest statute provides, *inter alia*, that no spent nuclear fuel may be transported within 100 miles of any "municipality populated by 10,000 or more." Because of Northwest's topography, the state statute would effectively preclude any transportation of spent nuclear fuel through the state. The federal statute would allow limited access through Northwest.

Question: Is the Northwest statute enforceable? Discuss all material issues.

Question Sixty-three

Dan Hauler was employed as a driver by XYZ Trucking Company. As he was hauling a load of lumber on a narrow, winding road, he stopped his truck to admire a particularly nice view next to a sign that stated: "State Law Prohibits Stopping Vehicles In This Area."

Patty Driver was driving her car on the same narrow, winding road. She came around a sharp curve and struck the rear of Hauler's truck. Paula Passenger, Driver's friend, was seriously injured in the accident. Driver was furious because Hauler's truck was stopped in the road. After attending to Passenger, she ran over to Hauler and, holding a tire iron over her head menacingly, she demanded an apology. Hauler managed to persuade Driver to put down the tire iron, but when she said disparaging words about Hauler, Hauler punched Driver and broke her nose.

Question: Discuss the potential claims that Driver, Passenger, Hauler, and XYZ have against each other. Do not discuss insurance claims, defenses, or damages.

Question Sixty-four

The Heber Chamber of Commerce authorized its part-time Executive Director, Bill Welsh, a well known promoter, to try to get a major sports franchise into Heber. Welsh contacted the Sioux City Sues basketball franchise owner, Dodge Ford, who was eager to sell the basketball club. Welsh said he needed a side broker's fee of 1%, since he had to moonlight as a promoter. Welsh disclosed the separate fee arrangement to the Chamber. Ford said he would agree to a limited brokerage fee for Welsh and would discuss a sale of his franchise to Heber provided that he and Heber reached an agreement on price and further provided that the transaction could be structured to minimize adverse tax consequences to Ford through a consulting agreement for a portion of the price.

Welsh wrote the following letter to Ford, who returned it signed.

To: Dodge Ford   May 1, 1986

You agree to pay 1% of the total sales price of any sports club sale I arrange with the Heber City Chamber of Commerce during the next 15 months.

/s/ Bill Welsh

Accepted.

/s/ Dodge Ford

After months of discussion Welsh had the following term sheet sent to Ford, which Ford signed and returned to Welsh.

To: Dodge Ford   January 10, 1988

A. *Sale of Franchise*

Sales price cash $2,000,000; $200,000 at closing, blance in one year to be escrowed at Zions Bank. Assume all debt of $4,000,000.

B. *Consulting Agreement* - Dodge Ford personally

- 2 years at $350,000 per year whether consult or not
- No other club ownership for 2 years
- Heber Chamber will decide if and when any services are needed.

/s/ Bill Welsh   /s/ Dodge Ford

A sales agreement and a consulting agreement were separately prepared and executed on March 1, 1988. Each contract was consistent with the terms set forth in the term sheet of January 10, 1988, but neither contract mentioned the other and each contained a standard, boiler-plate integration clause. At the closing, the Heber Chamber paid $200,000 to Ford.

In February 1989, Welsh called Ford and demanded payment of a brokerage fee under the terms of his May 1, 1986, letter agreement. Ford asked, "When will you pay my first year's consulting fees?" Welsh replied, "The Chamber has had a winning season so it won't need any services and so doesn't owe you any fees." Ford stated emotionally, "Well, to blazes with your finder's fee," and hung up.

On March 1, Zions delivered a check to Ford for $1,800,000 (plus accrued interest).

Ford comes to you for advice. Does Ford have an enforceable claim against Heber for payment of consulting fees? Does Welsh have an enforceable claim against Ford for payment of his broker's fee? If Ford cashes the check from Zions, what will be the effect, if any, on his claims against Heber and his obligations to Welsh? Discuss the issues, claims, and defenses, particularly those relating to formation and enforceability of these contracts.

Question Sixty-five

Alice acquired real property described as "everything north of the fence line up to Highway 40." Alice used all of the property so described for ten years and then sold it to Bill, using the same legal description.

Cathy owned the real property south of the fence line. Fifteen years after Bill purchased his property, he and Cathy verbally agreed that Cathy would buy all of Bill's property. Because of their agreement, and with Bill's consent, Cathy performed a survey of Bill's property and discovered that the fence line had been incorrectly placed 100 feet onto her property. Cathy then demanded that Bill reduce the purchase price accordingly to take into account the 100 feet already belonging to Cathy.

Question: Discuss the claims each party would make regarding the 100-foot-wide strip of real property immediately south of the fence line, and discuss whether Bill can now refuse to sell the property to Cathy. Do not discuss the possible adjustments to price.

Question Sixty-six

Bob and Brenda Buyer lived in a house in the country that had no utility services. They had electric lights powered by batteries that were recharged by a generator. One day their generator broke down, and they took it back to Sam Seller, the dealer they bought it from. Unfortunately, it was no longer under warranty, and it would be expensive to fix. Sam offered to rent them a generator while they decided whether to buy a new generator or fix the old one.

They mentioned to Sam that Brenda was often alone and would have to be able to start it by herself. She was a small woman. Sam said he had just the thing for them. He rented them a small generator, the Hercules Home 1000. After a couple of weeks the Buyers decided to buy a new generator.

They told Sam that they needed one with more power than the Hercules Home 1000. Sam said a heavy duty commercial model, the Hercules Power 2000, would be just the thing for them. It would cost $2,500. He would give them $1,000 as a trade-in for their old generator. Sam ordered one for them. It arrived a week later. Bob and Brenda paid $750 in addition to the trade-in, and agreed to pay the remaining $750 over the next three months.

The Buyers took the new generator home. Unfortunately, Brenda could not start it. Bob was just barely able to do so. Nevertheless they used the generator to charge their batteries that evening. When the batteries were charged they shut the generator off, and the switch broke.

The next day the Buyers took the Hercules Power 2000 back to Sam and told him they wanted their money back because Brenda could not start it. They also pointed out that the switch had broken the first time they used it, so they wanted to return the generator for that reason. Sam said no, a deal was a deal, and besides, he had had to specially order the generator. He said he would repair the switch under warranty, but that they would have to pay the rest of the $750 agreed to. They said they wanted their money back, and were certainly not going to pay him the other $750. Sam said in that case he would claim a security interest in the Hercules Power 2000, and he would keep it in his possession until it was paid for in full.

Six months have passed. The Buyers still do not have a generator, and Sam still has the Hercules Power 2000. The Buyers have come to see if there is anything you can do for them.

What rights do the Buyers have?

What causes of action do they have against Sam?

What are their chances of success?

Question Sixty-seven

Sam owned Blackacre and Whiteacre, two unimproved vacant tracts of land. The county assessor's records listed each tract as containing 10 acres. Without having seen either tract, but having checked the assessor's records, Bob telephoned Sam and said, "I offer to buy Blackacre and Whiteacre for $20,000, $10,000 now and $10,000 in one year." Sam responded, "O.K., I'll have the papers ready tomorrow." The following day Bob paid Sam $10,000, and the parties signed a land sale contract prepared by Sam's lawyer. The contract described the property as "Blackacre, containing 20 acres, more or less," and did not mention Whiteacre. The contract was otherwise consistent with oral communications between Bob and Sam.

The contract did not contain language making time of the essence.

During the next 12 months the following events occurred:

A. Bob sold his interest in the contract to Cal for $10,000. Cal notified Sam of his purchase.

B. The announcement of a proposed freeway increased land values in the area from $1,000 per acre to $3,000 per acre.

C. Bob, Sam, and Cal each learned that while Blackacre contained 10 acres, Whiteacre contained only 7 acres.

On the date the final payment was due, Cal tendered $7,000 to Sam and demanded deeds to Blackacre and Whiteacre. Sam rejected the tender and two days later notified Cal that the purchaser's interest in the contract was "terminated because of nonpayment."

Land values in the area are continuing to increase rapidly.

What rights and remedies, if any, does Cal have? Discuss.

Question Sixty-eight

The following question comes from the New Jersey Bar Exam for February 1986. The task was to write a brief either for the defendant or for the government, either in support of a motion to suppress evidence or in opposition to it.

Choose a side and write your own brief. Better still, if you have the time, try writing a brief for each side.

Walt Witker is a longtime government attorney employed by the United States Department of Defense. About a year ago he was suspected of being a homosexual. A Department of Defense investigator was assigned to monitor his activities. The investigator bugged Witker's apartment and his private government office, tapped his telephones, and set up remote television cameras to observe him through peep holes placed throughout his apartment and office. These efforts confirmed Witker's homosexual activities and disclosed contacts with suspicious persons.

On a recent evening at 10:00 PM, the investigator made an unannounced visit to Witker's apartment. For several hours he badgered, taunted, and humiliated Witker about his homosexual activities, repeatedly playing excerpts of the audio and video tapes acquired over the past year. The investigator chastised him for these activities and emphasized how vulnerable they made him to espionage efforts of foreign governments.

Finally, Witker broke down. He confided that he already had been blackmailed and had revealed defense secrets to a foreign agent. Upon the investigator's suggestion, he voluntarily wrote out a detailed statement of these events.

Witker was promptly indicted for espionage. He is making a motion to suppress each and all of the tapes, as well as the oral and written statements to the investigator.

Take your choice. Write the argument portion of a brief:

a) On behalf of Witker, in support of the motion to suppress;

or

b) On behalf of the government, in opposition to the motion to suppress. In either case, anticipate and meet the principal arguments of the other side.

Selected State Topics

Question Sixty-nine: Professional Responsibility

(Code of Professional Responsibility)

Father gave Son a $25,000 "stake in life" as a present for Son's college graduation, expressing the hope that Son would use it to start a business. Father sought Broker's recommendation of an attorney who could handle negotiations and legal matters in setting up a business venture and received the name of Lawyer, Broker's close friend. Father told Lawyer his objective and said that he would pay all the legal fees to get Son set up in some suitable venture. Lawyer agreed to assist. Father scheduled a meeting for Son and gave Lawyer a $3,000 retainer fee. Lawyer deposited it all in his business account, except for $300.00, which he kept as a present for Broker.

The next week Lawyer met with Son, who was accompanied by his former college roommate. Son and Roommate wanted to open a restaurant with Son's "stake" money as capital and Roommate as manager. Son, however, advised Lawyer that Father disliked Roommate and should not be told of his involvement until the restaurant was opened. Son desired to be a "silent" partner (he knew nothing about restaurants) and requested that Lawyer and Roommate set up the deal while Son took a vacation.

Lawyer and Roommate's attorney thereafter met several times to work out the deal. Father learned of Roommate's involvement when he received Lawyer's monthly accounting 30 days later: the time slips revealed Lawyer's meeting with Roommate. Father demanded that Lawyer extricate Son from the venture immediately. Lawyer notified Roommate's attorney that the deal was off.

Question: Discuss the ethical issues suggested by these facts and the principles governing their resolution under the Code of Professional Responsibility.

Question Seventy: Wills

(Uniform Probate Code)

In 1979, Walt Willwriter executed the following will: "Upon my death all my estate is to be divided as I have previously written out." The will was properly signed and witnessed. No attachments or further writings were with the will, nor were any subsequently found. In 1985, crippled by arthritis, Walt decided to change his will to leave his estate to his good friend Seth. He executed a new will to that effect, which although Walt did not expressly so state, was intended to revoke his previous will. This new will was witnessed only by his attorney.

Walt was unable to sign it himself, but did manage to put his initials ("W.W.") at the bottom of the will. In 1988, Walt died.

Question: You represent Walt's surviving spouse Sarah. Sarah believes she is entitled to all of Walt's estate and seeks your advice. Counsel Sarah on the validity of the two wills and any distributions to her of Walt's estate. Assume the Uniform Probate Code is in effect.

Question Seventy-one: Corporations

(Model Business Corporation Act)

The directors of Corporation issued 100,000 shares of common stock to Larry Landholder in exchange for a certain piece of property owned by Landholder. A few days later, the property was appraised at $10,000.

Question: Shareholder is concerned about the effect this transaction may have on the value of his stock in Corporation. He asks your advice whether he has any potential claims against the directors, and if so, on what theories. What is your advice?

Question Seventy-two: Domestic Relations

(Uniform Marriage and Divorce Act)

Herb and Wilma were married in 1970. They have one child, Charles. In 1987, Wilma passed the bar examination and joined a large firm. Her salary as a first-year associate was $60,000. Wilma filed a petition for dissolution of the marriage shortly after starting work, alleging adultery as grounds and naming Herb's boss as corespondent.

Wilma drafted a separation agreement giving Wilma full custody of Charles and providing no maintenance to Herb. Herb signed the agreement. Two weeks later Herb had a serious accident. He will be unable to work for five years.

Question: Herb comes to you for advice. Assuming Herb's state has enacted the Uniform Marriage and Divorce Act, advise Herb on the following:

1. Is the form of the petition for dissolution proper?

2. Is the maintenance provision in the separation agreement enforceable?

3. Is the child custody provision in the separation agreement enforceable?

4. How might the allegation of adultery affect the court's decision on custody?

Question Seventy-three: Professional Responsibility

(Code of Professional Responsibility)

Client has retained Andy Attorney to institute legal proceedings against Bill Bookkeeper, the former controller and auditor for the sole proprietorship owned by Client. Client believes that $40,000 has disappeared from his business accounts, over which Bill Bookkeeper had sole control.

Bookkeeper is represented by Pam Defender, a former public defender, now in private practice. Attorney advised Defender in writing that if Defender's client did not acknowledge liability and repay all of the money, Defender would ''be representing Bookkeeper not only in civil court but also in criminal court, as the entire file will be turned over to the D.A.'s office.''

Attorney's letter to Defender went unanswered, as did Attorney's phone calls to her. Exasperated, Attorney told Client to call Bookkeeper directly and let him know that they were considering criminal charges against him unless he repaid all of the money. Bookkeeper responded by offering $20,000 to Client to settle the case. Client rejected the offer.

Preparing for trial, Attorney decided to retain a fingerprint expert to prove that Bookkeeper's fingerprints were on certain critical documents. The fingerprint expert quoted a rate of $165.00 per hour, or 10% of the gross jury verdict. Attorney retained him for the percentage rate, believing that this would save money for Client. The expert, located out of town, stated that he also wanted Attorney to pay for his first-class airfare, a limousine to and from his hotel and court, and a two-bedroom suite in the city's finest hotel.

At trial, Attorney gave an impassioned closing argument, telling the jury that he had personally examined the evidence and was convinced of the justness of Client's cause. Attorney further told the jury that in his opinion Bookkeeper was unbelievable as a witness and knew that his case was weak because Bookkeeper had offered Client $20,000 to settle the case.

Question: Identify the ethical issues in Attorney's representation of Client and Pam Defender's representation of Bookkeeper. The Code of Professional Responsibility applies in Attorney's jurisdiction.

Question Seventy-four: Corporations

(New York Law)

DeskCo., a New York corporation, manufactures office furniture and is located in Poughkeepsie, New York. At a duly called meeting of its Board of Directors on January 12, 1988, DeskCo.'s independent certified public accountant reported that DeskCo. had total assets of $1,100,000 consisting of: (1) an office building, last appraised in February 1987 at $300,000; (2) plant, machinery, and equipment with a combined current fair market value of $300,000; (3) furniture inventory with a current fair market value of $100,000 and other inventory with a fair market value of $100,000; and (4) $300,000 cash. The accountant also reported that DeskCo.'s current liabilities totaled $200,000. On January 12, 1988, DeskCo.'s stated capital was $500,000, and DeskCo.'s certificate of incorporation contains no restrictions relevant to the declaration or payment of dividends.

Jones, one of the directors present at the meeting, knew that the office building next door to DeskCo.'s, which was comparable in all respects to the one owned by DeskCo., had been sold on January 8, 1988, for $100,000 after a lengthy search for a buyer. Jones also knew that half of DeskCo.'s furniture inventory, which was not insured, had been destroyed when the warehouse basement flooded during a rainstorm on the night of January 11, 1988. Neither the accountant nor any of DeskCo.'s other directors was aware of the sale of the adjoining building or of the flood damage, and Jones did not inform them of these matters.

Wright, another director of DeskCo., in reliance on the accountant's report, duly moved to declare a dividend of $200,000. The motion was seconded and carried by the unanimous vote of all ten of DeskCo.'s directors, including Jones.

DeskCo. also packages and distributes perfume. On January 20, 1988, DeskCo. entered into a written contract with GoodSmells, a local perfume manufacturer, which is not a shareholder of DeskCo., for the purchase of GoodSmells' entire 1,000 gallon inventory of "B"-type perfume for $50 per gallon. Delivery and payment were to be made on March 1, 1988.

On February 16, another perfume distributor offered GoodSmells $60 per gallon for its entire inventory of "B"-type perfume. On February 19, GoodSmells learned that DeskCo.'s certificate of incorporation states that DeskCo.'s sole corporate purpose is to manufacture furniture. That same day, GoodSmells informed DeskCo. that it would not deliver any perfume under its contract with DeskCo., contending that its contract with DeskCo. was invalid.

Blue, who lives in Poughkeepsie, is the president and majority shareholder of DeskCo. On December 4, 1987, Blue purchased a $10,000 diamond bracelet from Green, a local jeweler. Blue asked Green to take a promissory note for $10,000 in payment for the bracelet. Green knew that Blue was the president and majority shareholder of DeskCo. and, for that reason, accepted the note, which was payable in 30 days and which was signed "Blue."

On January 4, 1988, Blue refused Green's demand for payment of the note and Green duly commenced an action against Blue and DeskCo. to recover on the note. Blue and DeskCo. each served answers consisting of a general denial. Green then moved for an order of attachment against Blue and DeskCo.

In support of his motion, Green has offered as evidence the promissory note and an affidavit setting forth the foregoing pertinent facts. Green's affidavit also alleges that Green knows of no counterclaims by Blue or DeskCo. and that Green believes that Blue might transfer substantial assets to others with the intent to frustrate the enforcement of any judgment that Green might obtain. Blue and DeskCo. have not offered any evidence in opposition to the motion, but both contend that Green's motion should be denied as a matter of law.

(a) Did each of the directors of DeskCo. properly vote to declare a dividend?

(b) Was GoodSmell's contention concerning the invalidity of its contract with DeskCo. correct?

(c) How should the court rule on Green's motion against Blue and DeskCo. for an order of attachment?

Question Seventy-five:
Trusts/Property/Contracts

(California Law)

A was the owner in fee simple of a parcel of real property on which there was a building housing five tenants who carried on separate businesses in the building. In 1980, *A* entered into a new 10-year written lease with *B*, one of those tenants. In the lease, *A* convenanted to keep the leased premises "in good repair and condition throughout the term of this lease." Part of the property to the rear of the building consisted of a parking lot exclusively controlled and maintained by *A* for the convenience of his tenants and their customers.

A died in 1982, devising his entire estate to *T* in trust for the benefit of *A*'s daughters, who survived him. During the administration of the estate, *B*'s leased premises fell into disrepair, and although *B* demanded of *A*'s executor that repairs be made, nothing was done. In 1984, administration of *A*'s estate was completed and *T* undertook administration of the trust. *B* demanded that *T* make repairs; *T* refused. *B* then spent $1,500 on repairs to the leased premises.

After *T* became trustee, the surface of the parking lot developed several severe cracks, making use of the lot hazardous. Tenants complained to *T* about the parking lot, but *T* refused to repair it. *C*, a customer of one of the tenants, fell because of the hazardous condition of the parking lot and suffered permanently disabling injuries.

B sued *T* individually and as trustee for breach of covenant to repair leased premises. *C* sued *T* individually and as trustee in a personal injury action seeking damages that far exceeded the total of the trust assets.

1. What should the result be in each of these actions? Discuss.

2. Is *T* entitled to indemnification from the trust estate for any damages recovered against him individually? Discuss.

Question Seventy-six:
Wills/Torts/Procedure

(New York Law)

You are an associate in a New York law firm. The senior partner in the firm has given you a memorandum of his interview with a client, Richard Brown. The memorandum states:

Richard Brown is a New York domiciliary. In 1987, Richard's son, John, age 18, also a New York domiciliary, was attending college in State X. John was a brilliant student. In early October 1987, while John was a passenger in a car owned and driven by his friend Tom in State X, Tom collided with a tree while negligently attempting to pass another car. Tom is domiciled in New York, where his car is registered and insured. As a result of the accident, John sustained serious personal injuries. John was immediately flown to New York City to receive special medical attention.

While in the New York hospital, John asked the Brown family's attorney to prepare a will for him leaving everything he owned at his death, including any legal claims, to his brother, David, and his sister, Susan, equally. Inadvertently, the bequest to Susan was omitted from the will. The omission was discovered immediately after the will was duly executed by John. While still in the presence of his attorney and the witnesses, John, in his own handwriting, inserted the bequest to Susan above his signature and above the attestation clause of his will. Despite valiant medical efforts, John died ten days later, survived by his parents, Richard and Marilyn, his brother, David, and his sister, Susan.

The senior partner has instructed you to prepare a memorandum addressing the following questions:

(a) Is John's will, including the handwritten bequest to Susan, valid?

(b) What cause or causes of action can be maintained against Tom and who will benefit from any such action or actions?

(c) If Tom remains in State X, can any action be brought against Tom in New York Supreme Court?

Question Seventy-seven: Corporations

(Utah Bar Exam)

Mr. President, Ms. Veep, Mr. Secretary, and Ms. Shareholder decided to sell pieces of the Berlin Wall as novelties and in order to do so formed a corporation called Own a Piece of the Wall, Inc. ("O.P.W."). Mr. President, as the sole incorporator, prepared and signed articles of incorporation, which he mailed to the appropriate state agency with a check for the correct amount of filing fee. The articles of incorporation did not provide for a registered agent. The articles of incorporation named Mr. President, Ms. Veep, and Mr. Secretary as the original members of the board of directors.

The corporation was anxious to begin business while the market was hot so bylaws were not prepared, nor did the board of directors hold an organizational meeting. It was informally agreed that Mr. President would be president and general manager of the corporation, Ms. Veep would be vice-president, and

Mr. Secretary would be secretary. It was also informally agreed that the following would receive stock for the consideration shown:

Individual	Consideration	No. of Shares
Mr. President	$400 cash	400
Ms. Veep	$300 cash	300
Mr. Secretary	Typewriter given to corporation with an agreed value of $300, which he decided to keep at his home and also use for personal business	300
Ms. Shareholder	Agreement to perform future services with an agreed value of $300	300

No resolution of the board of directors was adopted reflecting the above informal agreements.

Mr. President engaged Mr. Jackhammer, a local contractor, to go to Berlin to cut pieces of the wall and ship them back for sale by O.P.W. To induce him to enter into the contract, Mr. President told him O.P.W. was an international company worth millions of dollars. A written contract was signed by Mr. Jackhammer and by Mr. President for O.P.W. The contract provided for payment to Mr. Jackhammer of $50,000 upon completion of the contract work.

Mr. President then took the $700 cash paid as consideration for the stock from the corporate bank account and flew to Berlin to oversee the wall cutting. While there, he used part of the money from the corporate account to buy souvenirs for his family. Unfortunately, there turned out to be very little demand for pieces of the wall, and sales by O.P.W. were very poor, so poor, in fact, that there was no money to pay Mr. Jackhammer for his work.

Mr. Jackhammer has sued the corporation, Mr. President, Ms. Veep, Mr. Secretary, and Ms. Shareholder because he has not been paid.

Assume O.P.W. is liable to Mr. Jackhammer on the contract for $50,000. Discuss legal theories under which Mr. President, Ms. Veep, Mr. Secretary, and Ms. Shareholder, or any of them, may be personally liable to Mr. Jackhammer on the contract.

Question Seventy-eight: Domestic Relations

(New York Law)

Hus and Wife, his wife, were married in Syracuse, New York, in 1970 and have continued to reside there. Their son, Chi, was born in 1978. In 1985, Wife was employed as a registered nurse with annual earnings of $25,000, and Hus was self-employed in a successful travel agency with annual earnings of $75,000. In February 1985, Hus and Wife agreed to separate, and Hus moved to his own apartment. Chi continued to reside with Wife, and Hus voluntarily made payments to Wife for the support of Wife and Chi.

In May 1985, Wife duly commenced an action for annulment against Hus on the ground of Hus's fraud. The action was reached for trial in September 1985. Wife's proof in support of her complaint established that Wife had married Hus in reliance on Hus's agreement to convert to Wife's religion; that following their marriage, Hus insisted on postponing his conversion until his aged mother died; that in May 1984, following the death of Hus's mother, when Wife again reminded Hus of his promise to convert to her religion, Hus told Wife for the first time that while he had intended to convert when he made the promise, he changed his mind after the marriage and decided that he would never convert. The proof also showed that Hus and Wife continued to reside together as man and wife until they separated in February 1985.

At the close of all the proof, Hus moved for judgment dismissing Wife's complaint. Wife cross-moved for a judgment of annulment against Hus and also for equitable distribution of the parties' marital property. The court (1) dismissed Wife's complaint, and (2) denied Wife's motion for equitable distribution. Wife did not appeal the rulings.

In November 1985, Hus and Wife duly entered into a separation agreement in which Hus agreed to pay Wife $150 weekly for her maintenance and $100 weekly for the support of Chi. The agreement also provided that their marital property would be divided equally and further provided that, in the event either party should seek a divorce in the future, the agreement would be incorporated but not merged into any judgment of divorce. The agreement was duly filed in the county clerk's office.

Hus and Wife continued to live apart, and in January 1987, Wife commenced an action for divorce against Hus on the ground that Hus and Wife had lived apart for over one year, pursuant to their separation agreement. After the action was commenced, Wife duly moved *pendente lite* for an order granting her temporary maintenance of $300 per week based on her affidavit that she was in financial need of such temporary maintenance. Hus's affidavit in opposition alleged that he had paid to Wife all of the agreed-upon amounts under the separation agreement, including the weekly payment to wife of $150 for her maintenance. The court (3) denied Wife's motion.

Hus opposed Wife's action for a divorce, and the proof at the trial in June 1987 established that Hus and Wife had lived separate and apart since February 1985; that Hus and Wife had entered into their separation agreement in November 1985; that Hus and Wife had substantially complied with the terms of their separation agreement but that on New Year's Eve, December 31, 1986, when Wife visited Hus at his residence, Hus and Wife had cohabited. At the close of the proof, the court (4) granted Wife a judgment of divorce. The court further ordered that their separation agreement be incorporated but not merged into the judgment of divorce.

In January 1988, Wife duly moved for an order increasing the amount Hus was obligated to pay Wife for the support of Chi from $100 per week to $200 per week. Wife's affidavit in support of her motion alleged the following facts:

(i) Hus had recently sold his travel agency to X Co., a nationwide travel business, for $250,000 cash;

(ii) Hus also received an employment contract with X Co. under which Hus would continue to manage the Syracuse branch of X Co.'s travel agency at an annual salary of $100,000 for ten years;

(iii) Wife continues to be employed as a registered nurse and still earns $25,000 annually; and

(iv) Hus has continued to make the payments to Wife for her support and the support of Chi as provided by their separation agreement and the judgment of divorce.

Hus did not controvert the facts alleged in Wife's affidavit, but Hus opposed Wife's motion for an increase in Chi's support.

(a) Were rulings numbered (1), (2), (3) and (4) correct?

(b) How should the court rule on Wife's pending motion for an increase in Chi's support?

Question Seventy-nine:
Community Property

(California Law)

In 1980, Harry and Wendy, a married couple, moved to California from State X where they had resided since their marriage in 1960. Under the laws of State X, a spouse's earnings are his or her separate property.

While married and residing in State X, Harry's accumulated earnings were used to purchase stock in Harry's name only and a residence in Harry's and Wendy's names as joint tenants. The residence was sold in 1980 and the proceeds of the sale were used to buy a California condominium, free and clear of indebtedness, in Harry's and Wendy's names as joint tenants.

Upon arriving in California, Harry purchased an auto repair business, using funds he had inherited. Each month, Harry withdrew from the proceeds of his repair business an amount equal to what he had been paid in his previous employment as an auto mechanic. He deposited the money in a checking account held jointly with Wendy. This account was used to meet all their monthly living expenses.

In 1982, Wendy was injured in a car accident caused by the negligence of Harry. Wendy used the insurance settlement she received for her injury to purchase savings bonds in her name.

In April 1985, Harry executed a will with a provision declaring the auto repair business to be community property.

In January 1987, Victor obtained a judgment against Wendy for an injury he suffered when she struck him during a heated argument at a condominium association meeting the prior year. Wendy's attendance at the meeting had been over Harry's strenuous objection.

Which of the following properties will be subject to execution in satisfaction of Victor's judgment against Wendy, and to what extent?

1. The savings bonds? Discuss.

2. The stock portfolio? Discuss.

3. The condominium? Discuss.

4. The auto repair business? Discuss.

Question Eighty: Trusts

(New York Law)

You are an associate in an Albany law firm. Yesterday you attended a meeting with a senior partner in your firm and Biz, a successful businessman. You learned that Biz is 35 years old and married Deb, his second wife, age 30, in 1983. There are no children of their marriage. Biz's first wife, Eve, died in 1981, and Ned, age 10, is the only child of Biz's marriage to Eve. Biz has requested your firm's advice with respect to the following matters.

The first matter relates to the will of Biz's mother, Mom. Biz's father, Dad, died in 1970. Under Dad's probated will, Dad established a $1,000,000 trust with income to Mom for life. Dad's will provided that the principal of the trust be paid to such persons as Mom may appoint at any time during her lifetime or by her will at her death.

Mom died last month, without having exercised the power of appointment during her lifetime. Her will has been admitted to probate. With respect to her power of appointment under Dad's will, Mom's will directs (i) that the principal of the trust be paid over to Biz and Big Bank, as trustees; (ii) that the income from the trust be paid to Biz for life; (iii) that, upon Biz's death, the trust continue to be held by Big Bank as sole trustee for the benefit of Biz's surviving children; and that (iv) the principal be paid over to Biz's children, in equal shares, when his youngest surviving child attains the age of 25.

The second matter relates to the preparation of a new will for Biz. Biz wants to provide for Deb during her lifetime but does not want his property to pass outright to Deb or to any member of Deb's family through her. Biz is also concerned that Deb would not provide for Ned in her will. Biz's net worth is approximately $2,000,000 and he proposes to leave his entire estate in trust, with the income to be paid to Deb during her lifetime. At Deb's death, Biz wants the principal of the trust to be paid to Biz's issue.

The senior partner has requested that you prepare a memorandum addressing the following questions:

(a) Is the trust provision contained in Mom's will a valid exercise of the power of appointment granted to her in Dad's will?

(b) If Mom's exercise of the power of appointment created a valid trust, may Biz properly serve as trustee of that trust?

(c) What rights, if any, would Deb have to reach the principal of the trust that Biz proposes to create in his new will?

(d) What are the tax consequences, if any, of creating the proposed trust in Biz's new will?

Bar Exam Essay Answers

Answer One: Real Property

Dear Mr. Jones:

Conclusion: For the reasons set out below, I believe that you are entitled to the rent for the month of September on the apartment now occupied by Ted Typical. You will not, however, be able to recover the rent for any period longer than a month.

Rule: Under the common law of real property, a leasehold is a nonfreehold estate. There are four kinds of leaseholds: (i) tenancy at sufferance, (ii) tenancy for a fixed term, (iii) tenancy at will, and (iv) periodic tenancy.

Definitions: A *tenancy for a term* (or a *tenancy for years*) ends at the end of the time period. A *tenancy at sufferance* arises where the lease period ends, and the tenant holds over. In most jurisdictions [cite local law], if the landlord continues to accept the tenant's rent, the tenancy becomes a periodic tenancy. It does not become another tenancy for a term. A *periodic tenancy* is a tenancy measured by the unit of time by which the tenant pays rent. A "month-to-month" tenancy is one form of periodic tenancy. (The *tenancy at will* is one where there is no fixed arrangement as to duration; in most jurisdictions, it automatically becomes a periodic tenancy on the payment of rent.)

Application: Here, you entered into a one-year lease with Ted Typical, rent payable every month on the first of the month. This was a tenancy for a term, a one-year term, to be precise. When Ted's lease expired, and you did not enter into a new lease, he continued to pay rent, and you continued to accept it, making his a periodic tenancy, or month-to-month.

Rule: Under the Statute of Frauds, an agreement for the sale or lease of land must be in writing, signed by the party to be charged. Without such a written agreement, no demand for rent or a sale price can be enforced, unless there is another tenancy, as well.

Application: Here, you did not enter into any new written lease with Ted Typical, whether for one year or for any other period. He has, as demonstrated above, only a month-to-month tenancy.

Conclusion 1: Therefore, you are not entitled to rent for the one-year term.

Conclusion 2: You can sue for and recover the rent for the month of September.

Rule: Under the common law of real property, where there is a periodic tenancy, the tenant must give the landlord timely notice of his intention to quit. Unless the common law rule is superseded by statute, the notice of termination must be given at least one rent-period in advance. (In some states there is a statutory number of days.) The landlord is entitled to collect rent for one rent-period.

Application: Here, Ted has given you only 15 days' notice of his intention to quit, namely, from August 15 to August 31, 1989.

Conclusion: Accordingly, Ted Typical has given you insufficient notice of his intention to quit. Therefore, under the common law rule, you may recover rent for the period of sufficient notice, to wit, one rent period, or the month of September.

I hope that this will be useful to you. Please do not hesitate to call me if you have any questions. I shall be happy to proceed on your behalf, if that is what you wish.

Yours very truly,

Can Candidate

A Note on Answering This Question

This is a straightforward question in real property. The temptation is to treat it as though it were simply a yes-no question or a short-answer question. The Model Paragraph system keeps you from falling into that trap. Set out the law carefully. Define all terms of art (here, the types of tenancies) and draw full and careful conclusions. The result will be a well-organized essay.

Study this example. After a day or two try to reproduce the answer on your own. Learn the law involved. It will come up again in a later essay in this book. Be prepared.

Answer Two: Criminal Procedure

1. The chief arguments in favor of suppression are that the interrogation was violative of sixth amendment rights and that the waivers of *Miranda* rights were not knowing and the confession was therefore not voluntary.

2. The chief arguments against suppression are that the prior criminal proceeding had ended, so that sixth amendment rights were in fact not violated, and that the facts support the conclusion that the waivers of *Miranda* rights were voluntary.

1. *Arguments in Favor of Suppressing the Confession.*

A. *Fifth Amendment and Sixth Amendment Rights.* Henault had previously invoked his right to counsel, in the breaking and entering case. He had remained in custody. Therefore his subsequent waiver of his *Miranda* rights in the interrogation by the Vermont investigators, made without counsel present, was violative of his right to counsel.

Under the sixth amendment to the constitution, as applied by the Supreme Court in *Edwards v. Arizona*, 451 U.S. 477 (1981) and *Arizona v. Robertson*, 486 U.S. 675 (1988), where a defendant who has already been convicted is still in custody, an earlier invocation of the right to counsel remains effective at the latter interrogation. The policy argument is that, wherever there is a possibility of state-coerced self-incrimination, the earlier invocation of the fifth amendment right to counsel must remain effective.

Here, this legal and constitutional argument depends on a number of facts not clear from the fact pattern. Did Henault previously invoke his fifth amendment right not to talk to the police without counsel, or did he simply invoke his sixth amendment right to counsel at arraignment? If he invoked his fifth amendment right not to talk to the police without counsel, does his invocation of that right remain effective after his conviction and sentencing on the charge in which the right to counsel was invoked, namely, the breaking and entering charge? Does it matter whether his appeals period has expired? Does the Public Defender who represented him in the breaking and entering case still represent him? The argument must be (i) that the same policy considerations will apply to require counsel for a person in custody on an unrelated offense as on the same offense, when he has once invoked his right to counsel, and (ii) that it does not matter whether or not the prosecution for the original offense has been completed.

Therefore, this argument will conclude, the confession must be suppressed.

B. *Miranda Rights.* Henault's waivers of his *Miranda* rights were not knowing and intelligent, and his confession was not voluntary.

Under the U.S. Constitution as applied by the Supreme Court in *Miranda v. Arizona*, 384 U.S. 436 (1966), the defendant in custody has the right to be told of his right to counsel and to waive that right. Such a waiver must be knowing and voluntary. The policy is that, before confessions or other incriminating statements made by a defendant can be used against him by the state in a criminal prosecution, it is imperative to assure that there was no coercion and that the defendant had a clear understanding of his right to remain silent, to answer questions only with an attorney present, to have an attorney provided if he cannot afford one, and to cease answering questions at any time. The "totality of the circumstances" test assures the reliability of the statements and the strict adherence of law enforcement officers to procedures designed to insure constitutional rights. Facts supporting an argument that Henault did not knowingly waive his rights include his youth, any possible language deficiency, his unfamiliarity with the American legal system, and the possible effects of his guilty plea in the other case. With respect to the voluntariness of his confession, it can be argued that being interrogated in a jail, by a "team" of investigators, is inherently coercive and will overbear the defendant's free will.

Therefore, it will be argued, the confession should be suppressed.

2. Arguments Against Suppressing the Confession.

A. *Fifth Amendment and Sixth Amendment Rights Under Edwards and Robertson.* The Supreme Court cases do not extend to this case. When the interrogation of Henault occurred, the earlier criminal proceeding was over. Even were he still represented by counsel, and even had he originally invoked his fifth amendment right to counsel in that earlier proceeding, nothing prohibits the interrogation here. The normal fifth amendment protection is the right not to answer questions without counsel present. A waiver of *Miranda* rights is effective. The standard "totality of circumstances" test is sufficient to protect the convicted and incarcerated defendant. To hold otherwise would be to hinder and restrict legitimate law enforcement investigations wherever the defendant in one case is suspected in another.

B. *Miranda Rights.* Assuming, then, that Henault could indeed waive his *Miranda* rights, it remains to be shown that these waivers were knowing and intelligent and that his confession was voluntary. Facts supporting the conclusion that his waivers were knowing and intelligent include the fact that he had only recently been through the criminal process, during which time his attorney had no doubt told him that he had an absolute right not to cooperate with police officers seeking information from him. Contrary to the suggestions above, the fact pattern provides no evidence whatsoever that he had any linguistic, mental, or emotional deficiency. In addition, the facts support the conclusion that his confession was voluntary. The investigators were solicitous of his rights, appropriately advising him of his rights not only once but a second time, during a break in the questioning. The setting was not unusually coercive.

Therefore, public policy interest in the prompt and just adjudication of criminal matters requires that the confession be admitted. Suppression would disserve the public interest.

A Note on Answering This Question

This question is legally easy, but is nonetheless difficult to answer well. It asks for two things that may appear to be hard to handle, the first being "policy arguments." As the model answer provided by the Vermont examiners makes clear, what the examiners here *mean* by "policy arguments" are merely arguments about the extent to which Supreme Court rulings ought or ought not to be extended into borderline situations. As to questioning the facts, asking for more facts, and so on, that is not too difficult to do. It requires thought, that's all. Lawyers are constantly asking their clients for more facts. Even appeals, where the issues are supposed to be entirely legal, often turn on the skillful use of the facts. The important point is just to *pay attention* to what the interrogatory asks and to provide an answer. Here, the interrogatory asks for "policy" and discussion of other facts. The model answer provides it. All you have to do, after all, is answer the question.

Answer Three: Contracts

Under the common law of contracts, a general requirement of enforceability for a contract is that the contractual promise in question be supported by consideration. The promise must be exchanged for a return promise or performance that is bargained for, as discussed in *Restatement (Second) of Contracts* sec. 71 and its commentary. Here, it is clear that the parties are not bargaining for an exchange. The intent of Uncle Ed is clearly to make a gift. Although it is subject to the condition of attendance at Acme, it is clearly not intended to purchase Andy's attendance at Acme. In fact, Uncle Ed intentionally avoided making any statements until after the decision to attend Acme was made. See 1 *Williston on Contracts* sec. 112. Therefore, it is not an enforceable contract but a giift.

Although not enforceable as a traditional contract, this particular promise may be enforceable under the doctrine of promissory estoppel. 1 *Williston on Contracts* sec. 140. Under the *Restatement (Second) of Contracts* sec. 90:

> A promise which the promisor should reasonably expect to induce action or forbearance on the part of the promisee or a third person and which does induce such action or forbearance is binding if injustice can be avoided only by enforcement of the promise. The remedy granted for breach may be limited as justice requires.

Here, section 90 can be applied. Uncle Ed clearly did make a promise. That promise is enforceable if there was actual reliance by the promisee that was foreseeable by the promisor. Farnsworth, *Contracts* sec. 2.19. It was (or should have been) foreseeable by Uncle Ed that Andy might reasonably be relying upon this promise in planning his financial arrangements for attending law school. Actual reliance is present to the extent that Andy did not seek financial aid in reliance upon this promise. Andy did not appear, however, to be relying on this promise in deciding to attend Acme Law School. Accordingly, this promise should be enforced only to the extent necessary to prevent injustice. Calimari and Perillo, *Contracts 3d*. sec. 6-6. This should call for enforcement during the time period that Andy has lost his opportunity to seek financial aid, likely to be only the remainder of the first year. There is probably no need to enforce this promise beyond the first year, since Andy has plenty of time to apply for financial aid during his second year, which is what he planned on doing originally. *See* comment b to *Restatement (Second) of Contracts* sec. 90.

Answer Four: Evidence

On timely objection, with statement of specific grounds:

1. Admissible.

2. If the niece satisfied the court of her competency her testimony should be admitted.

3. Inadmissable.

No error may be argued unless timely objection is made and the specific grounds are stated.

1. Under the Federal Rules of Evidence, all relevant evidence is admissible, and all evidence which is not relevant is not admissible. Rule 402, Fed.R.Evid. Relevant evidence is evidence that has any tendency to make the existence of any fact in issue more or less probable. Rule 401, Fed.R.Evid. Here, we do not know from the facts given whether Mrs. Joe was talking to Ed Willard about leaving the gas turned on on the stove at the bar or on some other stove. If in fact Mrs. Joe was referring to the stove at the bar, then the statement has a tendency to make a fact in issue more or less probable. Therefore, it is relevant.

"Hearsay" is a statement that is offered in evidence to prove the truth of the matter asserted, but is not made by the declarant while testifying at trial. *See* Rule 801(c), Fed.R.Evid. Under Rule 801(a)(2), Fed.R.Evid., an admission of a party is not hearsay. Admissions by a party-opponent are excluded from the definition of hearsay on the theory that their admissibility is the result of the adversary system. Fed.R.Evid. 801 advisory committee note. The expectation is that the party opponent can explain or deny the out-of-court statement. Here, the statement by Mrs. Joe that she left the gas stove on is obviously being offered for the truth of the matter asserted. But, as the statement is offered against Mrs. Joe, it is the admission of a party-opponent. Therefore, Ed Willard's testimony as to what Mrs. Joe said is both relevant evidence and excluded from the definition of hearsay. Therefore, it is admissible.

2. The same issues as in Part 1 are raised again. The new issue is whether Mrs. Joe's six-year-old niece is competent to testify.

Under the Federal Rules of Evidence, generally, all persons are competent to testify. Rule 601, Fed.R.Evid. *See also,* 2 J. Wigmore, *Wigmore on Evidence* sec. 509 (1979). A person must have personal knowledge of the facts, Rule 602, and must appreciate the nature and obligation of an oath to tell the truth. *See generally,* Rule 603, Fed.R.Evid. Therefore, if Mrs. Joe's niece satisfies the court that she appreciates the nature and obligation of an oath to tell the truth, she is competent to testify under the Federal Rules of Evidence. Therefore, the testimony should be admitted.

Under the common law, however, the competency of children was not presumed, and children were often disqualified. *See* 2 J. Wigmore, *Wigmore on Evidence* secs. 505 and 508 (1979). The modern trend is to abolish disqualification because of infancy. *Id.* sec. 509; Rule 602, Fed.R.Evid.

3. Nancy's statement to Fred Marsh raises the issue of double hearsay, hearsay upon hearsay. Under Rule 703, Fed.R.Evid., an expert can base his or her opinions or inferences upon facts or data that need not themselves be admissible in evidence if they are of a type reasonably relied upon by experts in the particular field. *See* Fed.R.Evid. 703, and advisory committee note. Here, Nancy's statement undoubtedly would not constitute the sort of material an incendiary expert would reasonably rely upon. Nancy was too far removed from the event to be reasonably reliable. Therefore, testimony concerning Nancy's statement to Fred Marsh would have to be excluded.

4. If error is raised on appeal to a ruling admitting evidence, a timely objection or motion to strike must have been made, or else no error may be argued on the admission of the evidence. *See* Fed.R.Evid. 103(a)(1). Furthermore, the specific grounds of an objection must be stated. The rationale is to alert the judge to the proper course of action and to enable opposing counsel to correct the error. Rule 103, advisory committee note, subdivision (a).

Answer Five: Torts

1. Defendant's motion for a directed verdict on Count One (negligence) is denied.

2. Defendant's motion for a directed verdict on Count Two (battery) is also denied.

In deciding a motion for a directed verdict, the court must view the evidence in the light most favorable to the nonmoving party, here, the plaintiff. The court must deny the motion where crucial issues of fact could be decided in favor of the nonmoving party. The court finds that crucial issues of fact would be decided in favor of the plaintiff. Therefore, defendant's motions for directed verdicts as to Count One (negligence) and Count Two (battery) are denied.

1. *Count One: Negligence.* Under the laws of this state, the elements of negligence are (i) duty of care, (ii) breach of that duty, (iii) actual cause, (iv) proximate cause, and (v) harm. *See* W. Prosser and W. Keeton, *Prosser and Keeton on the Law of Torts* sec. 30 (1984). The court decides whether there was a duty of care, as a matter of law. Actual and legal causation and damages are fact questions, for the jury. As to duty, although Dant owed Pace no duty to protect her from a wasp sting, once he undertook to do so by crushing the insect against her body, he owed her a duty to do so with care. Therefore, the court holds that Dant owed Pace a duty of care in crushing the wasp against her body.

As to causation and damages, the court finds that the evidence is so plain that Dant's blow caused bodily harm to Pace that the questions of causation and damages are withdrawn from the jury and decided in favor of the plaintiff.

As to the breach of duty (i.e., negligence), the court finds that the evidence could permit a jury to find that the defendant used more force in striking the wasp than would have been used by an ordinary person of reasonable prudence under the same circumstances.

Therefore, defendant's motion for a directed verdict is denied, and Count One is submitted to the jury to determine breach of duty (i.e., negligence) and, if there was a breach of duty, then the amount of damages.

2. *Count Two: Battery.* Under the laws of this state, the elements of battery are (i) intentional (ii) touching (iii) in a harmful or offensive manner (iv) without consent. The law implies a consent for one person to come to the aid of another to avoid imminent harm. There is no consent to force that exceeds the scope of the original consent.

Each of these elements is ordinarily a jury question. However, the evidence is so convincing in this case that the defendant did intentionally strike the plaintiff in a manner that caused harm, that the elements of intent, touching, and harm are withdrawn from the jury.

As to consent, the evidence plainly establishes that Pace gave no consent in fact. The jury may find for the plaintiff, however, either on the ground that the defendant was unreasonable to believe that he needed to take action to avoid the plaintiff's suffering injury, or on the ground that the force used exceeded the scope of the consent implied by the occasion.

Therefore, the motion for directed verdict as to Count Two is denied. The count is submitted to the jury to determine whether the defendant's action had implied consent and, if there was consent, whether the force used exceeded the scope of the consent. If there was no consent or if the consent given was exceeded, the jury will determine the damages suffered.

A Note on Answering This Question

This is a simple question. Writing a good answer, however, requires enormous patience. First, you have to distinguish the legal aspects of the question from the procedural ones. In discussing negligence, for example, you have to state that the duty of care is a question of law, for the court to decide, while the other elements are generally questions of fact, and in a jury trial are therefore for the jury, as trier of fact, to decide. Where, however, as here, the trial court finds the evidence on one or more of the elements to be conclusive, the court may withdraw any such issue from the jury and decide it as a matter of law.

Second, you have to examine the evidence for and against a positive conclusion on each element of the tort. That is the principal task in writing any essay on the law of torts: examining the facts in relation to one element at a time. Writing a torts essay means handling facts. It is always tempting to suppose, in addition, that if a fact pattern appears on a bar examination at all, then the correlation between the facts and the elements must be one-to-one. Resist the temptation to answer every question in the affirmative. Do not lose the points that come from carefully weighing the facts; decide only after careful examination whether or not the plaintiff can make out a *prima facie* case.

This question also demonstrates the importance of knowing not only the elements for each tort, but the defenses.

Answer Six: Federal Jurisdiction and Procedure

The district court may confer jurisdiction on the bankruptcy court.

Under the United States Constitution, art. VI, conflicting state laws may not interfere with the operation of federal law: "This Constitution, and the Laws of the United States . . . shall be the supreme Law of the Land; and the Judges in every State shall be bound thereby. . . ." A federal court is exclusive judge of its own jurisdiction. Under 28 U.S.C. sec. 1334(b), federal district courts have original but not exclusive jurisdiction of all civil proceedings arising under title 11, or arising in or related to cases under title 11. Under 28 U.S.C. secs. 157(b) and 157(c), bankruptcy judges may (with limited exceptions not relevant here) hear cases related to bankruptcy cases. A United States district court may refer matters to the bankruptcy court.

Here, the courts of the state of Nebraska may not interfere with the operation of the United States District Court, which may judge its own jurisdiction. The district court may take jurisdiction of specific matters related to the bankruptcy, here the foreclosure action, and refer them to the bankruptcy court. Therefore, Sam Second will fail in his argument that the district court cannot confer jurisdiction over the foreclosure action.

A Note on Answering This Question

This question requires more knowledge of procedure related to bankruptcy than a bar examination will usually ask. However, even without specific knowledge of bankruptcy procedures, a good answer is possible. Start with basic principles. Apply them to the facts. A lawyer-like answer will result.

Answer Seven: Constitutional Law

The federal district court may not overturn the ruling of the Nebraska court. The governing principle is the full faith and credit accorded to judgments.

Under the United States Constitution, art. IV, sec. 1, as interpreted by the Supreme Court in *Durfee v. Duke*, 375 U.S. 106 (1963), the federal district courts must accord full faith and credit to the judgments of state courts, even as to questions of jurisdiction, where the record indicates that the questions have been fully litigated and finally decided in the court that rendered the judgment. Here, it appears that the action to quiet title in Perelman was fully litigated in the Nebraska state court. It also appears that the question was finally decided: the Supreme Court of Nebraska affirmed the decision of the lower court. Therefore, the federal district court was not free to determine whether the Nebraska courts had jurisdiction.

Note, however, that the states themselves were not parties to the action. They were not bound by the determination. The states could otherwise determine the boundary between them.

A Note on Answering This Question

This is an intriguing little question. It deserves a careful and formal essay in answer. The temptation in writing an answer to such a short question is to treat it as though it were a short-answer question, not an essay, and to write one or two conclusory sentences, ignoring the application of law to the facts in the fact pattern. The sample answer given above demonstrates the proper procedure. Set out the principle of constitutional law that applies. Carefully demonstrate the way that the principle does or does not fit the facts. Draw a conclusion. Where, as here, there is a significant exception to the rule you have written down, note that exception in a short separate paragraph.

Answer Eight: Torts

Memorandum of Law

1. *Actor v. Cheapo*: Defendant's motion for summary judgment is granted [assuming that there is no evidence that Cheapo took any willful or wanton act against Actor]. Alternative: Defendant's motion for summary judgment is denied [assuming that there is insufficient evidence for the court to decide that Cheapo was not aware of the risk and, if aware, that he took reasonable measures to prevent harm].

2. *Worker v. Cheapo*: Defendant's motion for summary judgment is denied.

1. *Actor v. Cheapo.* Under the rules of civil procedure of this state, the court properly grants a motion for summary judgment where, upon consideration of the affidavits and other submissions in the case, it appears that there is no remaining triable issue of fact, and the case may be decided as a matter of law. The motion for summary judgment in the case of Ann Actor against Cheapo Movie Production Company (Cheapo) is granted.

Under the laws of this state, the elements of negligence are (i) duty of care, (ii) breach of that duty, (iii) actual cause, (iv) proximate cause, and (v) harm. *See* W. Prosser and W. Keeton, *Prosser and Keeton on the Law of Torts* sec. 30 (1984). A licensee is a person who is present on the premises for his own purposes and at the owner's sufferance. The landowner's duty of care to licensees is to warn them of traps and not willfully or wantonly injure them. Here, the circumstances posed a risk of which Cheapo was unaware. Accordingly, the overburdened bridge cannot be considered a "trap" in the legal sense. No evidence suggests that Cheapo took any willful or wanton act against Actor. Therefore, Cheapo is not liable to Actor, and the motion is granted.

[Alternatively: Motion denied. The evidence does not permit the court to say that Cheapo was not aware of the potential that the seemingly sturdy bridge would be overloaded. It also does not permit the court to say that Cheapo should not have provided a better fire escape, and that in any event, the use of the bridge for a mass exodus in case of fire was not foreseeable.]

2. *Worker v. Cheapo.* The motion for summary judgment is denied. Under the law of this state, an invitee is one who is present on the premises to provide a business benefit to the owner. The owner has a duty of care to invitees to warn them of risks the owner knew about or ought reasonably to have known about. Here, Worker was employed by a contracting company that was constructing the castle on the movie set owned by Cheapo. He was an invitee. Cheapo

accordingly owed Worker the duty of ordinary care, to warn him of risks Cheapo knew about or ought reasonably to have known about. Viewing the evidence most favorably to Worker, a jury could decide that Cheapo should have foreseen this accident and taken additional measures to prevent it. There is, accordingly, a triable issue of fact in the case. Therefore, the defendant's motion for summary judgment is denied.

A Note on Answering This Question

As in many torts questions, the candidate must argue that the definitions contained in the elements of the tort do or do not apply on the facts presented. Observe that the examiners would give credit to two different conclusions in the case *Actor v. Cheapo*. It is not that one answer is the "right" answer, and the other is "wrong." On the contrary, either answer is acceptable and will receive a good grade if it is carefully argued. The candidate must set out the applicable definition (here "licensee") and apply it carefully to the facts, then set out the applicable duty of care (here, "to warn of traps and not willfully or wantonly injure") and apply it carefully to the facts. [In states where the traditional distinctions between "licensees" and "invitees" are merely guides in deciding whether the defendant has behaved as a reasonable landowner, the candidate will so state.]

It is crucial for the candidate to keep in mind the procedural posture of the case and the applicable presumptions and burdens. In the case *Worker v. Cheapo*, the defendant is moving for summary judgment. The court may accordingly consider not merely the abstract question of whether a jury could find in favor of the plaintiff, but whether, *viewing the evidence most favorably to the plaintiff*, a jury could find in plaintiff's favor.

Answer Nine: Torts

These pleadings are not proper as they stand under the theory of *res ipsa loquitur*. Under the theory of *res ipsa loquitur*, where the instrumentality causing the injury is shown to be under the defendant's exclusive control and management, and the accident is one that in the ordinary course of affairs does not occur if those who have management or control over that instrumentality exercise ordinary care, then in the absence of evidence of negligence by the defendant, this constitutes by itself reasonable evidence that the accident arose from want of proper care. When an attorney pleads *res ipsa*, he does not, therefore, plead specific acts of negligence.

Here, however, the attorney pleaded specific acts of negligence: first, permitting the door to remain for many months without any effective retarder to sudden closing and, second, failing to repair or replace the retarder on the door when the defendant knew it was inoperative and had ample opportunity to repair it. Therefore, the attorney here cannot in the same count proceed under the theory of *res ipsa loquitur*.

However, in the federal courts, and in most state courts, plaintiff can plead alternative theories under different counts. Here, plaintiff might plead both negligence, using the allegations cited, and also *res ipsa loquitur*, in different counts.

A Note on Answering This Question

This question demonstrates again the importance of reading the interrogatory carefully before outlining the answer. This is not a question about whether a court should find negligence; it is also not a fact question. This is a *pleadings question*. The candidate who becomes deeply involved in the applicable theories of negligence or in the facts misses the point. The interrogatory asks only whether the pleadings are proper for *res ipsa loquitur*. Once the candidate carefully reads the interrogatory, answering the question is easy.

Answer Ten: Criminal Procedure

1. Smith must testify. His argument against "use" immunity will fail.

2. Smith's argument that his right to counsel will be violated also fails.

1. *Self-Incrimination and "Use" Immunity.* Under the fifth amendment to the Constitution, no one can be compelled to testify against himself. Under 18 U.S.C. sec. 6002, however, where a witness in a federal proceeding would otherwise refuse to testify, on the basis of his privilege against self-incrimination, he may be ordered to do so. However, no testimony or other information "compelled under the order (or any information directly or indirectly derived from such testimony or other information) may be used against the witness in any criminal case, except a prosecution for perjury, giving a false statement, or otherwise failing to comply with the order." In any possible retrial, the testimony may not be used directly or derivatively. The government bears the burden of proving that its case in a subsequent proceeding was derived from wholly independent sources. The grant of "use" immunity must, that is, under *Kastigar v. United States*, 406 U.S. 441 (1972), leave the witness in "substantially the same position as if the witness had claimed his privilege in the absence of a grant of immunity."

Here, the grant of "use" immunity must accordingly leave Smith in the same position he would have been in had he refused to testify. The transcript of the first trial contains a clear record of the evidence the government had obtained without the aid of Smith's compelled testimony. If the government has evidence that it had, but did not use, at the first trial, it should document that fact for the record, prior to Smith's testifying before the grand jury.

Because, however, Jones will act as the prosecutor twice, once before the grand jury investigating the actions of the union officials and again in the retrial of Smith, there is a danger of subtle and undetectable nonevidentiary use of Smith's grand jury testimony in the second trial. Under the rulings in such cases as *United States v. Schwimmer*, 882 F.2d 22 (2d Cir. 1989) and *United States v. Semkiw*, 712 F.2d 891 (3d Cir. 1983), the government may avoid this contamination by erecting a "Chinese wall" between prosecution teams. Smith may be compelled to testify, but Jones must then be barred from participation in any way in *either* the grand jury proceedings or the subsequent retrial of Smith.

Therefore, although there might otherwise be danger of self-incrimination in this situation, Smith's fifth amendment privilege against self-incrimination will be satisfied if he receives "use" immunity for his grand jury testimony, while at the same time Jones is prohibited from participating in any way in either the grand jury proceedings or the subsequent retrial of Smith.

2. *Right to Counsel.* Under the sixth amendment, "in all criminal prosecutions, the accused shall . . . have the assistance of counsel for his defense." Under the Supreme Court's decision in *Massiah v. United States*, 377 U.S. 201 (1964), secret prosecutorial interrogation of a defendant after an indictment is prohibited. Under the Supreme Court's ruling in *United States v. Mandujano*, 425 U.S. 564 (1976), however, with a grand jury appearance, the right to counsel extends only to guaranteeing the right to consult with the attorney outside the grand jury room. The witness who has a right to counsel cannot insist that the attorney accompany him into the grand jury room.

Here, Smith may argue that compelling him to testify before the grand jury is compelling "secret prosecutorial interrogation" after his indictment in his own case and that he therefore has a right to the assistance of counsel in the grand jury room. He will distinguish *Mandujano* on the grounds that no criminal proceedings had been instituted against Mandujano at the time he testified. Thus, Smith would argue that *Mandujano* does not apply to witnesses who are currently under indictment.

However, as noted above, Smith will receive "use" immunity for his testimony. The decisions in *Massiah* and *Mandujano* must both be distinguished from Smith's on that basis.

Therefore, Smith will fall within the general rule in *Mandujano*. The right to counsel guarantees only the right to consult with an attorney outside the grand jury room. Therefore, Smith's motion to quash the grand jury subpoena will fail.

A Note on Answering This Question

The candidate must demonstrate that he recognizes the fifth amendment privilege against self-incrimination and that he understands the meaning of "use" immunity. It is a foregone conclusion that Smith will have to testify before the grand jury. The candidate's job, therefore, is not to put up a futile argument that "use" immunity will be insufficient. On the contrary, what the candidate must do is demonstrate the various subtle ways in which the courts have assured that "use" immunity does not violate the fifth amendment rights of the defendant. There is insufficient evidence on the facts presented here to suppose that any other result is possible.

Likewise, there is no way Smith can succeed in quashing the subpoena on the grounds that he needs counsel in the grand jury room. The case law simply forecloses that line of argument. What the candidate must show is that he sees the problems and also how Smith's arguments will be answered.

Answer Eleven: Contracts

Buyer does not have an enforceable contract to purchase Greenacre from Seller.

Seller has made an effective offer. Buyer's acceptance will be effective if received before Seller revokes the offer. Under the common law of contracts, for an offer to be effective it must be clear, definite, and unequivocal. An offer can generally be revoked by the offeror at any time prior to acceptance. This is true even when the offer says it is irrevocable, unless consideration is given in exchange for the offeror's promise to keep the offer open (an "option"). Where the offeror specifies acceptance by a certain mode, e.g., wire, response by another means that is definite and does not vary the terms of the offer will constitute a valid acceptance if the offer has not been revoked at the time acceptance takes place.

Here, Seller's offer to sell Greenacre is clear, definite, and unequivocal. It can be revoked by Seller at any time, even though it says it is irrevocable. Buyer gave no consideration to Seller for holding the offer open. Seller's offer asks for reply by wire, but Buyer replied by letter. Buyer's letter of acceptance is definite, however, and does not vary the terms of the offer.

Therefore, Seller has made an effective, albeit revocable, offer. Buyer's letter of acceptance is effective if the offer has not been revoked when acceptance takes place.

Under the common law of contracts, all other things being equal, an offer is effective upon receipt, an acceptance is effective upon dispatch, and a revocation is effective upon receipt. However, where the acceptance is not communicated by the means specified by the offeror, the acceptance is effective upon receipt. Here, the telegram of revocation from Seller is effective upon receipt, Thursday, May 4. The Buyer accepted the offer by mail. The offeror, Seller, had specified that acceptance should be by wire, however. Therefore, the acceptance is effective on the day of receipt, Friday, May 5, rather than the day of dispatch, Thursday, May 4, as would normally be the case. Accordingly, the revocation of the offer was effective on May 4, one day before the acceptance, which became effective on May 5. Therefore, Buyer does not have an enforceable contract to purchase Greenacre from Seller.

Answer Twelve: Evidence

1. Stanley can testify as an expert regarding the trading.

2. Justice can introduce the charts that Stanley prepared.

1. *Admission of Expert Testimony.* Under Rule 702, Fed.R.Evid., "If scientific, technical, or other specialized knowledge will assist the trier of fact to understand the evidence or to determine a fact in issue, a witness qualified as an expert by knowledge, skill, experience, training, or education, may testify thereto in the form of an opinion or otherwise." The witness need not be in the same profession or trade, but may testify about the standard of care in a similar profession or trade, when the standard of care is the same in both. Qualification of an expert witness is within the discretion of the court. The weight to be accorded expert testimony is a matter for the trier of fact.

Here, Stanley, working only part-time as a broker, and not having actively traded stocks for ten years, will have his qualifications as an expert challenged. However, if Stanley is the manager of a large brokerage firm and is responsible for brokers who do trade stocks, he is probably qualified by experience and training to give an expert opinion in this case. Questions about his expertise would affect only the weight the jury gives to his opinion. Therefore, Stanley's expert testimony will be admissible.

2. *Admission of Charts*. Under the Federal Rules of Evidence, all relevant evidence is admissible unless excluded. Rule 402, Fed.R.Evid. Relevant evidence is "evidence having any tendency to make the existence of any fact that is of consequence to the determination of the action more probable or less probable than it would be without the evidence." Here, the charts are evidence of Slick's trades and of the Dow Jones Industrial Average and are certainly relevant to John's claim that Slick committed fraud in his account.

Under the Federal Rules of Evidence, charts and summaries are permissible to represent the "contents of voluminous writings, recordings, or photographs which cannot conveniently be examined in court." The originals or duplicates must be made available for examination or copying, or both, and the court may order them produced in court. Rule 1006, Fed.R.Evid. Therefore, the charts are admissible if the data themselves, presented in the charts, are admissible.

Under Rule 801(d), Fed.R.Evid., the *monthly brokerage statements* are not hearsay. They are admissions by Slick and therefore are not subject to a hearsay objection. Therefore, they are admissible.

If the court were to find the statements the brokerage firm sent out each month to be hearsay, however, they would nonetheless be admissible under the business records exception to the hearsay rule. Rule 803(6), Fed.R.Evid. It would be necessary for Justice to lay sufficient foundation, to include: (a) that the statements are memoranda, records, or data compilations (b) of acts or events (c) made at or near the time (d) from information transmitted by a person with knowledge (e) kept in the course of a regularly conducted business activity and (f) that it was the regular practice of that business to make the record. That foundation could be laid by testimony by the custodian of the records or by another qualified witness with sufficient knowledge.

Under Rule 803(17) of the Federal Rules of Evidence, "*market reports*, commercial publications, *market quotations*," and the like, generally used and relied upon by the public, are admissible as an exception to the hearsay rule. Here, the Dow Jones Industrial Averages are market reports and market quotations. Therefore, they are admissible.

Under Rule 902(6), Fed.R.Evid., *newspapers* are self-authenticating, and so admissible. (The likelihood of forgery of newspapers is slight.) Here the Dow Jones Industrial Averages were obtained from the *Wall Street Journal*, a newspaper. Therefore, the newspapers are admissible.

Therefore, as the data to be presented in the charts are admissible, the charts themselves are admissible.

Note that even were the charts not admissible, the expert could testify relying on documents not before the jury, but the opponent would have the right to introduce them into evidence.

A Note on Answering This Question

Making the outline for the answer to this type of question is easy. The interrogatory itself tells you that there will be at least two points in the outline, because the interrogatory has two parts: (i) Can Stanley testify as an expert regarding the trading? and (ii) Can Justice introduce as evidence the charts that Stanley prepared?

In the same way, the second of these two questions tells you, again, that there are at least two further questions. Stanley has prepared charts containing two different types of information: (i) daily stock trading in John's account, the numbers taken from John's monthly brokerage statements; and (ii) the Dow Jones Industrial Average for a two-month period, the data coming from the *Wall Street Journal*. The fact that the latter data come from a newspaper means that the answer must treat both the admissibility of the data and the admissibility of reports in newspapers. Therefore, answering the second of the two main questions (Can Justice introduce as evidence the charts Stanley prepared?) will require stating the rules regarding the admissibility of (i) the charts Stanley prepared (and stating the rules for admissibility of the data contained in those charts); (ii) monthly brokerage statements; (iii) market reports or market quotations; and (iv) newspapers.

You should recognize that you will use six or more rules of law to write the answer to this question. These rules of law form the outline for your answer. Once you have identified and listed those rules, all you need to do is to write a Model Paragraph for each one (Rule–Application–Conclusion).

Answer Thirteen: Real Property

Sara will prevail.

Under the statute of frauds, contracts for the sale of real property must be in writing. Statutes usually require that a conveyance be signed by the grantor in order to be enforceable. The signature of an agent is sufficient, provided, under the law in most states, that the agent in turn has written authorization. A contract for sale of real property must identify the property and include other essential terms.

Perch may argue that Sara orally agreed to the contract by saying, "It sounds okay. Please send me a copy." However, only Broker actually signed the contract. Sara did not. Nor is there any indication that Broker, as Sara's agent, had a written power of attorney. Therefore, the contract is unenforceable because it does not satisfy the statute of frauds.

Perch may also argue that "part performance" will satisfy the statute of frauds. Where another party has relied on the contract to his detriment, equity will sometimes recognize that the first party is estopped to avoid the contract. Here, part payment is not sufficient to constitute part performance. Two days is not long enough for sufficient detrimental reliance. Therefore, the signature being lacking, there is no other way in which the statute of frauds is satisfied. Nor will equity otherwise enforce the contract. Therefore, the contract is unenforceable.

A Note on Answering This Question

This question is short and straightforward. The trap to avoid is the temptation to treat it as though it were a short-answer question, rather than an essay question. First, as always in applying the Model Paragraph system, make sure to set out the full rule or rules, apply the rules to the facts, and draw full and clear conclusions. Second, where you are told to "discuss" the issues, you must state the full arguments on both sides and, where appropriate, apply each argument with its own rules to the facts, drawing the conflicting conclusions each side would draw. Here, that process is foreshortened. Nonetheless, you must take care to set out not only Sara's arguments, but also Perch's arguments. Stating only one side of a case is not "discussing" it.

Answer Fourteen: Federal Jurisdiction and Procedure

Scenario I

1. The Illinois court has subject matter jurisdiction, but not personal jurisdiction.

2. Defendant should file a motion to dismiss under Rule 12(b)(2) Fed.R.Civ.P.

3. Defendant should file a motion for change of venue, under 28 U.S.C. sec. 1404(a).

1. Jurisdiction consists of subject matter jurisdiction and personal jurisdiction. Under Title 28 U.S.C. sec. 1332, a district court has subject matter jurisdiction of all civil actions where the amount in controversy exceeds $50,000 and is between citizens of different states. Here, plaintiff seeks $67,000, which is more than $50,000, and the plaintiff is a citizen of Illinois, while the defendant is a citizen of Utah. Therefore, there is subject matter jurisdiction. However, to determine whether the federal district court may obtain personal jurisdiction of an out-of-state defendant requires answering two questions. First, does the state long-arm statute provide for jurisdiction? Second, if so, is application of the statute constitutional under the facts? Were there minimum contacts? Is the forum a fair one in which defendant will receive a full opportunity to be heard? *International Shoe Co. v. Washington*, 326 U.S. 310 (1945). In a contracts case, the court will look at the parties' negotiations, the terms of the contract, and the course of dealing. Making a contract may be sufficient contact to warrant personal jurisdiction.

Here, even assuming that the Illinois long-arm statute would reach the defendant, one must ask whether defendant had "minimum contacts" with the forum state. Although defendant's contacts with Illinois were limited to mail and telephone contact with plaintiff, nonetheless the court will examine prior negotiations, the terms of the contract, and defendant's interest in benefiting from the contact. In any event, even if the minimum contacts test is satisfied, the court will also have to be satisfied that assertion of personal jurisdiction here satisfied standards of fair play and substantial justice.

2. Under Rule 12(b)(2), Fed.R.Civ.P., defendant may move to dismiss for lack of jurisdiction over the person. Here, as noted above, the court may lack jurisdiction over defendant. Therefore, defendant should so move.

3. Under Title 28 U.S.C. sec. 1404(a), "a district court may transfer any civil action to any other district . . . where it might have been brought," for the convenience of parties and witnesses. Here, all witnesses to the failure of the equipment to perform, and plaintiff's sales representatives, are in Utah. Defendant may argue that the convenience of the parties and of most witnesses would justify transferring the action from Illinois to Utah. Therefore, the defendant should move for change of venue.

Scenario II

1. The court in Utah has both subject matter and personal jurisdiction.

2. No motions pursuant to Rule 12 should be made.

3. Defendant should file an answer to plaintiff's complaint. Defendant should assert a counterclaim.

4. Defendant may not litigate its claim against Box in this action.

1. Jurisdiction, as noted above for Scenario I, consists of subject matter jurisdiction and personal jurisdiction. A district court has subject matter jurisdiction in all civil actions where the amount in controversy exceeds $50,000 and the action is between citizens of different states. Here, those conditions are met. The court in Utah also may have personal jurisdiction of both parties. Plaintiff may submit itself to the court's jurisdiction. Defendant has its principal place of business in Utah. Therefore, the court has jurisdiction.

2. No motions should be made pursuant to Rule 12, Fed.R.Civ.P.

3. Defendant should file an answer to plaintiff's complaint, admitting or denying, as appropriate, the averments of the complaint. Under Rule 8(c), Fed.R.Civ.P., affirmative defenses such as failure of consideration and fraud must be specifically pleaded. Under Rule 11, Fed.R.Civ.P., every pleading of a party represented by an attorney "shall be signed by at least one attorney of record in his individual name, whose address shall be stated." The signature of the attorney constitutes his certificate that he has read the pleading, that there is good ground for it, and it is not interposed for delay.

Defendant should also assert a counterclaim pursuant to Rule 13, Fed.R.Civ.P., for the $7,500, given to plaintiff as a down payment. Under Rule 13(a), Fed.R.Civ.P., a pleading "shall state as a counterclaim any claim which at the time of serving the pleading the pleader has against any opposing party, if it arises out of the transaction or occurrence that is the subject matter of the opposing party's claim and does not require for its adjudication the presence of third parties of whom the court cannot acquire jurisdiction. . . ." This counterclaim is therefore compulsory. Accordingly, the court has jurisdiction even though the amount is less than $50,000.

4. Defendant may not litigate its claim against Box in this action in Utah. Under Rule 14, Fed.R.Civ.P., the third party defendant must be a party "who is or may be liable [to defendant] for all or part of plaintiff's claim" against defendant. That rule does not apply here. Under Rule 19, Fed.R.Civ.P. (Joinder of Persons Needed for Just Adjudication), joinder is only appropriate where complete relief between plaintiff and defendant cannot be accorded in the absence of the party to be joined or that party's claims and interest relating to the subject matter of the action. Neither requirement is met here. Accordingly, Box cannot be joined in this action in Utah.

Defendant may, however, move to have the suit transferred to Nebraska, so that the claim against Box may be tried at the same time. Under 28 U.S.C. sec. 1404, a district court may order a case transferred to any other district, for the convenience of the parties. Here, all other things being equal, joining Box may in fact simplify the case and serve the convenience of the parties. Therefore, defendant may move to have the suit transferred.

Answer Fifteen: Constitutional Law

The Court will probably find that operating a liquor store is not a strictly governmental function, and the petitioner states will therefore not prevail in avoiding federal taxes on the proceeds.

Under the U.S. Constitution, art. I, as interpreted by the Supreme Court in such cases as *Ohio v. Helvering*, 292 U.S. 360 (1934), *South Carolina v. United States*, 199 U.S. 437 (1905), and *New York v. United States*, 326 U.S. 572 (1946), the federal government may tax any function the states undertake on which the government would tax an individual or group. The sixteenth amendment, which permits the income tax, does not exempt the states. Although the federal government has not imposed an income tax on strictly governmental functions (Section 115 of the Internal Revenue Code (January 1990) exempts from "gross income" income derived from any public utility or the exercise of any essential governmental function accruing to a state), there is no prohibition on doing so.

Here, the states operate liquor stores. The states' *aim* in operating the liquor stores is to control liquor consumption. This is a governmental aim, pursuant to the police power. The aim, however, does not change the nature of the function. The federal government would tax an individual or group on the function of operating a liquor store. Therefore, the court will find the function taxable. The petitioner states are unlikely to prevail.

A Note on Answering This Question

The Model Paragraph form applies very neatly to this type of question. Indeed, having such a format in mind saves the writer from treating the question as either a short-answer question, on the one hand or, on the other, a philosophical disquisition of unlimited scope. Having set out the distinction between governmental and nongovernmental functions, one can quickly dispose of running a liquor store as obviously a nongovernmental function. The conclusion swiftly follows: the petitioner attorneys general are unlikely to prevail.

Answer Sixteen: Torts

1. Ted and Vince will sue one another for negligence. Ted will sue Frank and Chevrolet in strict liability, warranty, and negligence. Ted will sue Dr. Stanley and Forest Hospital in negligence. Vince will sue Frank and Chevrolet: if he was injured, he will have the same claims that Ted has. If the defective steering mechanism caused the accident, Vince may have an indemnity claim against Frank and Chevrolet for any damages he may have to pay to Ted. Vince will also have claims under warranty for the damage to his car. If Vince proves a case in strict liability against Chevrolet, Frank may have a claim for indemnification.

2. Contributory or comparative negligence [depending on state law], and violation of statutes are the principal defenses.

3. If Vince is liable to Ted, Ted will seek recovery for all of his damages, including amputation of his legs. The parties will seek actual and special damages.

4. The parties' chances for success will depend on the evidence each is able to produce, as will be set out below.

Ted v. Vince

Under the law of this state, the elements of negligence are (i) duty of care, (ii) breach of that duty, (iii) actual cause, (iv) proximate cause, and (v) harm.* [Violation of the speeding laws may be evidence of negligence, or may be *prima facie* negligence. This is a question of state law.] Driving too fast for road conditions is negligent. An argument might be made, in addition, that a driver has a non-delegable duty to maintain his steering mechanism in good working order. Here, if Vince was driving too fast, he might be found negligent. If the steering mechanism was not in good working order, he might also be found negligent on that basis.

Defenses. Under the law of this state . . . [set down the rule for contributory or comparative negligence]. Here, Ted was driving with a suspended license. However, there was no causal relationship between the suspended license and the accident. Therefore, it is not an effective defense. Otherwise, someone driving with a suspended license could never recover for the negligence of another, and would always be responsible for any accident, no matter how careful he was.

Second, state law requires that a driver who stops at an intersection stop behind the white line. Here, Ted does appear to have been negligent in not stopping behind the white line. However, again, there appears to be no causal relationship between the negligence and the accident. A negligent act is relevant only if it is the proximate cause of the accident. Depending on the facts introduced at trial, it may be that under these circumstances Ted would have been hit even if he had been behind the white line. The result might be different had Ted been hit from the side.

Third, if Ted was drunk that would constitute a violation of state law that would imply negligence in a proper case. However, here it is not clear that Ted was intoxicated within the meaning of state law. Even had he been intoxicated, moreover, there would not appear to be a causal connection between the intoxication and the accident. He was not moving when the accident happened. The only possible relationship between his intoxication and the accident would be that he had stopped over the white line.

Finally, Vince may argue that Ted's not having his seat belt fastened was negligence. As there is no relationship between the seat belt and the cause of the accident, this argument fails. At most, it may relate to the later question of mitigation of damages. Vince would have to show by expert testimony that Ted's injuries would have been reduced had he been buckled in.

Damages. Under the law of this state, a person who causes an injury is liable for any aggravation of that injury caused by subsequent medical malpractice. If Vince is liable to Ted, accordingly, he is liable for all of Ted's injuries, including the amputation of his legs. (See the paragraph directly above for discussion of mitigation of damages.)

Vince v. Ted

[Vince's car was damaged. It is not clear whether Vince was injured. Any claim of Vince against Ted for negligence would raise the same issues discussed above. State law rules for comparative or contributory negligence would apply.]

---

* See W. Prosser and W. Keeton, *Prosser and Keeton on the Law of Torts* sec. 30 (1984).

Ted v. Frank and Chevrolet

Strict Liability. Under the *Restatement (Second) of Torts*, sec. 402A (1965), the elements of a claim for strict products liability are (i) that the seller sold a product that was unreasonably dangerous for its intended use, (ii) that it reached the user in substantially the condition in which it was sold, and (iii) that the user was injured as a result. Applicability of this theory will rest on questions of fact, including whether the steering mechanism in fact failed.

Warranty. Under the U.C.C. as adopted in this state, sec. 2-318, a seller's implied warranties of merchantability and fitness for a particular purpose extend to any person who might be expected to be injured if the product is not as warranted.

Negligence. The elements of negligence are stated in paragraph one, page one of this answer. If Ted claims negligence, he will have to introduce evidence of negligence in manufacturing, designing, or inspecting the steering system.

Ted v. Dr. Stanley

The elements of negligence are as stated above, paragraph one, page one of this answer. The standard of care applicable to a physician is a national standard [unless state law is otherwise]. A physician will not be liable in negligence simply because hindsight shows that his decision was incorrect. Here, the surgeon will be expected to testify that Dr. Stanley's decision was incorrect and that in fact it was negligent. If he is liable, Dr. Stanley will be liable for the additional injuries Ted suffered because of that negligence. A tortfeasor takes the victim as he finds him. Dr. Stanley cannot assert a seat-belt defense or an intoxication defense. He is, however, only liable for aggravation of the injuries. Ted will have to show that his legs would not have been lost had Dr. Stanley not been negligent.

Dr. Stanley might also be negligent in failing to call on a more experienced physician for advice.

Although several defendants may be liable, Ted is entitled to only a single recovery for his injuries.

Ted v. Forest Hospital

Under the law of this state, the employer will be liable for the negligence of the employee, under a theory of *respondeat superior*. Here, it appears that Dr. Stanley was the employee of Forest Hospital. If that is true, and if Dr. Stanley is found negligent, Forest Hospital may be liable.

In addition, the hospital may also be liable in negligence for leaving an inexperienced resident on duty or for failing to have established procedures requiring residents to call on more experienced physicians when necessary.

Vince v. Frank and Chevrolet

If Vince was injured, he will have the same claims against Frank and Chevrolet that Ted has.

If the accident resulted from the defective steering mechanism, as opposed to Vince's negligent driving, Vince may have an indemnity claim against Frank and Chevrolet for any damages he may have to pay Ted. There is an implied agreement in the case of the sellers of the defective product. Vince will also have claims under warranty for the damage to his car.

Vince v. Dr. Stanley

[Whether there is such a claim is a matter for state law. There is no claim for indemnity where there is no express or implied agreement.]

Frank v. Chevrolet

In the event that Vince proves a case in strict product liability against Chevrolet, demonstrating that the defect existed when Chevrolet sent the car to Frank for sale, then Frank will have a claim for indemnification against Chevrolet. He will be entitled to recover any damages he has to pay Ted for his injuries or Vince for such part of his liability as is attributable to the defective steering.

Ted's Damages

Note that Ted will be entitled to recover for special damages under state law. He will recover all the actual costs that have resulted from the accident. These will include all past and future medical expenses, all past and future lost income, and other incidental expenses. He will also seek recovery for all past and future pain and suffering. In addition, of course, he will have a claim for damage to his car.

Answer Seventeen: Criminal Procedure

The court would probably admit the cocaine, the firearms, and the money. Depending on the facts, the court should either admit or refuse to admit the books and records.

"Protective Sweep." Under the fourth amendment to the United States Constitution, the people shall have a right to be safe in their houses, and no warrants shall issue but upon probable cause.

Exceptions to the requirement of a warrant include border searches, automobile searches, consent searches, searches made after hot pursuit, school searches, searches incident to a lawful arrest, and searches under exigent circumstances.

The arresting officers may make a "protective sweep" without a search warrant following a lawful arrest. When officers have arrested a person inside his residence, the "exigent circumstances" exception permits such a search to the extent necessary to protect the officers' safety. The officers must reasonably believe that there might be other persons on the premises who could pose a danger to them as they make the arrest.

Here, it could be argued in favor of the validity of the sweep that the officers were experienced officers who could "sense" a dangerous situation. Further, they knew from the affidavit that Ricardo employed persons to kill police officers. It is widely known, in addition, that drug dealers often possess weapons to protect themselves. Officer Berle's statement that he "wanted to see if anyone else was there" supports the assertion that the sweep was for the officers' safety.

It could be argued against the validity of the sweep, on the other hand, that the officers characterized it as "routine" rather than as resulting from fear for their safety. In addition, the fact that Ricardo was arrested and handcuffed in the doorway of his apartment suggests that he could have been arrested and taken into custody without the officers' entering the apartment.

Therefore, given all of the circumstances in this case, the court would most likely find the sweep permissible and admit any evidence found in plain view, that is, the cocaine, the guns, and the money.

Locked Room: Books and Records. Under the fourth amendment, whether consent to a search is voluntary is a question of fact, based on the totality of the circumstances surrounding the giving of consent. *Schneckloth v. Bustamonte,* 412 U.S. 218 (1973). No single factor is dispositive. Here, first, the verbal "O.K." by Ricardo argues in favor of consent. On the other hand, the officers told him that they would get a search warrant, if necessary, and that might have been perceived as a threat. In addition, Ricardo later refused to sign a consent form, and that, too, argues against consent.

Therefore, a trial court could find either that there was or was not consent to the search of the locked room. Accordingly, the court might or might not permit the books and records to be admitted.

Answer Eighteen: Contracts

B will seek rescission based on mutual mistake and frustration of purpose. S will argue that B assumed the risk.

Mutual Mistake. Under the *Restatement (Second) of Contracts* sec. 152 (1981), there are four requirements for mutual mistake warranting rescission of the contract:

1. Both parties must be mistaken at the time of the contract;
2. The mistake relates to a basic assumption on which the contract was made;
3. The mistake must have a material effect on the agreed exchange;
4. The party seeking relief must not bear the risk of the mistake.

Here, B can show that both parties were mistaken at the time of the contract, since neither one anticipated that the Great Marathon Amusement Park would go out of business. The mistake relates to a basic assumption on which the contract was made. The mistake will have a material effect on the agreed exchange. However, B may have difficulty in proving that he did not bear the risk of the mistake. The contract states that "S makes no other representations or warranties [other than that she is the owner of the real and personal property that is the subject matter of the sale]." Accordingly, S will argue that B assumed all risks other than those within S's narrow warranty.

Warranty Disclaimer and Risk of Mistake. Under the law in many states, in addition, warranty disclaimers such as those in S's contract have been held to mean that the buyer assumes the risk.

Frustration of Purpose. Under the *Restatement (Second) of Contracts* sec. 265 (1981), where the buyer finds that the major purpose of the transaction has been frustrated he may, unless he has assumed the risk, rescind the contract. Here, B may argue that the major purpose of the transaction was to have a stand adjacent to an operating amusement park. It seems that the frustration has been nearly total. He will argue that he is therefore entitled to rescind.

Here again, however, S will argue that B has assumed the risk.

Answer Nineteen: Contracts

1. Steps Cary should take:
   (a) Tender $500 to Mr. Pigeon.
   (b) Seek a temporary restraining order to prevent sale to Ms. Sotheby.
   (c) Seek a preliminary injunction.
   (d) Initiate a suit for specific performance.

2. Defenses that should be raised: Misrepresentation, mistake, unclean hands, unconscionability.

3. Cary will probably be able to obtain a temporary restraining order. Ultimately, however, he is unlikely to prevail.

1. *Steps Cary Should Take.* Under the common law of contracts, a contract requires offer and acceptance, a bargained-for exchange, and consideration. Under the statute of frauds, a contract for the sale of goods must be in writing, and signed by the party to be charged, in order to be enforceable. Here, Cary made an offer of $500 for the painting, and Mr. Pigeon agreed to sell him the painting. There was therefore consideration. The contract was in writing. Therefore, there is an enforceable contract.

Under the rules of civil procedure of this state, a party does not have to prove his case in order to obtain a temporary restraining order, but only that immediate and irreparable injury will result if an injunction does not immediately issue. Here, since the sale to Sotheby is expected to occur in a mere two days, the harm is imminent, and there is no time for an adversarial hearing. Therefore, a temporary restraining order *ex parte*, to preserve the status quo, is the appropriate interim action.

If he does not believe it will tip his hand, Cary may also tender the $500 to Mr. Pigeon and ask for the painting in accordance with the terms of the contract.

Under the rules of civil procedure of this state, a temporary restraining order is good only for . . . days. To obtain a preliminary injunction, a party must show irreparable harm plus likelihood of success on the merits. The injunction can issue only after notice and hearing.

Under the law of this state, where there is a breach of contract for the sale of unique goods, the aggrieved party may seek specific performance. Here, the painting is unique. Specific performance is therefore the remedy Cary should seek.

2. *Defenses.* Pigeon will raise the defenses of misrepresentation, mistake, unclean hands, and unconscionability.

The defense of misrepresentation is unlikely to prevail. Under the common law of contracts, silence as to a material fact is not misrepresentation in the absence of some positive duty to reveal the information not disclosed. Here, a court is unlikely to conclude that Cary had a duty to disclose to Pigeon his belief as to the value of the painting.

The defenses of mistake and unclean hands are likely to have greater success. Under the common law of contracts, a unilateral mistake will not afford the mistaken party the opportunity to avoid the contract. However, there is an exception to this rule where the nonmistaken party knew or should have known of the other party's misunderstanding, yet proceeded to take advantage of it. The remedy is rescission. Here, Pigeon was unilaterally mistaken about the value of the painting. It could probably be established that Cary was aware of Pigeon's mistake. Therefore, Pigeon may be able to rescind the contract.

Under the principles of equity, "he who seeks equity must do equity." This is the basis of the defense of unclean hands. Courts have held that one who comes to a court of equity seeking equitable relief like specific performance must have "clean hands." Here, Cary can be shown to have taken advantage of Pigeon's mistake and to have failed to disclose the real reason for his interest in the painting. Therefore, a court may well find that Cary does not have clean hands. It may therefore refuse to invoke specific performance.

A court may also find this contract "unconscionable" and refuse to enforce it.

3. *Likelihood of success.* Cary will probably succeed in obtaining a temporary restraining order, which does not require a showing of likelihood of success on the merits. On the merits, he is likely to lose.

Answer Twenty: Evidence

Evidence to Be Offered on Jane's Behalf

A. *Existence and Terms of the Contract.*

1. Jane will seek to prove the existence of the contract by (a) her oral testimony (i) regarding the April meeting, and (ii) regarding the terms of the contract, (b) her recollection of the written contract, and (c) her handwritten notes. She will also introduce evidence that the only copy of the contract was destroyed. (If Jane's memory does not permit her to testify fully on the contract, she can establish that the notes were made when she was at the meeting and the terms were fresh in her mind.) *See* Rule 803(5), Fed.R.Evid.

2. *Best Evidence Rule.* HECC will argue that under the best evidence rule, Fed.R.Evid. 1002, the only way to prove the contract is with the contract itself. Jane will counter that, first, the best evidence rule requires the original document to prove its contents, not its existence. Fed.R.Evid. 1002. Second, the rule does not require the original to prove the contents where the original is lost or destroyed (absent bad faith). Fed.R.Evid. 1004(1). Here, the original has been destroyed while in possession of the opposing party. Fed.R.Evid. 1004(3). Indeed, Jane's testimony and her notes are now the best evidence of the existence and terms of the contract. Therefore, Jane will argue, the best evidence rule does not preclude admission of Jane's oral testimony and notes to prove the terms of the contract.

Parol Evidence Rule. HECC will also argue that the oral testimony or handwritten notes violate the parol evidence rule, which provides that evidence of prior or contemporaneous oral statements inconsistent with a written contract cannot vary the terms of a written contract. Here, however, Jane will argue that her testimony is not inconsistent with, and is not offered to vary, the terms of the contract but, on the contrary, is offered to prove the existence and terms of the contract. Therefore, the parol evidence rule does not preclude admission of Jane's oral testimony and notes.

3. The court is likely to admit Jane's oral testimony on the formation of the contract. She may be able to use the notes to refresh her recollection. As to introducing them into evidence, however, HECC could argue that they are self-serving, and hearsay.

B. *Completion of the Contract.*

1. Jane will seek to testify about HECC's undertaking its contractual obligations, the manner in which it completed them, and her payment of the contract price.

   In addition, Jane will seek to have her business records showing the work performed and her payment to HECC admitted under the business records exception to the hearsay rule. Fed.R.Evid. 803(6).

2. HECC will not be successful in opposing admission of this testimony, provided that Jane can lay a proper foundation for introduction of the documents.

C. *The Leaks: Testimony and Photographs.*

1. Jane will seek to testify about the leaks. Under the Federal Rules of Evidence, relevant evidence is admissible unless otherwise excluded. Rule 401, Fed.R.Evid. Here, evidence about the leaks is relevant as it tends to prove breach of HECC's duties under the contract and the resulting damage to Jane. Fed.R.Evid. 401.

   In addition, Jane will seek to introduce the photographs documenting the damage. They are also relevant. Introduction of evidence like the photographs is at the discretion of the court; it will be permitted if the court finds sufficient foundation and rules that the evidence will aid the jury without causing undue prejudice.

2. HECC will argue that, absent the secretary's testimony in court, the photographs cannot be sufficiently authenticated under Rule 901 of the Federal Rules of Evidence. Jane, however, can testify from her own knowledge and observation that the photographs clearly and accurately represent the appearance of the roof and the internal structure at or just after the time of the leak. Fed.R.Evid. 901(a) and 901(b)(1).

3. Therefore, it is likely that both Jane's testimony and the photographs of the leak will be permitted into evidence as relevant.

D. *Expert Testimony of Alice Jones.*

1. Under Rule 702 of the Federal Rules of Evidence, an expert witness may be qualified as an expert by knowledge, skill, experience, training, or education. Here, Jane will seek to have Ms. Jones's testimony admitted under that rule, pointing to Ms. Jones's successful business and years of experience.

   Under Rule 704 of the Federal Rules of Evidence, testimony "in the form of an opinion or inference otherwise admissible is not objectionable because it embraces an ultimate issue to be decided by the trier of fact." Jane may offer Ms. Jones's testimony about negligence and breach of warranty, citing that rule.

2. HECC will attempt to have Ms. Jones's testimony excluded. It may perhaps argue that her lack of formal education disqualifies her. Rule 702

precludes that argument. HECC may also argue that Ms. Jones cannot in any event testify as to the ultimate issue to be decided. Rule 704 forecloses that argument.

3. Therefore, Ms. Jones's expert testimony will be admissible.

E. *Ms. Jones's Testimony Regarding Other Jobs and Whiskey Bottles.*

1. Jane will offer Ms. Jones's testimony regarding HECC's troubles on other jobs and regarding the whiskey bottles she found at this job site.

2. Under the Federal Rules of Evidence, hearsay is not admissible except as provided by the Rules. Rule 802, Fed.R.Evid. HECC will argue that Ms. Jones's testimony as to other jobs is hearsay.

Under the Federal Rules of Evidence, relevant evidence may be excluded if its probative value is outweighed by its prejudicial impact. Rule 403, Fed.R.Evid. HECC will argue that, absent other evidence linking the bottles to the HECC crew, Ms. Jones's testimony regarding the empty bottles is prejudicial and has only slight probative value and should be excluded.

3. Therefore, Ms. Jones's testimony as to the other jobs will probably be inadmissible as hearsay, and her testimony about the bottles will probably be inadmissible as prejudicial.

F. *Mr. Edwards's Admissions at the Settlement Conference.*

1. Jane will seek to introduce the statements of Mr. Edwards, president of HECC, the first, made at the conference table, that "some of [the] roofers like to have a couple of drinks with lunch," and, a second set overheard in his conversation with his attorney and not made at the table itself, that "I know the boys got drunk and botched the job, . . ." and so on. She will point out that the second set of statements was made in the hallway outside the meeting, not at the meeting.

2. HECC will object. Under Rule 408 of the Federal Rules of Evidence, evidence of "conduct or statements made in compromise negotiations" is inadmissible. As to the second statement, HECC will raise the lawyer-client privilege. In addition, HECC will argue that the second set of statements is excludable as hearsay.

However, only confidential communications are privileged. Here, Edwards and his attorney did not attempt to close the door, and so the second set of statements was disclosed to a third party. The statements do not constitute hearsay, since they are clearly party admissions under Rule 801(d) of the Federal Rules of Evidence.

3. Therefore, the first set of statements is inadmissible, as having been made in compromise negotiations. The second set of statements is admissible as party admissions not subject to privilege.

Answer Twenty-one: Real Property

In a race-notice jurisdiction, Sara will win.

Under the common law of real property, the first conveyance has a superior claim. "First in time is first in right." Personal delivery of a quitclaim deed is effective conveyance. Failure to record a deed at the time of conveyance has no effect on the deed's validity between the parties. Here, Sara, as first transferee, had prior claim to Blackacre at common law. She will win, unless Rich, as a subsequent purchaser for value without notice, can use the state recording statutes to overcome priority.

Under the recording statutes, subsequent purchasers are protected, but not donees. Under the "umbrella doctrine," however, the donee of a purchaser also achieves the status of a protected purchaser. Under a "race-notice" statute, a subsequent purchaser must also first duly record in order to overcome the claim of a transferee with common law priority. Here, the claims of Sara and Devo are unaffected by the notice statute. Sara has common law priority. Devo will take, if at all, through Rich's status, under the umbrella doctrine. Rich, however, as a subsequent purchaser, must also first duly record in order to overcome Sara's common law priority. It was in fact Sara who first recorded. Accordingly, Rich, and hence Devo, would lose. Therefore, under a race-notice statute, Sara should win.

If the recording statute were of the "notice" type, Rich would have taken clear of Sara's interest, so Devo as Rich's grantee would win.

Answer Twenty-two: Constitutional Law

1. Doug can be required to pay child support, unless he can successfully challenge the presumption of paternity as a denial of due process.

2. Doug cannot prevent his wife from having an abortion.

3. Neither the state nor a parent has the right to prevent or require a minor's abortion in the first trimester.

4. The abortion issue will not decide who obtains custody of the girl.

1. *Child Support.* Under the applicable provision of state law as given, there is a conclusive presumption of paternity as to children living in the same home with a husband and wife. However, under the United States Constitution as interpreted by the Supreme Court in such cases as *Cleveland Board of Education v. LeFleur*, 414 U.S. 632 (1974), a conclusive presumption regarding matters related to parenthood may deny procedural due process.

Here, both husband and wife agree that the girl might have other possible fathers. Such evidence could be evaluated at a hearing where all interested parties had notice and an opportunity to present evidence.

However, the time for bringing a paternity action has long since run. Doug may nonetheless seek to establish that he is the father if he wants to obtain custody of the child.

Therefore, barring a successful challenge to the presumption of paternity, Doug will be considered the father of the girl. His child-support obligations will follow in accordance with state law.

2. *Wife's Abortion.* Under the United States Constitution, as interpreted by the Supreme Court in *Roe v. Wade*, 410 U.S. 113 (1973), and *Planned Parenthood of Central Missouri v. Danforth*, 428 U.S. 52 (1976), a woman has a constitutional right to choose an abortion in consultation with her physician, in the first trimester. A state may not give to a husband any control over that decision. Here,

the wife has a right to choose to have an abortion in the first trimester, in consultation with her physician. The husband, Doug, has no control over that decision. Therefore, the state statute giving the husband veto power over the wife's abortion is unconstitutional, and Doug cannot prevent his wife, Debbie, from having an abortion.

3. *Girl's Abortion.* Under the Constitution as interpreted by the Supreme Court in cases dealing with the abortions of minors, including *Bellotti v. Baird*, 443 U.S. 622 (1979), the state may neither assert nor grant to the parents the right to prevent or require an abortion for a minor in the first trimester of pregnancy. Therefore, neither Debbie nor Doug, assuming he is found to be the father, can use the force of law to prevent or require an abortion for the girl.

Note that the Supreme Court has left it to the states to choose whether to enact statutes requiring parental consent or notification or, in appropriate cases, a so-called judicial by-pass, for a minor's abortion. *E.g., Hodgson v. Minnesota*, 110 S. Ct. 2926 (June 25, 1990). The fact pattern presents no information on the existence of such a state statute here. Nor, in view of the narrowness of the question presented, would such a statute alter the outcome of this case. In any event, it is clear that in this case both Doug and Debbie have in fact been notified.

4. *Determination of Custody.* Under the law of this state, the court must decide the custody question in the light of the "best interest of the child." The fact pattern states that both Doug and Debbie are fit to have custody. The court could and would take views on the abortion into account. In addition, the court would consider the length and strength of the relationship with the two parents. It will also consult the girl's preferences. However, since neither parent can compel a decision on the abortion, that issue will not be dispositive in deciding which one obtains custody of the girl.

Answer Twenty-three: Federal Jurisdiction and Procedure

1. The federal district court has both subject matter jurisdiction and personal jurisdiction of the parties. Venue is proper.

2. Neither the citizenship of the original parties, nor the impleading of a third-party defendant who is a citizen of Ohio, nor the naming of a "John Doe" defendant destroys diversity.

3. Counsel did not comply with Rule 11, Fed.R.Civ.P.

1. Jurisdiction consists of subject matter jurisdiction and personal jurisdiction. Under 28 U.S.C. sec. 1332, a district court has (diversity) subject matter jurisdiction of all civil actions where the amount in controversy exceeds $50,000, and is between citizens of different states. Married persons may be citizens of different states. Diane is a citizen of the District of Columbia. Bruce is a citizen of Ohio. The tow truck owner is a citizen of Pennsylvania. Therefore, the parties are all citizens of different states. The amount in controversy is not stated. Assuming that it exceeds $50,000, however, as diversity has been established, the district court will have jurisdiction.

2. Under the rules applicable to ancillary jurisdiction, the citizenship of a third-party defendant does not destroy diversity. Here the defendant tow truck

owner impleads the band bus driver, under Rule 14, Fed.R.Civ.P., and the third-party defendant is a citizen of Ohio. However, as he is a third-party defendant, his citizenship does not destroy diversity.

Under Fed.R.Civ.P. 10(a), all parties must be named. Only a named party served with process affects diversity. Here, "John Doe" is not named and was never served with process. Therefore, "John Doe" does not destroy diversity.

3. Under Rule 11, Fed.R.Civ.P., every pleading of a party represented by counsel must be signed by an attorney. His signature is a certificate by him that "he has read the pleading; that to the best of his knowledge, information, and belief, there is good ground to support it; and that it is not interposed for delay. . . ." Counsel is obliged to make a diligent and good faith inquiry into the facts of the case. Here, counsel made no independent inquiry into the facts of the citizenship of the bus owner, yet alleged in the pleadings that John Doe was not a citizen of Ohio. Therefore, counsel did not comply with Rule 11, Fed.R.Civ.P.

Answer Twenty-four: Torts

Answer to Interrogatory:

Ray-Mart is under a duty of care to light the side of the building where there is no walkway.

Where a customer comes onto the land of a business as an invitee, to do business there, the landholder owes a duty of care that extends to portions of the business premises not ordinarily open to the public, but not shut off to them, and where it is foreseeable that they will go.

Discussion

Under the law of this state, the elements of negligence are (i) duty of care, (ii) breach of that duty, (iii) actual cause, (iv) proximate cause, and (v) damages. *See* W. Prosser and W. Keeton, *Prosser and Keeton on the Law of Torts* sec. 30 (1984).

Under the traditional tort law of most jurisdictions, there are distinctions among those who are on the land (i) as trespassers, (ii) as licensees, and (iii) as invitees. Where a person enters the land of another without consent of the owner or other privilege he is a *trespasser*. Where he comes on the land by permission of the landowner, but to pursue a purpose of his own, he is a *licensee*. Where he enters the land of another for a business purpose that will benefit or concern the landowner, he is an *invitee*. The possessor of land owes a different duty of care to each. To the trespasser he owes, ordinarily, no duty to make his land safe or to warn of dangers he knows about. (The law is otherwise with respect to known and habitual trespassers.) To the licensee the landowner owes a duty to disclose and warn of any concealed dangerous condition of which he has notice. He does not need to make the land safe nor to inspect it for the benefit of the licensee. As to the invitee, the landowner owes the duty to warn of dangerous conditions of which he would learn with reasonable care. (Under the law of some states, [including New York State] these categories are now used only as guides, and the courts hold the possessor of land to the standard that is reasonable under the circumstances.) The person in possession of land owes a special duty to invitees only so long as they are on the part of the land onto which they have been invited.

Here, Connie Customer came on the land of the Ray-Mart store as an invitee, to do business. However, Ray-Mart will contend that when she entered the darkened area next to the building, she did so as a licensee. It was a portion of the business premises not ordinarily open to the public, at least after dark. In fact, Connie Customer will assert, however, that the area was not shut off to customers, as an area might be that is marked "Employees Only." The area next to the building was available to customers, since parking was allowed next to the building. During the day this portion of the business premises would have no physical hazards a customer could not see, and it would be completely safe. It was foreseeable, however, that as parking was allowed next to the building, it would also be used at night. Ray-Mart would have notice of the electrical meter mounted on the side of the building. It would have, accordingly, a duty to disclose and warn of this concealed dangerous condition.

Therefore, Ray-Mart's failure to provide proper lighting next to the buiding rises to active negligence.

A Note on Answering This Question

This is a straightforward negligence question. In such a question, all one need do, usually, is set out the elements of negligence, and then show how the facts do or do not fit. Here, the wrinkle is arguing for the appropriate duty of care, namely, the landowner's duty to an *invitee*.

Answer Twenty-five: Criminal Procedure

1. Defendant has two potentially successful arguments on appeal: (a) that the prosecution's summation was clearly prejudicial, and (b) that the exclusion of his psychiatrist's testimony was clearly erroneous.

2. Defendant has arguments that he should raise, but that are unlikely to prevail: that the questioning of Pureheart was prejudicial, that the jury was suspect, and that the indictment was suspect.

I. *Double Jeopardy.*
Under the fifth amendment double-jeopardy clause, made applicable to the states through the fourteenth amendment, *Benton v. Maryland*, 395 U.S. 784 (1969), no one may be tried, or "put in jeopardy," for the same offense more than once. Double jeopardy requires that each element of the two offenses be the same.

Here, "simple assault" is defined as "attempting to cause or knowingly causing bodily injury to another." This offense does not contain the same elements as "sexual assault." The latter offense contains no requirement of intent to cause bodily injury or causing bodily injury. The former has no sexual element and no age limit. The two offenses do not match element for element. They are not the same. Nor is one a lesser included offense of the other. There is no identity, therefore, and there is no merger.

Therefore, defendant's argument that there was double jeopardy will fail.

II. *Fundamental Fairness of Indictment and Trial.*

    A. *The Indictment.* In a case where the prosecutor abuses his discretion or relies on the hearsay of newspaper reports, the defendant should argue for reversal. Here, the prosecutor decided to prosecute for "sexual assault" only after the matter received a great deal of publicity. Absent a showing of impropriety, however, which the fact pattern does not suggest, there is no reversible error here.

    B. *The Jury.* Where a defendant can demonstrate that publicity has resulted in influence on the jury during trial, this is grounds for reversal. Here, the defendant should examine the record of *voir dire* and attempt to discover any influence on the jury during the trial. Absent a showing of influence on the jury causing prejudice, defendant cannot obtain a new trial.

III. *Defendant's Right to Confrontation.* Under the sixth amendment, the defendant in a criminal trial has the right to confront the witnesses against him.

Here, the defendant was not present at the taking of Pureheart's testimony. Only the judge, the prosecutor, and defense counsel were present. Defendant, however, is unlikely to succeed in a challenge to this procedure.

First, although the right to cross-examine the witness is absolute, the nature and extent of cross-examination is within the judge's discretion. Without showing that the judge abused his discretion, the defendant cannot succeed. Given evidence that the confrontation would have caused damage to a child witness, defendant cannot succeed.

In addition, here, the interview was preserved on videotape. This is enough to allow the jury to weigh the veracity, competence, and completeness of Pureheart's testimony.

Therefore, no challenge to Pureheart's testimony will prevail.

IV. *Rejection of the Psychiatrist's Testimony.* The defendant in a criminal case has an absolute right to present evidence that he did not, indeed, could not, commit the crime. This right extends to the presentation of relevant evidence that is merely circumstantial. Under Rule 704 of the Federal Rules of Evidence, testimony may not be excluded merely because it "embraces the ultimate issue to be decided by the jury."

Here, however, the court excluded the testimony of defendant's psychiatrist that defendant "was psychologically incapable of committing a sexual assault on Pureheart." This is relevant evidence, albeit opinion. If, as might be anticipated, the psychiatrist's testimony would be treated as "expert" testimony, or even if it were not, it should have been admitted.

Therefore, the ruling of the court excluding the testimony of defendant's psychiatrist was clearly erroneous. Defendant may argue that it constitutes reversible error.

V. *Prosecutor's Summation.* It is error for the prosecutor to state an opinion, either about the character of the defendant, the veracity or character of the witnesses, or about the outcome of the case. Here, the prosecutor violated every part of this rule. His arguments were prejudicial. There is, therefore, a strong argument for reversal.

Answer Twenty-six:
Contracts—U.C.C.

The sample machine was the basis of the bargain and creates an express warranty, which has not been disclaimed. The buyer may revoke acceptance where discovery of the nonconformity was necessarily delayed.

Creation of Warranties. Under the U.C.C., an express warranty is created by any sample or model that is made part of the basis of the bargain. That warranty guarantees that the goods as delivered shall conform to the sample or model. Under U.C.C. sec. 2-313, "[a]ny sample or model which is made part of the basis of the bargain creates an express warranty that the whole of the goods shall conform to the sample or model." Here, the prototype was an important part of the selling process. Therefore, it appears that the prototype has been made part of the basis of the bargain between Alpha and NCM. Therefore, there was an express warranty that the machines would conform to the quality and performance of the prototype.

In addition, express warranties have not been disclaimed, only implied warranties.

Disclaimer of Warranties. Under the U.C.C., although with the right language and conspicuousness both express and implied warranties can be disclaimed, nonetheless, disclaimer of warranties is not favored. Under U.C.C. sec. 2-316(1), "words or conduct relevant to the creation of an express warranty and words or conduct tending to negate or limit warranty shall be construed wherever reasonable as consistent with each other, but . . . negation or limitation is inoperative to the extent that such construction is unreasonable." Here, there was no disclaimer of the express warranty created by the prototype computerized cash register that NCM furnished to Alpha. Therefore, the express warranty that the prototype created is one on which Alpha can rely in an action against NCM.

Right to Reject. Under U.C.C. sec. 2-601, where there has been a breach of warranty, the buyer may have the right to reject the goods. Where the goods have already been accepted, the buyer may reject only if (1) objection is made in a timely fashion upon discovery of the defect, and discovery was delayed by the inherent difficulties of discovery, and (2) the defect substantially impairs the value of the goods to the buyer. U.C.C. sec. 2-608. Here, it would be expected to take some time to discover that the new machines did not conform to the prototype. Visual inspection alone would not suffice. Nonconformity, however, would "substantially impair" the value of the goods to Alpha. Therefore, it appears that Alpha would have a right to reject the goods.

Answer Twenty-seven: Evidence

A. The trial court was correct.

B. The trial court was incorrect.

C. The trial court was correct.

D. The trial court was incorrect.

E. The trial court acted permissibly. The court may examine the witness. All parties may cross-examine the witness.

A. Under settled doctrine in the field of evidence, a witness may refresh his memory by using a writing while he is testifying. C. McCormick, *McCormick on Evidence* sec. 9 (3d ed. 1984). Under Rule 612 of the Federal Rules of Evidence, the adverse party is entitled to examine the document, to cross-examine the witness on it, and to introduce into evidence those portions that relate to the witness's testimony. The witness need not have prepared the document; the writing can have been prepared by another. *Johnston v. Earle*, 313 F.2d 686, 688 (9th Cir. 1962). The only restriction is that the document must in fact refresh the witness's recollection. *See generally* M. Graham, *Handbook of Federal Evidence* sec. 612.2.

Here, Dan's testimony seems to be his own, and his recollection seems to have been refreshed by the summary he consulted.

Therefore, the trial judge was correct in permitting Dan to use the summary to aid his testimony.

B. Under Rule 407 of the Federal Rules of Evidence, evidence of subsequent remedial measures is inadmissible to prove negligence or culpable conduct. However, evidence of subsequent remedial measures may be admitted when it is offered for another purpose, such as proof of ownership, control, or the feasibility of precautionary measures, if these issues are controverted, or for impeachment. Rule 407, Fed.R.Evid. Here, Dan had testified that nothing more could have been done to make the work area safer. That is, the feasibility of precautionary measures was in issue. Therefore, evidence of subsequent remedial measures would be admissible here either for impeachment or because the feasibility of such measures was controverted. The court incorrectly sustained the objection to Peter's attorney's question. The court should instruct the jury that this evidence cannot be used to establish culpability.

C. Under Rule 701, Fed.R.Evid., the opinion of a lay witness is admissible if the opinion is "rationally based on the perception of the witness and [is] helpful to a clear understanding of his testimony or the determination of a fact in issue." Here, the speed of the forklift Peter was operating was within Frank's perception, and Peter's carelessness is in issue. Therefore, Frank's testimony on the speed of the forklift is admissible. The court correctly ruled.

D. Under Rule 802 of the Federal Rules of Evidence, hearsay is not admissible except as provided by rule. Under Rule 801(c), hearsay is "a statement, other than one made by the declarant while testifying at the trial or hearing, offered in evidence to prove the truth of the matter asserted." Under the definition in Rule 801(a), a "statement" is an oral or a written assertion, or nonverbal conduct intended as an assertion. Here, Wendy was not asked merely about the fact that the letter was written: that is not hearsay. She was asked about the statements in the letter. Those statements are being offered for the truth of the matter asserted in them. The statements in the letter are hearsay. Therefore, the court was incorrect to admit Wendy's testimony as to that hearsay.

E. Under Rule 614(a), Fed.R.Evid., a court on its own motion may call a witness. Because the practice constitutes an intrusion upon the adversarial system, however, the practice should be used sparingly and with caution. *See, e.g., United States v. Ostrer*, 422 F. Supp. 93, 103 n.11 (S.D.N.Y. 1976). Under Rule 614(b), the court may itself question the witness. Under Rule 614(a), all parties may cross-examine the witness called by the court. Therefore, the court acted permissibly in calling a witness. The procedures are specified in Rule 614.

A Note on Answering This Question

This is a typical bar examination question testing knowledge of the law of evidence. The fact pattern and the interrogatories break the question up for you, so that you can see immediately exactly how many principal rules of law you will need to state and apply in order to answer the question. The outline for your answer will have as many points as there are parts to the question, here, five. Next to each number on your outline you will put a word or two to remind you of the principal rule of law you will state in writing your answer. Here is what your outline for this question might look like:

A. Refreshing recollection rule.

B. Subsequent remedial measures: when admissible.

C. Lay witness opinion rule.

D. Hearsay rule.

E. Court calls witness: rule and procedure.

Each paragraph in the essay is a straightforward model paragraph: *Rule–Application–Conclusion.*

Evidence questions are often just this easy to organize. What makes evidence questions difficult to answer well is that there are so many different rules and exceptions to rules. It is difficult for many students to choose the right rule to apply to the facts. Is this a case where the hearsay rule applies, or one of the exceptions? Are subsequent remedial measures inadmissible, the general rule, or is this one of the exceptions? In contrast with, for example, tort law, evidence questions require more thought in choosing the applicable rule and less effort, relatively speaking, in applying the rule to the facts. To see that this is true, compare the length of the paragraphs in the answer to this question with the lengths of the parts in the answers to torts questions or constitutional law questions.

Answer Twenty-eight: Real Property

Judy, the wife, is entitled to the farm.

Under the law of real property, a deed must be delivered in order to convey title. Delivery of the deed is a question of the intent of the grantor and is determined from facts and circumstances. Here, Mary never exercised the right of entry to the safe-deposit box in which John placed the deed. The box was used only by John. There is no evidence that Mary had control of the contents of the box or that the deed was delivered to her in any way. Here, in addition, the note was evidence of John's intent that no delivery of the deed should take place during his lifetime. Rather, the deed was to be delivered only after his death. Therefore, given the facts, there was no effective delivery of the deed.

Where land does not pass by deed it may pass by will. Here, under the residuary clause of the will, the property passed to the wife, Judy. Therefore, Judy is entitled to the farm.

A Note on Answering This Question

The bar candidate can also argue a strong case for the contrary result.

Answer Twenty-nine: Real Property

1. The two basic alternative approaches for implementing my client's plan are (A) private land-use planning through (i) the covenant running with the land, (ii) the equitable servitude, and (iii) the defeasible estate; and (B) public land-use devices, most likely a zoning ordinance.

2. The disadvantages of the private devices are that they can only be enforced by the owners who benefit from them and can therefore also be dispensed with. The disadvantages of the public devices are that they are dependent, in inception and in enforcement, on local politics.

Under the real property law of this state, there are three principal private land-use planning devices:

(i) the covenant running with the land;

(ii) the equitable servitude;

(iii) the defeasible estate
  (a) the fee simple determinable;
  (b) the fee subject to condition subsequent.

The public device is zoning for preservation of the character of the neighborhood, often called aesthetic zoning.

Making a covenant or servitude bind successor owners requires making the covenant "run with the land" or the servitude, so that successors will have notice, and equity will bind them. The requirements are

(a) the understanding must be a binding promise;

(b) the parties must intend that it bind successors;

(c) it must "touch or concern" the land.

The equitable servitude is enforceable by equitable remedies when it meets these requirements and it is otherwise equitable to enforce it. In addition, if the covenant (as distinguished from the servitude) is to run with the land, there must be "horizontal" privity between the parties to the original covenant, and "vertical" privity between the original parties and their respective successors. Here, there must be "horizontal" privity between the grantor and the grantee. There must also be "vertical" privity between Mr. Longstaff and his successor on one side of the transaction and his buyer and the buyer's successor on the other.

The third private alternative is the defeasible estate. Under the common law of real property, land can be conveyed so as to provide for divestiture in the event of failure to meet restictions. Under the fee simple determinable ("to A and his heirs, so long as all buildings on the property are erected and maintained in conformity with . . . .") the land will automatically revert to the grantor. The law does not favor automatic reversion. Under the fee simple subject to a condition subsequent ("To A and his heirs, but if buildings on the property are erected or maintained not in conformity with . . . or as approved by . . . then Adolphus Longstaff and his heirs may reenter"), the grantor is given the choice of reentering. Only holders of the future interests can enforce the restriction.

The disadvantages of the private arrangement are that (1) only the parties who are owners benefiting from it can enforce it, and (2) accordingly, interested parties can dispense with it. Private land-use restrictions can also be eliminated by legislation limiting time for use covenants or servitudes. They can disappear through changes in the neighborhood or neglect. By and large, however, as long as the people in The Horns want these arrangements, the restrictions can continue to be enforced.

Under the real property law of this state, a municipality may enact a zoning ordinance, and this zoning includes aesthetic or architectural zoning. [State laws differ.] Constitutional attacks on aesthetic zoning have argued that it is not within the police power of local government, and therefore invalid, and that it is an inverse condemnation, a "taking" of private property, for which compensation must be paid to the owner.

Here, in view of the value of these properties, aesthetic zoning will probably be upheld. It will be argued that preserving appearances maintains property values. Maintaining property values is a legitimate use of local police power. A valid exercise of the police power would not be a "taking" even if, contrary to the situation here, it in fact did diminish property values. This is especially true where the police power is used to forestall a nuisance. It could be argued that asphalt shingles in The Horns would be a nuisance.

The principal disadvantage of aesthetic zoning is that it is bureaucratic and political both in its creation and in its survival. In this case, probably, local authority can be persuaded to enact aesthetic zoning. Local authority, however, can thereafter (1) grant variances from the zoning requirements, (2) grant special use permits that dispense with the zoning requirements, and (3) amend the favorable zoning or repeal it entirely.

Both private and public devices require some sort of authority to make aesthetic judgments, an architectural agency for the public devices, a committee for the private ones. This may seem cumbersome to the client. There is also some possibility in the case of covenants, servitudes, or defeasible estates, of the argument's being made that owners cannot delegate their enforcement power to a committee. This argument has not been successful elsewhere. The leading case is *Neponsit Property Owners' Association v. Emigrant Industrial Savings Bank*, 278 N.Y. 248; 15 N.E.2d 793 (1938).

A Note on Answering This Question

This is a classic memo-writing question. It asks: What are the alternatives, and what are the disadvantages of each? The temptation to be vague and shapeless in answering is very powerful. Only careful attention to structure keeps the writer from wandering off the topic. Notice that in the first paragraphs of this essay, the alternatives are set out vertically, rather than being included as normal parts of the paragraph. Remember to set out vertically anything that you particularly want the grader to notice, whether the elements of a tort, the remedies available to a seller under Article 2 of the U.C.C. or, here, the three main private land-use planning devices.

Answer Thirty: Federal Jurisdiction and Procedure

Assuming that the court properly took jurisdiction over the matter, AAA may move for relief from the default judgment under Rule 60(b). In addition, AAA may have to seek temporary relief in the nature of a restraining order preventing execution of the judgment.

Under Rule 55, Fed.R.Civ.P., when a party against whom a judgment is sought fails to plead or defend, judgment by default can be entered against him either by the clerk of the court or by the court itself. Entry of default, or a judgment by default, may be set aside for good cause shown in accordance with Rule 60(b). If service of process is improper or insufficient, a default may be set aside. Under Rule 4(h)(1), service upon a corporation is made by delivering a copy of the summons and complaint to an officer, managing or general agent, or any other agent authorized to receive process. Here, Mary, the receptionist, was not one of these designated persons who could be served as representing AAA. There is no evidence that service was made in accordance with Rule 4(c), according to the law of the state in which the district court is held. Therefore, service of process was not proper.

Where a party has cause for a motion to set aside a default judgment under Rule 60(b), the motion must be made within a reasonable time, generally not more than one year after the judgment. (A party may also, where necessary, file an independent action for relief from a judgment or order.)

Under Rule 60(b), a motion to set aside a default judgment on such grounds as mistake, neglect, or voidability of the judgment "does not affect the finality of a judgment or suspend its operation." A party may have to seek temporary relief in the nature of a restraining order, or similar order of the court, preventing execution on the judgment. Rule 59(b), providing for a new trial or amendment of judgments, does not apply here because motions under Rule 59(b) must be served not later than 10 days after entry of judgment. Therefore, AAA may have to seek temporary relief in the nature of a restraining order preventing execution of the judgment.

Under 28 U.S.C. sec. 1332, a district court has subject matter (diversity) jurisdiction of all civil actions where the amount in controversy exceeds $50,000, and the parties are citizens of different states. Subject matter jurisdiction may be raised at any time. Here, the action is on a promissory note. The facts do not indicate that diversity of citizenship exists between the parties. Therefore, it may be that the court lacks subject matter jurisdiction.

Answer Thirty-one: Constitutional Law

The issues on appeal are whether the actions of the Neuter Racing Association, Inc. constitute state action and, if so, whether they have denied David Driver's right to due process under the 14th amendment.

State Action. Under the due process clause of the fourteenth amendment of the United States Constitution, no state shall deny due process of law. In order to have a cause of action under the due process clause of the fourteenth amendment, plaintiff must first demonstrate that there was state action. *Blum v. Yaretsky*, 457 U.S. 991 (1982). Where a state extensively regulates a private association, it may be possible to demonstrate sufficient state involvement to constitute state action. The state must be so intertwined in the private action that it can be said to be responsible for the violation of the right to due process. The aggrieved party must demonstrate a close nexus between the state and the loss or deprivation of which he complains.

Here, none of the following is sufficient to support a claim of state action: (i) below-market rents; (ii) substantial financial assistance; (iii) leasing relationship; (iv) neutral enforcement of state regulations. Nor is conducting horse racing "traditionally and exclusively reserved to the state." It would not constitute a public function. *Jackson v. Metropolitan Edison Co.*, 419 U.S. 345 (1974).

Here, however, David Driver can argue that the Ewin revocation policy had in fact been specifically approved by the Racing Commission. *Cf. Moose Lodge No. 107 v. Irvis*, 407 U.S. 163 (1972). He can also argue that the revocation was provoked by the second suspension order issued by the racing judge and the judge's call for further action. The state is responsible for the racing judge, who is arguably implementing a state policy.

Due Process. Under the fourteenth amendment, the citizen has a right not to be deprived of a substantial liberty or property interest by the state without due process of law. His right to pursue his occupation is a "liberty" and "property" interest. *Bd. of Regents v. Roth*, 408 U.S. 564 (1972). In determining the procedures required to ensure fairness, the courts will balance the interest affected, the risk of error, and the probable value of the procedures requested against the government's interest in administrative efficiency and cost savings. To be protected in his interest, the claimant must have a legitimate claim of entitlement to it.

Here, David Driver can argue that he has a property interest in his privilege to race at Ewin and in the continued exercise of his racing license. He can argue that deprivation of these interests requires, as is usual where the interest is substantial, a hearing and a statement of reasons. He can argue that providing these elements of due process will impose only a minimal burden on the state.

A Note on Answering This Question

This question, again, demonstrates the importance of dealing with the most fundamental questions in the outline of the subject area. Before treating the deprivation of due process, determine whether or not there is state action. That is how any fourteenth amendment due process question must be structured.

Notice, too, that the fact pattern in a Constitutional Law question rarely gives enough facts to support a definite conclusion. The case law, in addition, can be read and argued in a number of ways. Accordingly, the *Application* part of a Constitutional Law essay is often of the form, "Here, [petitioner/plaintiff/appellant] *can argue* that . . . ." The candidate is applying the law to the facts not in order to come to a conclusion but in order to show that on these facts the party in question has an argument.

Answer Thirty-two: Torts

Dear Personal Representative:

You have asked me for an opinion on whether Mr. Pail's estate should bring an action against Short Peninsular Railroad (SPR).

Under the law of this state, the elements of negligence are (i) duty of care, (ii) breach of that duty, (iii) actual cause, (iv) proximate cause, and (v) harm. *See* W. Prosser and W. Keeton, *Prosser and Keeton on the Law of Torts* sec. 30 (1984). Whether there was a duty of care is for the court to decide, because this is a question of law. The court will look at the relationship of the parties, and at how close the defendant was to the plaintiff in space, time, and logical connection. The court will ask whether the defendant could have foreseen that his acts posed some danger to the plaintiff. Here, SPR had no statutory duty to erect or maintain the fence between Farmer Plow's pasture and the railroad's right of way. However, once the damage its own negligence caused to the fence was brought to SPR's attention, it had a duty to repair the fence. A reasonable railroad would have foreseen that a fence that had been erected to keep livestock off the railroad right of way would also keep the livestock off an adjacent highway. Moreover, a reasonable railroad would have foreseen that an escaping animal could pose a risk not only to itself and to users of the railroad, but also to users of the highway. Therefore, a court will probably decide that SPR had a duty of care to a person using the highway, and that under these circumstances SPR breached that duty.

Under the law of this state, the plaintiff has the burden of proving that the negligence of the defendant was the actual cause of the harm complained of. Plaintiff also has the burden of proving that the negligence of the defendant was the proximate cause of the harm complained of.* *Id.* sec. 42. In a trial to a jury, these are jury questions. Plaintiff must prove, that is, that "but for" defendant's negligence the harm would not have occurred. Plaintiff must also prove that the injury occurred as a natural and probable consequence of the negligent act, among other things, without intervention of new independent causes that a reasonable defendant should not have foreseen. There may be more than one proximate cause. The existence of intervening negligence does not relieve the party responsible for the first proximate cause of liability for the damage.

Here, plaintiff can prove that SPR's negligence was the cause-in-fact of Pail's death. "But for" the negligent loading of the crate, Plow's fence would not have been broken, Tex would not have escaped, Duts would not have hit Tex, and Pail would not have been gored. In addition, plaintiff must prove proximate causation: that the death occurred as a natural and probable and even foreseeable consequence of SPR's negligent act. In this case, it can be argued that the freakish sequence of events between the negligent loading of the crate and Tex's death lunge at Pail could simply not have been foreseen. This is, however, a question for the jury. A jury could find that SPR should have foreseen the events that occurred. Therefore, plaintiff may be able to prove to the jury that SPR's negligence was both the actual and the legal cause of Pail's injuries and death.

(The model answer provided by the bar examiners states: "An applicant should recognize that there may be more than one proximate cause and that interven-

---

* State law regarding the scope and definition of proximate causation varies.

ing negligence does not relieve the one responsible for the first proximate cause from liability.")

A Note On Answering This Question

In 20 minutes the candidate can discuss only negligence law. Were the time limit 45 minutes or more, however, the candidate would have time to discuss the differences between an action for personal injuries and an action for wrongful death, treating (i) the elements of each, (ii) damages, and (iii) whether the recovery becomes an asset of the estate or passes to the distributees under the laws of intestacy.

Answer Thirty-three:
Criminal Procedure

1. The glasscutter is admissible, because it was obtained pursuant to a stop and frisk based on reasonable suspicion.

   The jewelry and silverware are not admissible because they were obtained without a warrant. The search and seizure come neither within the automobile exception to the warrant requirement nor within the exception for a search incident to a lawful arrest.

2. The statement given to the detectives is inadmissible because obtained in violation of Denton's fifth and sixth amendment rights.

1. The Glasscutter. Under the fourth amendment to the Constitution, the people shall have a right to be safe in their houses, and no warrants shall issue but upon probable cause. Exceptions to the requirement of a warrant include border searches, automobile searches, consent searches, searches made after hot pursuit, school searches, stop and frisk searches incident to a lawful arrest, and searches under exigent circumstances. A "stop and frisk" is justified where the police officer has formed a reasonable suspicion about a person's activities. The frisk is a "pat-down" search for weapons. *Terry v. Ohio*, 392 U.S. 1 (1968). Where evidence is seized in an impermissible search and seizure, constitutional principles prohibit its admission into evidence.

Here, the police had received a telephone call about a burglary. The officer who responded found the defendant, Denton, in front of the house. His standing there so shortly after the call was enough for the officer to form a "reasonable suspicion." Therefore, the officer could "stop and frisk" Denton. Accordingly, the search was permissible, and the glass cutter may be admitted into evidence.

The Jewelry and Silverware. The police may seize evidence from an automobile without a warrant when the circumstances fall within the "automobile exception" to the warrant requirement. The suspect must be in or near the car and able to reach what is in it, and the police must have had a reasonable suspicion to stop him. *Michigan v. Long*, 463 U.S. 1032 (1983). Here, however, Denton was outside the car, which was, in fact, locked. He was merely walking towards it. Therefore, the evidence does not fall within the automobile exception to the warrant requirement. It was improperly seized. Therefore, it is inadmissible in evidence.

The police may also seize evidence without a warrant when the seizure is incident to a lawful arrest. The evidence must be within the immediate reach and control of the arrestee. *New York v. Belton*, 453 U.S. 454 (1981). Here, although Denton was legally arrested, again, the contents of the car were not available to him. The car was locked. Its contents were not within his immediate reach and control. Accordingly, the jewelry and silverware do not fall within the exception to the warrant requirement for a search incident to a lawful arrest. Therefore, again, the jewelry and silverware are inadmissible in evidence.

2. *The Statement to the Detectives.* Under the sixth amendment, as soon as an arrestee asks for an attorney, all questioning must stop until an attorney is provided. *Miranda v. Arizona*, 384 U.S. 436 (1966). The fact that a defendant is read his *Miranda* rights again after he has asked for representation does not nullify his request for counsel. Nor does the fact that the second set of questions, following the new reading of the *Miranda* rights, is on a charge different from the charge as to which the defendant requested counsel.

Here, Denton applied for a public defender to represent him in the burglary charge. That was a request for counsel. The fact that the detectives investigating the Silvertown homicide read Denton his *Miranda* rights again does not nullify the first request for counsel. Nor does the fact that the second set of questions was on a charge different from the first. In addition, because Denton was in jail, the custodial element is influential. His statement regarding the Springfield homicide is a violation of Denton's sixth amendment rights. Therefore, it is inadmissible.

Answer Thirty-four: Contracts

If the brochure was not an offer, there is no contract. If the court finds there was an offer, however, Agency will assert mistake, illusory contract, and indefiniteness.

Formation of Contract. Under the laws of this state, a valid contract requires offer, acceptance, and consideration.

The Offer: Under the common law of contracts, the offer transfers to the other party the power to create a contract or "seal the deal." An offer must be distinguished from negotiations, which do not give the other person the power to create a contract by saying "I accept."

Here, the argument in favor of treating the brochure as an offer is that it contains numerous specific details that suggest that it in fact is an offer. One could argue that it transfers to another the power to create a contract because Paula could "seal the deal" by saying "I accept." The Agency will argue, however, that the brochure is not an offer, but instead a negotiation. On this theory, the brochure would be like a price list, which is usually treated as a preliminary negotiation. The brochure merely invited Paula to make an offer. In that event, Paula's January 23 letter would be considered an offer. Although it did not list many terms, it did invite the Agency to accept. Furthermore, full details are not required for a contract. The court can fill them in or, as here, the parties may incorporate terms from the negotiations into the contract by reference.

The Acceptance: Under the common law of contracts, a contract requires not just an offer, but also an acceptance. An acceptance is the exercise by the offeree of the power to create a contract. The offeror is the master of his offer. In common law (i.e., in non-U.C.C. cases), an acceptance has to be the "mirror image" of the offer. A "nonconforming" acceptance will usually be viewed as either an outright rejection or a counteroffer and rejection. Once an offer is rejected by an offeree, the offer is "dead." The offeree cannot thereafter accept it.

Under the rule in virtually all jurisdictions, the "mailbox" rule, an acceptance is effective on dispatch.

Here, assuming that the brochure was an offer, Paula will argue that she accepted the offer on January 23 when she sent Agency a letter reserving a seat. Paula will use the mailbox rule to support her argument that the acceptance was valid upon dispatch (Jan. 23), rather than upon receipt (Jan. 27). Paula will argue that she and Agency have formed a contract.

If a court decides that the brochure was not an offer, then it will find no acceptance and no contract. Although Paula's letter could be an offer, Agency never accepted. Indeed, in its January 25 telephone call, Agency expressly rejected Paula's offer to take a tour for $500.

Consideration: A contract requires an offer, acceptance, and consideration. If there is an offer and acceptance, then consideration should not be a problem. Paula can be viewed as exchanging a promise to pay money for Agency's promise to provide a tour. This is valid consideration. (See below, however, for an illusory contract defense.)

Contract Defenses: The Mistake Defense: If a court finds that Agency made the offer and Paula accepted it on January 23, Agency will raise a mistake defense. Agency mistakenly listed the price of the tour as $500 rather than $5,000. Agency will try to be released from the contract on the basis of this unilateral mistake.

Traditionally, the courts have been reluctant to release a party from a contract on the basis of a unilateral mistake. Furthermore, the courts typically won't release a party if the innocent party has relied on the mistake. Here, Agency's first hurdle is to convince the court that Paula has not relied on the mistaken offer to her detriment. Agency should argue that Paula has only lost 10 days of planning and that she can find another tour.

Agency could also argue that Paula knew or should have known that there was a mistake in the offer, that $500 is very cheap. Paula will argue that $500 is not unreasonable, that traveling in South America might be very cheap, and that it was a short tour.

The Illusory Contract Defense: The contract gave Agency the right to "refuse or discontinue service to anyone." Agency would argue that the contract is illusory because it had a "free way out": it could simply refuse to honor the contract. If a court followed the traditional approach, *Strong v. Sheffield*, 144 N.Y. 392, 39 N.E. 330 (1895), this argument might work.

It is more likely, however, that a court would read into this provision a "good faith" requirement. If Agency has to exercise its power in good faith, then it does not have a free way out, and the contract is not illusory.

The Indefiniteness Defense: A contract will be enforced only if its terms are definite enough so that a court can determine exactly what there is to enforce. Agency can argue that this contract is too indefinite to be enforced. It does not give a specific itinerary or specify which hotels and meals are to be provided. A court could not determine from the "Contract" what Agency promised.

Many courts would reject this defense. Courts have enforced contracts that have very sketchy details, particularly where the plaintiff is seeking monetary damages rather than specific performance.

Answer Thirty-five: Evidence

1. The testimony of Dennis may be admissible.

2. Some certification or authorization from the State of California may be required for the fingerprint records to be admissible. Sgt. Smart will probably be allowed to testify about her findings without the fingerprint records being in evidence.

1. *Testimony Regarding the November 19 Incident.* Under the Federal Rules of Evidence, all relevant evidence is admissible unless excluded. Rule 401, Fed.R.Evid. Relevant evidence is "evidence having a tendency to make the existence of any fact that is of consequence to the action more probable or less probable." Rule 401, Fed.R.Evid. Evidence of other crimes, wrongs, or acts is not admissible to prove character, but it may be admissible for other purposes, including motive, opportunity, plan, or knowledge. Rule 404(b), Fed.R.Evid. The court must, however, weigh the probative value of relevant evidence against its tendency to prejudice the defendant unfairly. Rule 403, Fed.R.Evid. Evidence that goes to prove an element of the crime is admissible. Evidence that goes to general disposition or that is unfairly prejudicial is not admissible.

Here, Dennis's testimony that Lewis was in Mervyn's on Lake Street on November 19, attempted to return a coat for cash, and fled, may tend to show that Lewis had stolen from Mervyn's in the past. Thus, the evidence is prejudicial. However, it arguably tends to show opportunity, knowledge and mode of operation, and so to prove an element of the present crime.

Therefore, Dennis's testimony may be admissible.

2. *California Fingerprint Records.* Under Rule 402, Fed.R.Evid., evidence must be relevant. Here, evidence of Lewis's fingerprints on the hanger goes directly to the element of Lewis's intent to deceive or permanently deprive, an element of theft. Therefore, the fingerprint evidence is relevant.

Under Rule 702, Fed.R.Evid., testimony of experts, if it will assist the trier of fact to understand the evidence or to determine a fact in issue, may be presented in the form of opinion or otherwise. A fingerprint record is arguably admissible as a self-authenticating document under certain conditions. Under Rule 902, Fed.R.Evid., extrinsic evidence of authenticity as a condition precedent to admissibility is not required for (i) domestic public documents under seal, (ii) domestic public documents not under seal with appropriate authentication, and (iii) certified copies of public records.

Here, the facts do not state that the fingerprint records are either authenticated or certified.

Therefore, some certification or authorization from the State of California may be required for the fingerprint records to be admitted in evidence.

Even without such certification or authorization, the expert could testify as to her findings. Under Rules 702 and 703, Fed.R.Evid., facts or data used by a properly qualified expert in forming an opinion need not be in evidence if they are of a type reasonably relied on by experts in the witness's field of expertise.

Here, the fingerprint records may be of that type.

Therefore, Sgt. Smart will probably be allowed to testify about her findings, without the fingerprint records being in evidence.

*Answer Thirty-six: Real Property**

1. As matters stand, the buyers cannot acquire marketable title. Under the laws of this state, property taxes automatically accrue as a lien against real property on _____ and are payable by _____ of each year. If not paid when due, the real property is sold to the county on a preliminary tax sale for the amount of the taxes. The owner then has _____ years within which to redeem the property by paying the amount of the taxes together with interest, penalties, and costs. If not redeemed, the county will sell the property in the _____ th year, typically during the month of _____, at a public auction to the highest bidder. There is no right of redemption from such a sale and the purchaser would receive a fee simple title with priority over all other interests. Here, since the title report is more than one year old, it is impossible to tell whether the property was redeemed from the preliminary tax sales or whether it was sold in the interim to a new owner. An updated title report should be ordered at once to determine present ownership. Even if the taxes were paid and the property redeemed, title is vested in the name of the 17-year-old minor child of the sellers. She has no legal capacity to execute a deed. A guardian must first be appointed for her. The guardian will need an appropriate court order to execute the deed on her behalf.

2. The judgment for $1,150 is now more than eight years old, and unless the updated title report shows it was renewed, the judgment is now void [subject to state law].

3. The $500 judgment, which is still within its statutory life of _____ years, was docketed while the sellers had title and unless otherwise paid will have to be paid at closing.

4. It appears and would be presumed that the deed of trust for $20,000 was executed by the sellers prior to conveying title to their daughter and would be a valid lien against the real property. The balance owing would be paid at closing.

5. The judgment for $2,000 was docketed more than five years after the sellers conveyed title to their minor child. Unless the judgment creditor could prove that the conveyance to the daughter was without consideration and in fraud of creditors in existence as of February 1983, the judgment would not be a lien on this real property. It is likely this judgment creditor was not a creditor of the sellers more than _____ years previous to its being docketed, and it likely would not be a lien. The title company would probably remove this exception if asked to do so.

6. The updated title report would be necessary to determine the validity of the mechanics lien. A lien claimant must commence legal action to foreclose the lien within _____ months after the performance of the last labor, delivery of the last material, or suspension of work for a period of _____ days. At the very latest, this would be _____. If the updated report fails to show the commencement of legal action and the recording of a *lis pendens*, the lien would be void and could be ignored.

7. Sewer assessments certified to the county are treated the same as property taxes and would have to be paid at closing.

---

* There is great variation among the laws of the various states. Know your own law. Fill in the blanks accordingly, or write different answers to conform to the law in your state.

A. In the absence of a contrary written agreement, the seller has no obligation to pay the buyers' document preparation fee. This is the obligation of the buyers. If not permitted by HUD, it would have to be deleted by the mortgage company.

B. The same as "A" above.

C. Discount points are a common problem, and provision for their payment is typically made in the earnest money sales agreement. Here the agreement is silent on this point. Since loan discount points relate to the buyers' loan, the seller has no legal obligation to pay them. However, from a practical standpoint the seller may wish to do so rather than lose the sale. HUD regulations prevent the buyer from paying them. It is unlikely they will be waived by the mortgage company. The sellers would have the right to abort the sale if the buyers insisted that the sellers pay the discount points. The sellers could also abort if the buyers tried to make the sellers pay either or both the document preparation fee and the tax service fee.

Answer Thirty-seven: Torts

1. M.D. Parker has causes of action against Chrysler in negligence, warranty, and strict liability. [State law may provide additional causes of action, such as willful and wanton misconduct.] M.D. Parker has a cause of action against Trucker Juan in negligence. [Again, state law may provide additional causes of action.]

2. All of the defendants would probably cross-claim against all of the others, claiming that the conduct of one or more of the other defendants proximately caused or contributed to the injuries. Defendants will deny that they were negligent, and assert the statute of limitations, contributory or comparative negligence [depending on state law], and that the injuries were caused by a superseding cause, whether Trucker Tew or any other actor whose acts were subsequent to those of each defendant. Trucker Tew and Trucker Juan may seek to justify their actions on the grounds of emergency.

I. *M.D. Parker's Causes of Action*

   A. *Against Chrysler Corporation*

      1. *Negligence.* M.D. probably has a cause of action against Chrysler for negligence, based upon Chrysler's failure to correct the known defect in the gas gauge. Under the common law of torts, the elements of negligence are (i) duty of care, (ii) breach of duty, (iii) actual cause, (iv) proximate cause, and (v) damages. *See* W. Prosser and W. Keeton, *Prosser and Keeton on the Law of Torts* sec. 30 (1984). If a manufacturer knows, or by using reasonable diligence, should know, of a defect, there is a duty to take appropriate corrective action to avoid injury or damage to consumers. Here, M.D. must show duty, breach, cause in fact, proximate cause, and injury.

      2. *Willful and Wanton Misconduct.* [Depending on state law, punitive damages may be available.]

      3. *Warranty.* Under the law of contracts [subject to modification by state law], a manufacturer, by placing goods on the market and failing to issue a recall, impliedly represents to the public that the goods are suitable and safe for their intended use. Under the Uniform Commercial Code, unless such warranties are disclaimed in accordance with the

Code, the manufacturer impliedly warrants the merchantability of all goods sold, and the fitness for an intended purpose of all those sold with the purpose in mind. U.C.C. sec. 2-314. Here, Chrysler expected that the product would be used with an assumption of safety. Chrysler could imagine that a defective gas gauge might expose passengers to severe injury where the automobile ran out of gas and stalled. Therefore, although the exact facts of this case could not have been anticipated, nonetheless, injury to passengers was foreseeable. Therefore, M.D. Parker may be able to establish a cause of action in warranty.

In addition, if the company's advertising stressed quality and safety, plaintiff may have a cause of action for breach of express warranty.

4. *Strict Product Liability.* Under Section 402(A), *Restatement (Second) of Torts*, (1965), a party selling a product in a defective condition that is unreasonably dangerous to the consumer is liable for physical harm caused thereby if (a) the seller is engaged in the business of selling that type of product and (b) the product is expected to and does reach the consumer without substantial change in the condition in which it was sold.

Here, the Chrysler LeBaron was manufactured by Chrysler Corporation, which was in the business of selling automobiles, and reached the consumer in a defective condition, without substantial change in the condition in which it was sold.

Therefore, plaintiff has a cause of action against Chrysler in strict product liability.

B. *Against Trucker Juan.*

1. *Negligence.* Trucker Juan (and D.P. Tile, if Trucker Juan is operating as an employee) is subject to an action in negligence. Under the tort law of this state, violation of the law may suffice to establish negligence *per se*. There may be a basis for negligence *per se* where a statute protects a certain class of persons against injury and such a person has suffered injury as a result of violation of the statute.

Here, arguably, Trucker Juan was negligent *per se* in operating in violation of the statutory load limits. [Such conduct may be subject to punitive damages, depending on state law, if it rises to the level of "willful and wanton conduct" and "reckless disregard of the safety of others."]

Therefore, I would consider filing actions against both Trucker Juan Martinez as an independent contractor (or agent or employee, or both) of D.P. Tile, and against D.P. Tile on a theory of *respondeat superior*: (a) as responsible for Trucker Juan's actions: and (b) as responsible for the actions of the dock superintendent who knew of the violation.

In addition, if plaintiff can establish by competent expert testimony that driving along Soldier Summit with only parking lights on was below the acceptable standard of care and caused the injury to M.D. Parker, then an additional action lies against Trucker Juan and, potentially, D.P. Tile.

2. *Causation.* Under the law of this state, plaintiff in negligence must show that defendant's actions were the proximate cause of his injuries and that such injuries were reasonably foreseeable.* Could Trucker Juan, for example, have completely avoided the accident if he had been driving at a safe speed with his headlights on? Without the intervening

---

* State law on proximate causation varies.

actions of Trucker Tew, Trucker Juan could in any event have swerved and avoided the accident. However, a jury may find that it was Trucker Juan's negligent operation of his vehicle that caused him to have an unreasonably short time to react to a dangerous condition. It might be found to be foreseeable that in reacting quickly he would have to collide with the object in front of him, a vehicle in another lane, or one behind him. Therefore, based on the facts of this case, if Trucker Juan's breach of the standard of care appears to have been related to the resulting damage to other motorists in a foreseeable way, the necessary causation will have been shown.

II. *Cross-claims and Defenses.*

  A. *Cross-claims.* Each of the defendants would probably cross-claim against all of the others. Each one could attempt to show that another defendant was the proximate cause of the injuries. In particular, they would allege that the actions of Trucker Juan and Trucker Tew were intervening superseding causes, either decreasing or entirely shielding the other defendants from liability.

  B. *Defenses.* Defendants will all deny that they were negligent and that their conduct was the proximate cause of M.D. Parker's injuries. Defendants will argue one or more of the following defenses:

  1. *Statute of Limitations.* [Depending upon applicable state law], the statute of limitations on most of M.D. Parker's causes of action may have run on December 1, 1989, or thereabouts.

  2. *Joint and Several Liability.* [State applicable state law.]

  3. *Contributory or Comparative Negligence.* [State applicable state law.] The defendants will allege that M.D. Parker was negligent in not wearing a seat belt and in not moving his vehicle to the right-hand side of the road, or turning on his emergency flashers or parking lights, especially in view of the weather.

  4. *Superseding Cause.* The defendants, Chrysler, D.P. Tile and Trucker Juan, in particular, will allege that the subsequent negligent acts of a third person caused the injuries. Under the tort law of this state, prior negligence is not superseded if subsequent negligent conduct is foreseeable, as with negligent medical care following an accident. Trucker Juan may be on firm ground in arguing that "but for" the negligent actions of Trucker Tew, Trucker Juan could completely have avoided the accident.

Answer Thirty-eight: Contracts

Seller has an enforceable claim against Buyer for the $200,000 owed under the purchase agreement. Seller also has an enforceable claim for the $100,000 owed under the consulting agreement. The covenant not to compete is unenforceable. Following is a discussion of the relevant issues.

Consideration. Under the common law, formation of a contract requires offer, acceptance, and consideration. Consideration is any benefit to the promisor or detriment to the promisee. Here, Buyer and Seller had agreed that the total purchase price for the Stratosphere was to be $400,000 and that, for tax reasons, $100,000 of that amount was to be paid in the form of consulting fees. Therefore, even though two separate agreements were prepared and signed, the parties intended that there was to be only a single contract. Therefore, the consideration for the consulting agreement was, at least in part, the sale of the Stratosphere.

Definiteness/Statute of Frauds. Under the statute of frauds, a contract that cannot be performed within one year must be in writing, and signed by the party to be charged. Here, Buyer might argue that the consulting agreement was unenforceable due to a lack of definiteness of terms, particularly with respect to the nature of the consulting services to be performed. However, the consulting agreement identifies the parties and the amount to be paid, and it indicates that the amount was to be paid in exchange for "consulting services." This would probably be sufficient to satisfy the statute of frauds. It would be appropriate for the court to consider extrinsic evidence to determine the intent of the parties as to the nature and extent of the services to be performed. Moreover, since Buyer drafted the agreement, it should be construed against him.

Covenant Not to Compete. Under the law of this state, a covenant not to compete is enforceable if it is supported by consideration, if there was no bad faith in the negotiation of the contract, if the covenant is necessary to protect the good will of the business, and if it is reasonable in its restrictions as to time and area. Here, it is questionable whether the covenant was necessary to protect the good will of the Stratosphere. More important, the covenant is completely unrestricted as to time and area. Even were it enforceable, moreover, it is doubtful that Seller breached it. Seller's new club is a substantial distance away from the Stratosphere. Only the fact that many of the same bands that used to play at the Stratosphere are now playing at Seller's new club suggests that the new club is in fact in competition with the Stratosphere. Therefore, it is likely that the covenant not to compete contained in the consulting agreement is unenforceable here.

Answer Thirty-nine: Real Property

Memorandum

TO: Les Orr

FROM: Bar Candidate

Re: Lisa Lott

For the reasons discussed at length below, I have concluded that it is unlikely that you will have to lease or sell your property to Lisa Lott.

Leasehold interest in your property. A leasehold is a nonfreehold estate. There are four kinds of leaseholds. The differences are relevant here: (i) tenancy at sufferance; (ii) tenancy for a fixed term; (iii) tenancy at will; and (iv) periodic tenancy. A *tenancy for a term* (or *tenancy for years*) ends at the end of the time period, one or more years or a fraction of a year. A *tenancy at sufferance* arises where the lease period ends and the tenant wrongfully holds over. In most jurisdictions [cite local law], if the landlord continues to accept tenant's rent, the tenancy becomes a periodic tenancy. A *periodic tenancy* is a tenancy measured by the unit of time by which the tenant pays rent. (The *tenancy at will* is one in which there is no fixed arrangement as to duration; in most jurisdictions, it automatically becomes a periodic tenancy on the payment of rent.)

Here, you entered into a written lease with Lisa Lott for a period of three years, with rent payable monthly, on the first day of the month, and failure to pay by the 10th constituting default. This was a tenancy for a term, and the term was three years. When the term ended, had Ms. Lott simply remained in possession, she would have been a tenant at sufferance. As you accepted her rent payment on July 1, 1988, Ms. Lott became a tenant with a periodic tenancy, here, month-to-month.

As to Lott's late payment of rent, August 12, 1990, had there been a renewal of the three-year periodic tenancy, subject to the same conditions as the original agreement, then Lott would be in default, since her payment came in more than ten days after the first day of the month.

Under the statute of frauds, however, an agreement for the sale or lease of land must be in writing, signed by the party to be charged. Here, there was no written agreement for two or three years, or for any period of years. Ms. Lott did not renew; she made a counteroffer of two years. Hence, Lott is not in default.

However, under a periodic tenancy, the landlord may give the tenant a timely notice to quit. Unless the common law is superseded by statute, notice of termination must be given at least one rent-period in advance. (In some states there is a statutory number of days.) Here, the rent period is monthly. You notified Ms. Lott on or about August 12, 1988, that she should quit the premises no later than September 15, 1988. You gave Ms. Lott more than 30 days' notice. Therefore, your notice of termination was timely and effective, and Ms. Lott must leave no later than September 15, 1988.

Option to buy the property. Under contract law, here applicable to the option to buy your property, an option is an irrevocable offer. That offer may have a fixed term, at the end of which it expires. In most jurisdictions, an option to purchase in a lease that expires does not carry over into a subsequent periodic tenancy. Here, the original agreement with Ms. Lott provided for her option to buy the property during the lease term, at fair market value. Ms. Lott did not in fact choose to exercise her option during the lease term. Therefore, the option to buy expired.

The option was in any event to buy the property at fair market value. That figure has not been determined. The amount proposed by Ms. Lott is $75,000, by her own admission, more than fair market value, since she stated, "which is more than it is presently worth." Therefore, Ms. Lott has not attempted to exercise the option, either before or after it expired.

Conclusion. It is most likely that a court will find that you have a month-to-month lease arrangement with Ms. Lott and that you have given sufficient notice of terminating it.

A Note on Answering This Question

At first glance, this question appears to be reasonably difficult, since it contains both landlord-tenant and contract issues. However, by taking the main topics one at a time and handling them with short Model Paragraphs, one can make brisk work of the essay. In fact, most of it is just close reading of the agreement, together with common sense. Notice that whenever a fact pattern sets out the words of a contract, a statute, or any other legal document, your first task as a lawyer is to interpret that document.

The main topics here, in order, are (i) the types of tenancies, and especially the type Ms. Lott now has, namely, month-to-month; (ii) the nonrenewal of the periodic tenancy, for two or three years; (iii) the right of the landlord to give the tenant in a month-to-month tenancy timely notice to quit; (iv) the fact that an option is an irrevocable offer with a, usually, fixed term, the term in this case having expired. Q.E.D. It turns out to be quite simple, if one just takes the main topics apart and handles them one after the other.

Answer Forty: Evidence

The issues:

1. Whether scientific expert testimony is admissible where the technique from which it results is neither generally accepted in the scientific community nor shown to be inherently reliable.

2. Whether an expert witness testifying in a criminal case may be permitted to express an opinion on the ultimate issue in the case.

3. Whether a witness not meeting the criteria of Rule 615, Fed.R.Evid., should be permitted to remain at prosecution table during a criminal trial. Whether his presence is prejudicial to the defendant.

1. Under Rule 702, Fed.R.Evid., expert testimony is admissible if it will "assist the trier of fact to understand the evidence or to determine a fact in issue." Some courts hold that scientific evidence for which a foundation has not been properly laid is necessarily unreliable and therefore should not be admitted. Other courts have held that inadequate foundation only affects the probative value of the evidence, not its admissibility. There are two common tests. The first is the *Frye* test, in which the proponent of the evidence must show "general acceptance of the principle or technique [upon which the testimony is based] in the scientific community." *Frye v. United States*, 293 F. 1013, 1014 (D.C. Cir. 1923). The modern trend, however, abandons exclusive reliance on *Frye* and suggests that "inherent reliability," rather than "general acceptance," should be the touchstone for determining admissibility of such evidence. Here, the method described by Dr. Itall has clearly not been shown to be generally accepted. It has not yet even been published. Some showing of inherent reliability would be needed for the results to be admissible. Here, it appears from the statement of facts that no such showing was made. Therefore, the foundation for the evidence being inadequate, the evidence would have to be excluded.

Because this evidentiary error affected the outcome of the case, and because the error cannot be called harmless, the conviction must be reversed.

2. An expert, here Dr. Itall, may express an opinion on the ultimate issue of the case. Under Rule 704, Fed.R.Evid., testimony from an expert on the ultimate issue to be decided by the trier of fact is permitted. Such opinion evidence does not necessarily invade the province of the jury because the jury is not required to accept the opinion of the witness. Here, Dr. Itall was an expert witness. He could therefore be permitted to testify that Betty Small was molested and that Ralph Malph was the molester, both points going to the ultimate issue in the case. This was admissible evidence. (Note, however, that in criminal cases, many courts have determined that Rule 704 opinion evidence may be so prejudicial, confusing, and misleading as to be inadmissible under Rule 403. The trend is against allowing expert testimony on the guilt of a criminal defendant.)

3. Unless he met one of the exceptions under Rule 615, Dr. Itall should have been excluded from the courtroom. Rule 615 requires exclusion of witnesses on the motion of either party or an order of the court. It does not authorize the exclusion of (1) "a party who is a natural person, or (2) an officer or employee of a party who is not a natural person designated as its representative by its attorney, or (3) a person whose presence is shown by a party to be essential to the presentation of his cause." Here, the doctor was not a party to the action. Nor

was he designated as a representative by the prosecution. No showing was made that his presence was essential to presentation of the case. Therefore, Dr. Itall should have been excluded from the trial proceedings.

The fact that Dr. Itall was not excluded does not automatically mean that the defendant was prejudiced by his presence. Here, a strong argument could be made, however, that such prejudice may have resulted. As noted in the fact pattern, Dr. Itall was able to form his opinion after he heard the testimony of the other witnesses. This may mean that his opinion from the interviews he had with Small alone was incomplete. If so, his presence during the trial may arguably have been prejudicial to the defendant.

Answer Forty-one: Federal Jurisdiction and Procedure

1. Amanda's remedies are (i) motions to the court for orders to compel discovery and (ii) motions for sanctions.
2. Ben may move for an order limiting discovery.

Under the Federal Rules of Civil Procedure, the parties "may obtain discovery regarding any matter, not privileged, which is relevant to the subject matter involved in the pending action," unless limited by court order. Rule 26, Fed.R.Civ.P. This includes claims or defenses of any party. Rule 26(b)(1), Fed.R.Civ.P. The information sought need not itself be admissible at trial if it may reasonably lead to the discovery of admissible evidence. The purpose is to allow a broad search for facts, the names of witnesses, and any other matter that may aid a party. *England v. Aetna Life Ins. Co.*, 139 F.2d 469 (2d Cir. 1943).

Interrogatories. Under Rule 33 of the Federal Rules of Civil Procedure, interrogatories may be directed to parties and may be served upon any party after commencement of the action or service upon the defendant of a summons and complaint. The party receiving interrogatories has 30 days to answer. If he does not answer an interrogatory, the party submitting the interrogatories may move for an order to compel response, under Rule 37(a), Fed.R.Civ.P. Here, Ben failed to respond to Amanda's interrogatories. Therefore, Amanda may move for an order of the court compelling Ben's responses, pursuant to Rule 37(a).

Production of Documents. Under Rule 34, Fed.R.Civ.P., a party may serve any other party with a request for production or inspection of documents within the scope of Rule 26. The request should describe the documents with "reasonable particularity." Responses are due within 30 days. Here, Ben has failed to respond to Amanda's requests for document production. Therefore, Amanda may move for an order of the court compelling Ben's responses. Rule 37(a)(2).

Sanctions. Sanctions under Rule 37 for failure to comply with an order to provide discovery include the following:

a. An order that the matters regarding which the order was made or any other designated facts shall be taken as established;

b. An order refusing to allow the disobedient party to support or oppose designated claims;

c. An order striking out pleadings or parts thereof;

d. An order treating as contempt of court the failure to obey any orders except an order to submit to a physical or mental examination;

e. An order requiring the party or his attorney who refuses to comply to pay expenses, including attorney's fees, caused by the failure (in appropriate circumstances). Rule 37(b)(2). Here, should Ben not comply with a court order compelling discovery, the court might impose one or more of these sanctions.

Rule 37(b)(2). Here, should Ben not comply with a court order compelling discovery, the court might impose one or more of these sanctions.

Protective Orders. Under Rule 26(b)(1), the court may limit discovery by order where it is unreasonably cumulative, duplicative, burdensome, or expensive, considering all the factors in the case. The party seeking a protective order must show good cause, demonstrating that justice requires the order, to protect a person from annoyance, embarrassment, oppression, or undue burden or expense. Rule 26(c), Fed.R.Civ.P. Here, some of Amanda's requests for discovery are described as "very broad, somewhat unclear," and requesting informatrion and documents that "may not be admissible in evidence." These characteristics do not alone qualify for a protective order under Rule 26. Therefore, unless Ben can meet the criteria in Rule 26 for a protective order, the court will compel response to all of Amanda's requests for discovery.

Answer Forty-two: Constitutional Law

If the facts support my client's contentions, he may have a good case alleging fourteenth amendment violations: denial of equal protection and denial of due process.

A. *Threshold Questions*

1. *Case or Controversy; Discrimination; Property.* The Supreme Court has held that certain professional expectations are rights, not privileges, and that as rights they are "property rights" subject to protection under the fourteenth amendment. If the practice of law is a "property right," then it is subject to fourteenth amendment protection.

   Under the equal protection clause of the fourteenth amendment as interpreted by the Supreme Court, a two-tiered analysis is applied. Where state action affects a "fundamental interest" or applies to a "suspect classification," it is subject to "strict scrutiny," and the burden is on the state to justify the discrimination and to show that the regulation is as narrowly drafted as possible. Here, Attorney Smith alleges that his right to practice law has been abridged on the basis of race, which is a "suspect classification." Therefore, any state practice that affects him solely because he is a member of that "suspect classification" is subject to judicial "strict scrutiny."

2. *State Action.* Under the various Supreme Court rulings interpreting the fourteenth amendment, a group need not be an agency of the state to engage in "state action" and so be subject to fourteenth amendment scrutiny. Where a group is subject to regulation and where it is, as here, the only vehicle for admission to an important public function, the courts may find enough "significant state involvement" to characterize its actions as state actions.

3. *Exhaustion of Administrative Remedies.* Under the applicable precedents, it is normally necessary to exhaust administrative remedies before seeking judicial redress. However, where it is futile to seek administrative redress, the exhaustion of administrative remedies is waived. Here, Smith would argue that the Bar's failing to provide the requested information makes further proceedings in that agency futile.

B. *Denial of Due Process*

Assuming that Attorney Smith can persuade the court that the action of the Bar is "state action," the matter presents several questions of violation of the due process clause of the fourteenth amendment.

1. Where there is a "property" interest involved, the state cannot deprive the citizen of property without due process. If the practice of law is a property right, then the state must employ due process in denying that right to a citizen. Attorney Smith may argue that the Bar's refusal to provide him with information has no justification and is a deprivation of due process.

2. Where there is a "property" interest involved, the state cannot act arbitrarily in denying that right, but must have established criteria that can be applied objectively, or in any event, fairly. Here, Attorney Smith can argue that the examination involves procedures that either permit or encourage arbitrary action.

3. The burden is on the state agency that denies a "property right" to show that there is a connection between the standards it uses and the exercise of the right. Here, Attorney Smith can argue that there is no clear connection between the test he took and the practice of law.

C. *Denial of Equal Protection*

Under the equal protection clause of the fourteenth amendment, as interpreted by the Supreme Court, where state action affects a "fundamental interest" or applies to a "suspect classification," it is subject to "strict scrutiny." Provided that the plaintiff can show discriminatory intent, the burden is on the state to justify discrimination and to show that the action or regulation is as narrowly constrained as possible. Here, Attorney Smith will argue that the action of the Bar is "state action," that it affects a "property right," and that it is being applied with discriminatory intent in a discriminatory manner. Race is always a "suspect classification." He will have to show discriminatory intent. Assuming he can do so, he will argue that the burden is on the state to justify its refusal to produce the information he requested.

A different question arises when and if the Bar does produce the information Attorney Smith asked for. He must then show that his examination was different from that given to the others or that it was graded differently from those of the others, in either event with discriminatory intent. He must also show that if he had been graded fairly he could have passed.

D. *Conclusion*

Attorney Smith must show that the practice of law is a "property right," that the Bar is an agency of the state or that there was significant state involvement, and that there has been discrimination against him in violation of the equal protection and due process clauses of the fourteenth amendment. As race is always a "suspect classification," the applicable standard will be "strict scrutiny." The burden will be on the Bar to produce evidence to show that the test was reasonable in itself and that it was not applied to Smith's case in a discriminatory manner.

A Note on Answering This Question

This question takes in large areas of constitutional law. Writing the essay requires keeping a firm and disciplined hand on the pen. It is especially important to remember always to go to the most fundamental questions in the area of law. In a constitutional question, the candidate must always, without exception, treat the threshold issues. Standing is often the threshold issue. Here, the three threshold issues are case or controversy, state action, and exhaustion of administrative remedies.

Answer Forty-three: Criminal Procedure

Memorandum in Support of Motion to Suppress

I. *Fourth Amendment Guarantees*

Under the fourth amendment to the United States Constitution, and the constitution of this state, with only certain narrow exceptions, warrantless searches and seizures are condemned. A citizen's right to be free from unreasonable searches and seizures is protected and guaranteed both by the fourth amendment and by the provisions of the constitution of this state:

The right of the people to be secure in their persons, houses, papers, and effects against unreasonable searches and seizures shall not be violated; and no warrant shall issue but upon probable cause supported by oath or affirmation, and particularly describing the place to be searched and the person or things to be seized.

There are recognized exceptions: a search incident to a lawful arrest, a consent search, an inventory search, an automobile search, a school search, a border search, and an open or plain view search. A warrantless search is also permitted when exigent or emergency conditions do not permit law enforcement personnel to obtain a warrant.

Where material is seized in an unpermitted search or seizure, it cannot be used against the defendant in that case but must be suppressed.

Each step of the encounter with defendant needs to be scrutinized in light of the fourth amendment standard.

A. *The Stop*

Under the fourth amendment, vehicle stops are "seizures" subject to fourth amendment protections. There are three bases for stopping a vehicle: (1) stop incident to a traffic violation, (2) stop pursuant to a reasonable suspicion, and (3) stop pursuant to a uniform stop procedure. *Delaware v. Prouse*, 440 U.S. 648 (1979).

Here, this stop could not be justified as incident to a lawful detention for a traffic violation. There was no evidence of any traffic violation. Rather, Patrolman followed the vehicle only because he had a "gut feeling" there was criminal activity going on.

Under state law, a peace officer may stop any person in a public place when he has a reasonable suspicion to believe that he has committed or is in the act of committing or is attempting to commit a crime, and he may demand the person's name and address and an explanation of his actions. A "gut feeling" does not meet the constitutional standard of "reasonable suspicion" to support a stop. Therefore, since the stop here was not based on a traffic violation, and was not supported by a threshold "reasonable suspicion," and was also not part of any sort of uniform procedure, it occurred in violation of fourth amendment guarantees.

B. *The Encounter Between Patrolman and Defendant*

When a person believes he is not free to leave, a seizure occurs. *Terry v. Ohio*, 392 U.S. 1 (1968). It is proper to ask for license and registration from a stopped motorist, but the right to frisk is restricted. A *Terry*-type frisk is not a search; a frisk is a "pat down" for weapons or instruments that might be a hazard to the officer.

Here, the *Terry*-type "pat-down" is impermissible. The defendant was nervous and shaky. So would anyone be who was stopped by the police. There is no indication that the defendant would threaten the officer in any way.

Therefore, the "pat-down" was in violation of the fourth amendment, and the evidence seized as a result must be suppressed.

C. *The Canister*

Until possession of an object is shown to be a violation of the law, in itself, possession does not form the basis for arrest, or for search and seizure. When Patrolman felt a small hard object in defendant's pocket, he might have been justified in asking defendant to remove it. He was not justified in opening it. Therefore, the opening of the canister was impermissible, and the search was warrantless and unconstitutional. The seized marijuana must accordingly be suppressed.

D. *The Vehicle Search*

1. *The Content Search.* The owner and driver of a vehicle has standing to assert his rights against unlawful searches and seizures. His expectation of privacy in the interior of the vehicle cannot be abrogated by a passenger having no proprietary interest. The passenger lacks standing to consent to a search. Here, Patrolman saw the license and registration. He knew that Driver, not the passenger, was the owner of the vehicle. Driver never consented, and in fact strenuously objected. Patrolman relied exclusively on the passenger's consent to the search. Therefore, no effective consent was obtained. The search was constitutionally impermissible. The seized material must be suppressed.

2. *The Inventory Search.* An inventory search of an automobile is permissible in order to ensure the welfare and safety of law enforcement personnel and in order to protect the police from false claims of theft. Here, the arrest did not occur until after the search. The search could neither have protected the arresting officer nor assured that a person arrested would make no false claims of theft. Therefore, the inventory search in this case was not incident to a lawful arrest. It is not otherwise permitted. Therefore, it is unconstitutional, and the set of scales produced by this search must be suppressed.

II. *The "Good Faith" Exception*

Under the Supreme Court's ruling in *United States v. Leon*, 468 U.S. 897 (1984), the exclusionary rule:

does not bar the use in the prosecution's case-in-chief of evidence obtained by officers acting in reasonable reliance on a search warrant issued by a detached and neutral magistrate but ultimately found to be unsupported by probable cause.

468 U.S. at 900. This "good faith" exception to the exclusionary rule constitutes a major limitation on the privacy protections afforded by the fourth amendment. However, the overwhelming majority of federal and state courts considering related issues have held that *Leon's* good faith exception does not apply to warrantless searches and warrantless arrests. Here, the entire case rests on warrantless searches and seizures. There was no application for a warrant. There was no magistrate. Therefore, the "good faith exception" argument is inapplicable in this case.

III. *Conclusion*

Suppression of evidence is the necessary and appropriate remedy where law enforcement personnel violate state and federal safeguards regarding search and seizure. This rule, requiring suppression of the evidence seized, deters officers from violating citizens' privacy rights. Here, the discovery of the marijuana, the scales, and the cocaine, all resulted from constitutionally impermissible seizures. No exception to the warrant requirement is applicable here. There was no application for a warrant, and there was no warrant. Accordingly, all evidence seized must be suppressed.

Answer Forty-four: Torts

1. The Bartons may seek relief in damages or injunctive relief, alleging nuisance or trespass, or both.

2. The procedural requirements in this state for bringing an action in damages are . . . .* The procedural requirements for obtaining a temporary restraining order are . . . .* The requirements for obtaining a preliminary injunction are. . . . * Permanent injunction . . . .*

3. In the equitable action the court will balance the interests of the parties, and the relative hardships, weighing the fact, among others, that the Bartons moved to the nuisance. In the action for damages, the defendants will challenge the proof of proximate causation, and assert that there is no "nuisance," and no "trespass." Other possible defenses, depending on the facts, and on state law, are privilege, consent, and governmental immunity.

1. Under the law of this state, plaintiffs in an action in trespass or nuisance may seek either relief in damages or injunctive relief. Damages will be available for personal injury, including physical and emotional injury, as well as for diminution in the value of the property. Damages are available up to the date of cessation of the wrongful activity. Injunctive relief may be in the form of a temporary restraining order, a preliminary injunction, or a permanent injunction.

2. [The candidate should state all of the procedural requirements under state law for bringing an action for damages or for injunctive relief: the form of the complaint, filing and service of summons and complaint; how service is effected; whether the rules permit service by mail; proof of service, time periods; whether the complaint must contain the request for a jury trial. The candidate must also

---

* Complete with requirements of your own state.

state the requirements for a temporary restraining order (usually (i) the threat of immediate and irreparable injury and (ii) the basis of the complaint), and the time periods for dissolution or modification; the time periods and requirements for preliminary injunction and for permanent injunction.]

3. *Nuisance.* Under the law of [state], a nuisance is an unreasonable activity or condition on the defendant's land that substantially or unreasonably interferes with the plaintiff's use or enjoyment of his land. A private person may bring a private action in nuisance where he can show that he suffers an injury different from any injury to the public at large. He must show that a nuisance exists and that it in fact causes substantial harm. He may seek injunctive relief, damages, or both. (See para. 1.)

Defenses: Defendants here can assert, first, that their conduct does not constitute a "nuisance," in that it does not unreasonably interfere with the Bartons' enjoyment of their property. The outcome will depend on proof of facts at trial. It will to some extent be a matter of degree and will depend on the entent to which the trier of fact finds that the noise and smoke interfere with the Bartons' reasonable enjoyment of their property.

In the suit for *injunctive relief*, defendants will assert that a balancing of the hardships in equity will not justify imposition of equitable relief. The court can deny equitable relief if it finds that the hardship to the defendants outweighs the hardship to the plaintiffs.

In a suit in nuisance for *injunctive relief*, it is a defense that the plaintiff took possession of his property after the alleged nuisance came into being (he "came to the nuisance"). This is not generally a full defense. Plaintiffs can argue that the nuisance is intermittent, and that they did not know it existed when they moved.

In the action for *damages*, defendants will argue that the plaintiffs cannot prove proximate causation. They will argue that Mr. Barton's health problems were a preexisting condition, not the result of the conduct of the school. In response, plaintiffs will argue that the conduct of the school was the proximate cause of additional problems.

Trespass: Under the law of this state, trespass is an intentional invasion, or causing to be invaded, of the plaintiff's property, whether by a person or by an object.

Defenses: Here, the defendants will claim that there is no "trespass," alleging that the smoke and noise do not cause sufficient physical impact upon the property to constitute a trespass. This is a question for the trier of fact.

As to both nuisance and trespass, defendants may, depending upon state law, argue for a privilege of necessity, consent by the plaintiffs and, because the tuition of some students is paid by the municipality, governmental immunity.

Prospects for Obtaining Relief: The outcome of the case in damages will depend on the facts.

As to injunctive relief, the plaintiffs are unlikely to obtain a temporary restraining order, since they probably cannot demonstrate that they would suffer immediate and irreparable harm without one. They might, however, obtain a preliminary injunction, depending upon how the court weighs the potential harm to the town against the seriousness of the harm to the plaintiffs if the conduct is allowed to continue.

Other Causes of Action: Plaintiffs may also investigate the possibility of claims under federal, state, or local environmental laws or regulations. In addition, depending on the facts, they may be able to assert claims against the seller or broker of the real estate, for fraud or misrepresentation in connection with the sale of the property.

A Note on Answering This Question

This is an extremely difficult question to handle. The law is simple enough; however, there are so many different issues (both legal and procedural), that it is easy to get lost.

The model answer takes each part of the interrogatory separately, and numbers the parts of the answer to correspond to the interrogatories. Remember that when it is hard for you to keep straight what is going on in an answer, it is at least as hard for the grader to do so.

Next, the model answer treats nuisance separately from trespass, although so far as the injunctive relief available is concerned, the same considerations apply to both causes of action. That is exactly the type of overlap that causes so many organizational problems here. Nonetheless, what the model answer does is to treat the legal defenses to nuisance *and* the defenses to injunctive relief under any theory together. Thus, the first paragraph under part 3 of the model answer sets out the definition of nuisance and the remedies available. Then, in a separately labeled section, called "Defenses," the model answer covers the two principal legal defenses to nuisance (that there is no "nuisance," and that the plaintiffs cannot prove proximate causation, because they had preexisting health problems) *and* the defenses to injunctive relief.

Next, the model answer sets out the definition of trespass and the legal defenses to trespass.

Finally, in mop-up paragraphs, the model answer handles prospects for obtaining relief and possible other causes of action.

The trick here is to find one simple way through the question and follow it consistently. Here, the model answer separated nuisance from trespass and considered legal and equitable remedies under each one. The alternative would have been to separate injunctive relief from damages, then handle both nuisance and trespass under each heading. Either way works. The main thing is just to be consistent and clear.

Answer Forty-five: Contracts

1. Parks may sue to enforce the original contract with Dodd.

2. Parks may sue to enforce the second contract with Dodd, should suit on the original contract fail, or should the second contract be found to be a "substituted contract," or a promise modifying a duty under an executory contract.

1. *Dodd's First Promise to Parks.* Under the *Restatement (Second) of Contracts* sec. 110(1)(b) (1981), a contract to pay the debt of another must ordinarily be in writing to be enforceable. As with all other contracts, there must be offer, acceptance, and consideration, as part of a bargained-for exchange. A promise to forbear asserting a claim is consideration. *Cf. id.* sec. 71(3)(a). Here, there was a writing, the original letter from Dodd to Parks, so the writing requirement is satisfied. Parks promised to forbear bringing civil action against Dodd's son, so there is consideration. Dodd requested Parks' promise, and Parks gave it in

exchange for Dodd's promise, so there was a bargained-for exchange. Therefore, there is an enforceable contract between Dodd and Parks, in which Dodd agreed to reimburse Parks for "all medical bills" incurred as a result of the accident.

Whether Parks may sue on the original contract, however, depends upon whether Parks's second agreement with Dodd constituted a "substituted contract" or an "accord," and possibly on whether Dodd can successfully argue that the original contract was modified.

2. *Dodd's Second Promise.* Substituted Contract or Accord: Under the *Restatement (Second) of Contracts* sec. 279 (1981), where there is a substituted contract, the original obligation to pay is discharged. A substituted contract requires consideration. *Id.* sec. 278 comment c; sec. 279 comment b. Ordinarily performance of a duty already owed to the promisor ("pre-existing duty") is not consideration. *Id.* sec. 73.

Here, Dodd's promise to pay on the first of next month constituted a promise to do something Dodd was not already obligated to do. Arguably, accordingly there was valid consideration, and so there may have been a substituted contract. If so, therefore, the original obligation was discharged. Parks could sue Dodd only on the substituted contract, for $800.

Under the *Restatement (Second) of Contracts* sec. 281, in the case of an accord, as contrasted with a substituted contract, the original duty to pay may merely be suspended pending performance of the accord, which is an agreement, depending on the intention of the parties. Normally, there is no discharge until performance. The accord is the agreement. Performance is satisfaction. An unexecuted accord does not discharge the first contract; only performance does.

On this theory, since an unexecuted accord merely suspends the duty owed, Parks could sue Dodd on the original contract (for $1,500) or on the accord (for $800).

Promise Modifying a Duty Under an Executory Contract: Under the *Restatement (Second) of Contracts* sec. 89(a), a promise modifying a duty under a contract that has not fully been performed on either side is binding where the modification is fair and equitable in view of circumstances not anticipated by the parties when the contract was made. There must be an objectively demonstrable reason for seeking modification. Ordinarily, Section 89 modifications involve a frustrating event that may be unanticipated, even though it is foreseeable as a remote possibility.

Here, Dodd could argue that in making the original agreement to pay "all medical bills," she did not foresee a total of $1,500. She could argue that to hold her to paying the full amount would be unfair and inequitable, but to modify her duty so that $800 would satisfy it is "fair and equitable in view of circumstances not anticipated by the parties when the contract was made."

Answer Forty-six: Real Property

A. Uzer is entitled to use the property without interference from Oaner. He is required to grant to Oaner only a 20-foot easement, specified by Uzer, for access to the street.

Oaner will fail in his suit for equitable relief designating a 60-foot-wide easement across Uzer's property.

Under the common law of real property, an easement is an irrevocable grant of a non-possessory right from a landowner to another person, whereby the latter is permitted to use the land of the former in a way spelled out in the grant. An easement may be granted by deed. An easement may also arise out of necessity, as where landlocked land would, without the easement, not have access to a public road. Here, Oaner granted land on the public street to Byer, expressly reserving an easement for a right of way from the landlocked parcel he retained over the land conveyed. Had there not in fact been an easement in the deed, an easement by necessity would have arisen. Oaner's remaining land was landlocked. Oaner needed to cross the land conveyed in order to reach the public way. Therefore, there was an easement by deed but, even without the deed, there would have been an easement by necessity.

While Oaner is entitled to an easement of some size, he is not entitled to one more than 20 feet in width. Under the statute of frauds, any grant of an interest in land must be in writing, signed by the party to be charged, in order to be effective. Failing such an express grant, local ordinances will govern the size of the easement. The owner of the servient tenement may satisfy the easement in any reasonable manner that would not overburden the servient tenement. Here, there is no indication in the deed as to the size of the easement. The local zoning ordinance permits a minimum 20-foot-wide right of way to a landlocked parcel. Oaner has no right to any easement of any particular width. Indeed, even if there were an argument for granting Oaner an easement of more than minimum width, since one must come to equity with clean hands, Oaner, who refused to designate the easement and tried to hold out for a higher price for his land, would not have clean hands and would be unlikely to obtain equitable relief. Therefore, Oaner is entitled only to a 20-foot easement, the minimum permitted under the local zoning ordinance.

Oaner is, however, entitled to that 20-foot easement. His rights have not been extinguished. Under the common law of real property, the owner of a servient tenement can ordinarily extinguish an easement by adverse use for the prescriptive period. However, the owner of a servient tenement cannot extinguish an easement by necessity by conveyance to a bona fide purchaser without notice. The facts making the easement an easement by necessity are also sufficient to give the purchaser notice. Here, Uzer had erected a fence around the perimeter of his property in 1983, and it remains there now. This does not fulfill this state's prescriptive period for extinguishing an easement by adverse use, even were that possible where the easement is an easement by necessity. In addition, there is an easement by necessity. Uzer should have been on notice of the easement. Therefore, the easement was not extinguished by adverse use. In addition, therefore, whether or not Uzer had notice, by whatever means, of the easement, nonetheless, even if he were entirely without notice, that would not extinguish the easement.

Oaner is not entitled to equitable relief. Under the rules of procedure of this jurisdiction, to obtain an injunction a party must demonstrate irreparable harm and the unavailability of relief in damages, and that he will, further, most likely prevail on the merits, and that the balance of the equities favors him. One who makes a claim for equitable relief must show clean hands. "He who seeks equity must do equity."

Here, Oaner does not have relief in damages available to him. However, he cannot demonstrate irreparable harm, nor do the equities favor him. Oaner's conduct in threatening to withhold designation of the easement until Byer would pay more than market value for Oaner's landlocked parcel disqualifies Oaner from obtaining equitable relief, since he does not have "clean hands." The most that can be obtained is that Uzer will have to dismantle 20 feet of his fence on two sides of the property, permitting Oaner to use a 20-foot-wide right of way. Oaner is not entitled to further equitable relief.

B. EASEMENT

Grantor reserves to himself, his heirs, successors and assigns a right of way over the lands conveyed hereby to Grantee, for vehicular and pedestrian traffic between Forest Avenue and the remaining lands of Grantor. The right of way granted shall be permitted in accordance with the highest and best use permitted by any applicable zoning regulations. If such regulations do not exist, Oaner reserves an easement up to fifty feet in width across Grantee's lands. . . .

Answer Forty-seven: Evidence

Although it is relevant, Victor's testimony might be inadmissible, as not presenting circumstances sufficiently similar to those in Peter's case.

Under the Federal Rules of Evidence, all relevant evidence is admissible, except as otherwise provided. Rule 402, Fed.R.Evid. Evidence is relevant if it has any tendency to make the existence of any fact that is of consequence to the determination of the action more probable or less probable than it would be without that evidence. Rule 401, Fed.R.Evid. Relevant evidence may be excluded if, among other grounds, its probative value is substantially outweighed by the danger of unfair prejudice, confusing the issues, or misleading the jury. Rule 403, Fed.R.Evid. Evidence of other injuries from use of a product will be sufficiently probative only if the circumstances are substantially similar to those at issue, how similar depending largely on the purpose for which the evidence is offered. C. McCormick, *McCormick on Evidence* sec. 200 (3d ed. 1984). Evidence of other injuries has been held admissible to show (i) that the defendant knew or should have known of the danger, (ii) that the product is actually defective, (iii) that it was actually the cause of the injury, and (iv) that the defendant's conduct actually created a risk to the plaintiff. When the evidence is offered to show that the defendant was on notice of the danger, the similarity in the circumstances and nature of the injuries can be less than otherwise. It must be such as to call defendant's attention to the defect.

Here, neither the injuries nor the surrounding circumstances of Victor's use of the product are similar to plaintiff's. First, Victor did not suffer the same injuries: his baldness was only partial, and he did not get a scaly rash. Second, the way Victor used Homebrew is different: he used the product for several years, while Peter used it only a few days. Third, the circumstances are different. The pattern of Victor's baldness suggests that it is genetic. Peter's injuries, in contrast, suggest environmental causes. Therefore, Victor's experience would not alert Derrick to any potential danger in Homebrew.

Therefore, if Victor's testimony is offered to show that Derrick was on notice that Homebrew shampoo was a dangerous product, it is not likely to be admitted.

A Note on Answering This Question

This question is largely a test of common sense. It is therefore uncommonly difficult. Students tend to squelch their common-sensical feeling that there is something wrong with Victor's proposed testimony. There *is* something wrong with it. Students, however, tend to want to find a complex rule to apply, ignoring the fact that relevance is the first and most important issue with respect to *any* evidence that any party may offer. Never underestimate the simplicity of the question. Never discuss complex issues until you have handled the basics.

Answer Forty-eight: Constitutional Law

The court would probably hold FEPCA to be a constitutional exercise of the commerce power.

Under the commerce clause of the Constitution, art. I, sec. 8, as interpreted by the Supreme Court in *McCulloch v. Maryland*, 17 U.S. 316 (1819), Congress has not only power to regulate interstate commerce itself, but also power to adopt legislation that is "necessary and proper" for the effective regulation of interstate commerce. Under the affectation doctrine, Congress has power to regulate local activities if it can rationally conclude that such activity has a substantial effect on interstate commerce, regardless of whether the effect is direct or indirect. *Wickard v. Filburn*, 317 U.S. 111 (1942); *Katzenbach v. McClung*, 379 U.S. 294 (1964); *Perez v. United States*, 402 U.S. 146 (1971). In determining whether there is a substantial effect, Congress may consider the aggregate effect of all the regulated activities, even though the contribution of any particular activity is minimal. The court will not probe behind the congressional purpose. If there is a rational basis for the law, there is commerce power.

Under the supremacy clause, art. VI, Congress has the power to preempt state law when the federal statute is in outright conflict with state law. Federal legislation also preempts the field when Congress expresses a clear intent to preempt in enacting the federal statute, where compliance with both federal and state law is impossible, and where Congress has legislated in a field so extensively as to occupy the entire field of regulation, leaving no possibility that state legislation could supplement federal legislation. *Rice v. Santa Fe Elevator Corp.*, 331 U.S. 218, 229–30 (1947); *Hines v. Davidowitz*, 312 U.S. 52, 67 (1941).

Here, Congress could rationally conclude that local activity burning fuels with higher sulphur content has a substantial effect on interstate commerce. Arguably, the cumulative effect of the health hazards of these fuels could affect the movement of persons and goods. Pollution crosses state lines and pollution control at the point of emission makes sense. Therefore, FEPCA is arguably a proper exercise of the commerce power.

As to preemption, here, the federal law preempts the field because it is impossible to comply with federal and state law at the same time. The court would therefore find that FEPCA had preempted state law. The fact that Congress may have sought to achieve social welfare objectives through FEPCA is not relevant. See *Hodel v. Virginia Surface Mining and Reclamation Ass'n.*, 452 U.S. 264 (1981).

Answer Forty-nine: Real Property

Dear Mr. Owens's Attorney:

Mr. Byer has retained me in the matter of his purchase of the land now owned by your client Mr. Owens.

Contrary to Mr. Owens's view, this is not a transaction in which "time is of the essence." Under the real property law of this state, time is "of the essence" only where that is clearly so stated in the original contract between the buyer and seller of real property and executed by both parties. Here, the original contract was dated June 1, 1986, and provided that closing of title would take place "on or before September 1, 1986." There was no mention in the original contract of time being "of the essence." On the contrary, the expression used was "on or about," clearly indicating that time was, in fact, not of the essence. Your client's certified letter dated August 25, 1986, contained the first mention of time being "of the essence." That letter was not part of the contract for the sale of the property. Your client's telegram dated August 26, 1986, while it changes the date suggested for closing, again states that time is "of the essence." That telegram, too, is not part of the original contract between the parties. There is nothing in this matter that is part of the contract except the contract itself. The contract, as noted above, says nothing about time as "of the essence." Therefore, it is not the case that time is of the essence in this matter. Law and custom allow Mr. Byer to take an additional two weeks.

Mr. Byer fully intends to perform. He will be prepared to do so within a reasonable time, as soon as he is able to raise the funds. Under the law of real property of this state, two weeks is not so long as to represent a violation of a contract for the sale of land. Here, Byer asks for two weeks beyond the last demand of Mr. Owens—September 1 or September 2. Such a delay is well within that permitted by the custom and law of this jurisdiction. Therefore, Mr. Byer should be permitted the two additional weeks that he asks.

On Mr. Byer's behalf, I must respectfully draw to your attention certain ways in which the deed Mr. Owens proposes to deliver falls short of the "good and marketable title, free and clear of all liens and encumbrances" for which Mr. Byer has contracted. Insofar as the title is not marketable, Mr. Owens has breached the contract.

Under the real property law of this jurisdiction, an easement affects the marketability of title and makes title not "free of all liens and encumbrances." Here, however, Mr. Owens's recorded deed provides for reservation unto Mr. Owens's grantor of "a right of way from Main Street to the rear of the property for public access to Babbling Brook for fishing and other recreational purposes." Surely public access across the land for the grantor is an encumbrance. Therefore, this easement is an encumbrance such as to make title "not free of all liens and encumbrances." Therefore, Mr. Owens is in breach of the contract for sale of the land.

In addition, my client has undertaken an examination of the land. We note that the physical description in the deed is inaccurate. The deed states "from the edge of Main Street North 30° West 200 feet to Babbling Brook." In fact, however, it is 220 feet from Main Street to Babbling Brook. The deed should so state.

On Mr. Byer's behalf I must accordingly note that while we are still interested in closing, at mid-September, nonetheless, there are already ways in which Mr. Owens has breached the contract. Accordingly, we also must ask for an abatement in the contract price.

Yours very truly,

Can Candidate

Answer Fifty: Contracts

Cotton Basics has breached the implied warranty of merchantability, and Toto's may reject the goods or revoke acceptance, return the goods, and "cover." (If, however, the disclaimer of warranty is found to be part of the contract, Toto's must pay.)

Under the law of this state, a contract requires offer, acceptance, and consideration. Here, Toto's original letter is an offer to buy tee shirts. (The contract is for less than $500 and so need not be in writing. However, this letter would in any event satisfy the statute of frauds, since it is signed by the party to be charged, Toto.) Cotton Basics' confirmation acts as an acceptance, even though it states an additional term, the warranty disclaimer, that was not part of the offer. Therefore, there was an enforceable contract.

Toto's Argument. Under the U.C.C. as adopted in this state, sec. 2-207 (Battle of the Forms), between two merchants, terms additional to or different from those of the original agreement become part of the agreement unless:

1. The offer expressly limits acceptance to the terms of the offer;
2. The new terms "materially alter" the contract;
3. Notice of objection is given within a reasonable time.

Here, neither (1) nor (3) is applicable. Therefore, the disclaimer of warranty will become part of the contract unless it "materially alters" it.

Under U.C.C. secs. 2-314(1) and 2-104(1), in the absence of explicit disclaimer, an implied warranty of merchantability accompanies the sale of goods by a merchant. That is, the buyer can expect the goods to be of a quality comparable to that generally acceptable in the trade. U.C.C. sec. 2-314(2)(c). Here, the standard shrinkage rate for tee shirts like those Toto's ordered is 8–10%, and Toto's could expect the tee shirts to fall within that range. The shirts actually had a shrinkage rate of 15%. Therefore, there was a breach of the implied warranty of merchantability.

Cotton Basics has included a disclaimer of all warranties, including merchantability, on the bottom of its invoice. If this disclaimer is valid, Toto's has no claim against Cotton Basics and will have to pay for the tee shirts. If the disclaimer materially alters the contract, however, it does not become part of the contract. Toto's may argue here that the disclaimer did not become part of the contract.

Under the U.C.C., a term will be considered to materially alter a contract if it results in unfair surprise or hardship. A clause that negates the standard warranty of merchantability may be considered to impose a hardship on the unsuspecting buyer, and not to be one that he or she would customarily expect to find on an invoice. Therefore, it is likely that a court would find that this clause materially alters the contract. It would not, therefore, be part of the parties' agreement. Therefore, there is an implied warranty of merchantability.

Therefore, Cotton Basics would have breached the implied warranty of merchantability by sending goods that did not meet the standard of the trade.

Remedies. Under the U.C.C., secs. 2-607(2) and 2-608(1), a buyer can revoke acceptance of goods and reject the goods if pre-acceptance discovery was difficult and the nonconformity substantially impairs the value of the contract. Here, the defect was shrinkage after washing, which could not be discovered until after the goods were washed. Therefore, Toto's may either reject the goods or, if Toto's is deemed to have already accepted the goods, Toto's may revoke its acceptance. Toto's may then choose from among the U.C.C. buyer's remedies. Toto's may return the goods and seek damages in the amount of the difference between the contract price and the market price at the time Toto's learned of the breach. U.C.C. sec. 2-712.

Cotton Basics' Argument. Under the U.C.C., sec. 2-207, if the term does not materially alter the contract, it will become part of the contract. Under the U.C.C., secs. 2-316(2) and 2-201(10), however, it is clearly provided that to disclaim an implied warranty of merchantability, the writing must be conspicuous and must mention the word "merchantability." Here, Cotton Basics has complied with both requirements, and the disclaimer would be effective, if it is part of the contract at all. Therefore, if the disclaimer is part of the contract, Cotton Basics has not disclaimed any warranties that it has in fact made. Cotton Basics would have the U.C.C. seller's remedies available to it. Toto's would have to pay for the tee shirts.

However, it is more likely that the court will find that the disclaimer of the warranty is not part of the contract.

Answer Fifty-one: Torts

Draft Opinion

Plaintiff brings this action for products liability alleging negligence, strict liability in tort, and breach of implied warranty, and seeking to recover substantial economic damages sustained in consequence of the bursting of a water pipe manufactured and installed by the defendant.

Under the applicable rules of civil procedure, the court properly grants a motion for summary judgment where, on the basis of the pleadings, depositions, answers to interrogatories, and admissions on file, together with the affidavits, if any, the court determines that there remains no triable issue of material fact, and where the question may be decided as a matter of law. *Cf.* Rule 56(c), Fed.R.Civ.P. Here there is no dispute regarding any material facts, and this court will decide the case on motion for summary judgment.

1. *Negligence.* Under [state] law, in order to make out a *prima facie* case in negligence, plaintiff must show (i) duty of care, (ii) breach of duty, (iii) actual cause, (iv) proximate cause, and (v) damages. *See* W. Prosser and W. Keeton, *Prosser and Keeton on the Law of Torts* sec. 30 (1984). Here, there is no evidence of defendant's breach of duty or negligence.

Under the doctrine of *res ipsa loquitur*, directed verdict and summary judgment may not be granted to defendant where plaintiff shows (i) that the injury would not have occurred in the absence of some negligence, (ii) that the defendant was in exclusive control of the injury-producing item, and (iii) that plaintiff is free of contributory negligence.

Here, this court is satisfied that an injury of this sort would not occur in the absence of some negligence. The pipe that caused the injury was in the sole control of the defendant, which manufactured and installed it. Plaintiff is clearly free of contributory negligence. Therefore, the court must deny the motion for summary judgment on Count I. It will be for the jury to determine whether it will make the permissible inference of defendant's negligence that may arise under the doctrine of *res ipsa loquitur.*

2. *Strict Product Liability.* Under [state] law, in order to make out a *prima facie* case for strict liability in tort and avoid summary judgment, plaintiff must show (i) a defective condition in the product rendering it unreasonably dangerous, and which existed at the time the product left defendant's hands; (ii) causation; and (iii) damages. Defectiveness is determined according to ordinary consumer expectations, taking into account the feasibility and cost of remedying the defect. Here, consumers do not expect pipes to burst. Therefore, using this standard, the pipe was defective. In view of the fact that the pipe was manufactured and installed by defendant, plaintiff has satisfied its burden of showing that the defect existed when the pipe left defendant's hands. [The laws of the various jurisdictions differ as to whether purely economic damage may be recovered under a theory of strict liability in tort. Under the *Restatement (Second) of Torts* sec. 402A (1965), recovery is limited to personal injuries suffered by consumers or users of unreasonably dangerous products; there is no recovery for economic injuries. Where purely economic injury cannot be recovered, defendant's motion as to Count II will be granted.]

3. *Breach of Implied Warranties.* Under the Uniform Commercial Code as adopted in this state, a seller impliedly warrants the merchantability of his product: it is suitable for the purposes for which such products are commonly used. In certain instances, in addition, the seller makes another implied warranty: that the product is suited to the particular purpose for which the buyer intends to use it and of which the seller has notice. Here, pipes do not ordinarily break. A pipe that does break is not suitable for its ordinary purpose. Therefore, there was breach of the warranty of merchantability.

As to the implied warranty of fitness for a particular purpose, while the equipment in the building was special, there is no indication that the pipe was specially chosen for that purpose.

With respect to both types of implied warranties, it is privity that causes the problem. There is a modern trend in products liability law under which courts have refused to enforce implied warranties in the absence of privity between the defendant and the plaintiff. The earlier abrogation of the privity requirement is recognized as a historical aberration incident to the development of the doctrine of strict liability in tort, which emerged from the doctrine of negligence and warranty. [Court either follows, or declines to follow, this trend, and decides with respect to Count III, accordingly.]

A Note on Answering This Question

The bar examiners asked for a "draft opinion deciding the motion." They did not ask for an ordinary bar examination essay or for anything else. Notice, accordingly, the numerous indications that this essay answer is in fact a draft judicial opinion. Be very careful to give the examiners what they have asked for.

The interrogatory divides the question into the three separate parts: negligence; strict liability; and breach of implied warranties. All the writer has to do is apply the model paragraph form, slightly modified, and go through each one. This question is so easy to organize that it is much easier to answer than it appears. Incidentally, more than one outcome is acceptable.

Answer Fifty-two: Criminal Law

1. The elements of murder are (i) a voluntary act, (ii) with malice aforethought; (iii) which act actually and proximately caused the death of another human being. "Malignant heart" murder occurs where defendant's conduct manifested extreme indifference to human life.

2. Denise will raise the defense of self-defense.

1. THE ELEMENTS OF MURDER.

Under the common law of crimes, murder is the voluntary killing of another human being with malice aforethought. J. Dressler, *Understanding Criminal Law* sec. 31.02 (1987); W. LaFave and A. Scott, *Criminal Law* sec. 7.1 (2d ed. 1986).

(i) *Voluntary Act.* Under the common law of crimes, although exceptions exist, ordinarily no person is guilty of a crime unless he commits a voluntary act. J. Dressler, *supra* at 65; W. LaFave and A. Scott, *supra* at 195. An act is voluntary if it is the result of a willed contraction of a muscle. J. Dressler, *supra* at 67.

Here, although Denise acted under some emotional pressure, the act of throwing the stone was voluntary, in this sense of the term.

Therefore, Denise's act was "voluntary" for purposes of proving murder.

(ii) *Mens Rea.* Under the common law of crimes, "malice aforethought," the *mens rea* element of murder, exists if one person kills another with any of four mental states:

1. Intent to kill a human being

2. Intent to inflict grievous bodily injury

3. Reckless disregard for the value of human life

4. Intent to commit a felony during which a death results

J. Dressler, *supra* at 449; W. LaFave and A. Scott, *supra* at 605.

Here, the prosecutor might assert any of the first three forms of malice.

Here, regarding the first two forms of malice, we cannot tell from the fact pattern what Denise's intention was. She may have thrown the stone to slow the rapist down, so she could flee. Or she may have intended either to kill him or, at the least, to inflict grievous bodily injury on him. "Grievous bodily injury" is "injury that imperils life" or that "is likely to be attended with dangerous or fatal consequences." *Wellar v. People*, 30 Mich. 16, 19–20 (1874); *People v. Crenshaw*, 298 Ill. 412, 416, 131 N.E. 576, 577 (1921).

Under the common law of crimes, although some courts speak of "transferred intent," the only mental state required is the intent to kill or seriously injure *a human being*. J. Dressler, *supra* sec. 10.06; R. Perkins and R. Boyce, *Criminal Law* 921 (3d ed. 1982). Here, assuming proof of the requisite intent for the sake of argument, it does not affect the analysis that the jogger, not the rapist, is the one who died. Therefore, the prosecutor need not be concerned about "transferred intent."

Under the common law of crimes, "malignant heart" or "depraved heart" murder occurs where the defendant's conduct was reckless, that is, he consciously took a substantial unjustified risk to the safety of another, thereby manifesting extreme indifference to human life. J. Dressler, *supra* sec. 31.06; W. LaFave and A. Scott, *supra* sec. 74. Here, the argument would be that when Denise threw the rock she must have seen the jogger, and that the act of throwing the rock in his direction was extremely reckless. However, even if the jogger was visible, the recklessness claim will fail because Denise will succeed in asserting the defense of self-defense. (See below.)

(iii) *Causation.* Under the common law of crimes, for the defendant to be guilty of any crime, his act must actually and proximately have caused the harm. J. Dressler, *supra* sec. 158; W. LaFave and A. Scott, *supra* sec. 3.12.

Here, causation is clear. But for Denise's act, the jogger would not have died. Nor is there any evidence of any intervening cause (such as bad medical care) that affected the result. Therefore, the prosecution can prove causation.

2. DEFENSE: SELF-DEFENSE.

Under the common law of crimes, a person is justified in using deadly force if (1) the actor is not the aggressor; and (2) he reasonably believes that such force is necessary to combat imminent, unlawful force likely to cause death or great bodily harm. [Jurisdictions differ in the obligation to retreat to any known area of safety before using deadly force.] J. Dressler, *supra* sec. 18.02.

Here, Denise was not the aggressor. She was about to be raped and was being threatened with a deadly weapon. She was threatened by imminent unlawful force likely to cause death or grievous bodily injury. She even attempted to retreat, but she was pursued. Therefore, under the circumstances, Denise acted justifiably. Therefore, she will succeed in the defense of self-defense.

A Note on Answering This Question

This question concerns the most serious crime, murder, and the most important defense, self-defense. It asks you to apply common law principles. Most bar examination questions ask you to apply the law of one state. Before leaving this question, make sure that you know the applicable definitions for the state to whose bar you are seeking admission. The definitions of the most common crimes and the elements of the most important defenses are standard fare on bar examination essays. In addition, you will use the definition of "murder" again in another essay in this book.

Answer Fifty-three: Evidence

1. Jack can prevent Mary from testifying that he admitted robbing the bank, by asserting the privilege for spousal communications.

2. Jack can prevent Mary from testifying to his bad reputation for truthfulness and honesty.

3. Jack cannot prevent Mary's other testimony.

Under Rule 801(d)(2)(a), Fed.R.Evid., an admission by a party opponent is not hearsay. In this criminal prosecution, Jack's statement that he robbed the bank is an admission by a party opponent. Therefore, his statement would not be excluded by the hearsay rule.

However, under the federal common law of evidence, as applied in criminal cases, Rule 501, Fed.R.Evid., confidential marital communications are privileged. Here, Jack's telling Mary while they were married that he robbed the bank is a confidential communication. Therefore, Jack should be able to prevent Mary from testifying that he told her he robbed the bank.

Jack should be able to prevent Mary from testifying as to his bad reputation as to truthfulness and honesty. Under Rule 404(a), Fed.R.Evid., evidence of a person's character or a trait of his character is not admissible for the purpose of proving that he acted in conformity therewith on a particular occasion, unless it falls within one of three exceptions: character of accused; character of victim; character of witness. Here, Mary's testimony does not qualify under the exception for character of the accused, Rule 404(a)(1), because that exception only allows the prosecutor to use such evidence in rebuttal to similar defense evidence. Here, Mary is the first prosecution witness. Accordingly, there cannot have been any prior defense evidence introduced. Nor does Mary's testifying to Jack's bad reputation qualify under the exception for the character of a witness. Rule 404(a)(3), Fed.R.Evid. Jack has not been, and, as a criminal defendant, need never be, a witness in this trial. Therefore, Mary's testimony about Jack's bad reputation is inadmissible.

Note that the privilege for marital communications applies only to Jack's admission to Mary that he robbed the bank. None of Mary's other proposed testimony involves confidential communications.

Answer Fifty-four: *Constitutional Law*

1. Washington can argue (a) his supporters' first amendment right to express support; (b) his first amendment right to speak to the crowd; (c) that the regulation is unreasonable; and (d) that it is overbroad on its face.

2. The outcome will depend on the facts. The Washington supporters will prevail if the gathering will not impede movement for an unreasonable time.

Under the first amendment to the United States Constitution, the Washington supporters have the clear right to express their support for their candidate by gathering for his homecoming. The first amendment also protects Mr. Washington's right to speak to the crowd. Indeed, political expression lies at the core of first amendment values. *Buckley v. Valeo*, 424 U.S. 1 (1976); *Williams v. Rhodes*, 393 U.S. 23 (1968). The first amendment has been applied to the states through the due process clause of the fourteenth amendment. *Gitlow v. New York*, 268 U.S. 652 (1925).

Here, although these activities are clearly protected by the first amendment, the State does have the power to preserve the property under its control for the use to which it was lawfully dedicated. *Greer v. Spock*, 424 U.S. 828, 836 (1976);

Adderley v. Florida, 385 U.S. 39, 47 (1966). The extent to which the government may limit public access to its property depends on whether the property is a public forum. *Cornelius v. NAACP Legal Defense and Educ. Fund, Inc.*, 473 U.S. 788 (1985); *Perry Educ. Ass'n. v. Perry Local Educators' Ass'n.* 460 U.S. 37, 44 (1983). Some public properties, such as sidewalks, streets, and parks, are clearly public forums. *Haque v. CIO*, 307 U.S. 496 (1939). With respect to other properties, such as military bases, jails, and libraries, the government has a stronger interest in preserving the normal function of the public facilities. *See Greer* and *Adderley, supra.*

Large regional airports, such as the Mt. Vernon International Airport in this case, are generally considered to be public forums. An airport terminal is much like a city street. Both are lined by shops, restaurants, newsstands, and other businesses. Travelers and other members of the public may go as they please without paying any fee. Thus, the nature and purpose of an airport make it an appropriate place for the communication of ideas. Courts that have considered the question have determined that airports are public forums. *E.g., U.S. Southwest Afr./Namibia Trade Cultural Council v. United States*, 708 F.2d 760, 764–66 (D.C. Cir. 1983); *Fernandez v. Limmer*, 663 F.2d 619, 626–27 (5th Cir. 1981); *Kuszynski v. Oakland*, 479 F.2d 1130 (9th Cir. 1973).

In a public forum, the State may not ban activity protected by the first amendment. The State may, however, impose reasonable time, place, and manner restrictions on such activity. *Airport Comm'rs v. Jews for Jesus*, 482 U.S. 569 (1987). A time, place, and manner restriction on speech in a public forum is reasonable only if (1) it is content-neutral, (2) it is narrowly tailored to meet significant government interests, and (3) it leaves open ample alternative channels of communication. *Perry Educ. Ass'n.* at 45.

Here, the Airport regulation is probably not a reasonable time, place, and manner restriction even though the Airport regulation is, on its face, content-neutral. Moreover, the State has a significant interest in the smooth operation of its airport, and there are certainly ample alternative channels of communication for the Washington supporters and for Mr. Washington. However, the regulation is not narrowly tailored. It prohibits all gatherings of more than 200 people regardless of the impact on the smooth operation of the Airport that such gatherings may or may not have. Moreover, the prohibition applies to the entire Airport, without respect to whether or not any congestion problem may or may not be present in a given area or at a given time.

As a restriction of first amendment rights, the regulation is subject to "facial" attack as well as attack as applied. Under the first amendment overbreadth doctrine, an individual whose own speech or conduct may be prohibited is permitted to challenge a statute on its face "because it also threatens others not before the court—those who desire to engage in legally protected expression but who may refrain from doing so rather than risk prosecution or undertake to have the law declared partially invalid." *Brockett v. Spokane Arcades, Inc.*, 472 U.S. 491, 503 (1985). A statute may be invalidated on its face, however, only if the overbreadth is "substantial." "There must be a realistic danger that the statute itself will significantly compromise recognized first amendment protection of parties not before the Court for it to be facially challenged on overbreadth grounds." *Members of City Council v. Taxpayers for Vincent*, 466 U.S. 789, 801 (1984). Large airplanes hold more than 200 people, there is no time or gate distinction, and there is no showing that more than 200 people could not, at some times and places in the Airport, be accommodated. Thus, Washington supporters can argue the statute significantly compromises a gathering for 201 people. Arguments on the other side are that this crowd is expected to be many more than

200 (i.e., 500) and could be larger. The gathering could be expected to impede pedestrian traffic at the gate for over 15 minutes, and perhaps much longer.

The outcome of the case will depend on the facts. The Washington supporters will prevail if the court finds that the gathering will not impede movement for an unreasonable time.

Answer Fifty-five: Contracts—U.C.C.

Owens cannot cancel the contract with Timbertrack. Depending on the facts, he may have a right to write to Timbertrack demanding assurances of performance.

Anticipatory Repudiation. Under the U.C.C., a party may treat a contract as having been breached upon learning that the other party does not intend to perform its obligations under the contract. U.C.C. sec. 2-609.

Here, Owens has heard from a competitor that Timbertrack is in financial difficulty and has failed to make timely deliveries of the bicycle that is the subject of the Timbertrack/Cycle City contract. However, Timbertrack has fully performed its contract with Cycle City and has not given Cycle City any reason to anticipate that it will not make the September 1 shipment.

Demand for Assurances. Under U.C.C. sec. 2-609, upon receiving "reasonable grounds for insecurity," one party may demand adequate assurances of performance from the other. Here, rather than treat the contract as breached, Cycle City should send a letter to Timbertrack demanding adequate assurances of performance. If no response is given within 30 days, or if an inadequate response is given, the demanding party may then treat the contract as repudiated and resort to its remedies under the Code. At that point, Cycle City would be excused from further performance under the contract (and would be able to purchase the bikes from Fast Freddie's).

In addition, during the 30-day period, Cycle City could suspend its own performance under the contract. Whether Cycle City has a right to demand adequate assurances of performance is a question of fact and depends on the commercial reasonableness of the action. The adequacy of Timbertrack's response also depends on the facts and circumstances. Here, Cycle City has learned from an apparently reputable source that Timbertrack has been unable to fulfill its contract with another buyer. In light of the fact that Timbertrack is a new business, it may be reasonable for Cycle City to demand adequate assurances.

Should Cycle City nonetheless advise Timbertrack that it considers the contract breached, Cycle City would itself probably be held liable for damages for breach of contract. Assuming that Timbertrack could not mitigate its damages by selling the bikes elsewhere, damages would be the difference between the contract price and the market price at the time and place for delivery.

It should be noted, moreover, that the U.C.C. implies an obligation of good faith in every contract. Cycle City will not be permitted to use its knowledge of Timbertrack's difficulties simply as an excuse to repudiate its contract with Timbertrack solely in order to avoid the contract.

Answer Fifty-six: Real Property

Memorandum

To: Judge Examiner

From: Bar Candidate

Re: *Watchful v. Homeowner and Borough of Meadow View*

Under the rules of civil procedure of this state, this court may grant summary judgment where, taking all of the affidavits and other materials in the case together, it appears that there is no material issue of fact to be tried, and judgment may issue as a matter of law. Here, the court may find that the applicable standard on which to judge the original actions of the Borough of Meadow View building inspector in granting Homeowners a permit is abuse of discretion and that there was no abuse of discretion in approving a permit for the Homeowners' addition to their house. The court may further find that although plaintiff in this suit has standing to seek enforcement of the Meadow View zoning ordinance, the facts do not present a proper case for exercise of that judicial power. Therefore, the court may grant summary judgment for the defendants.

The Homeowners' addition is arguably permissible under the ordinance. Under the United States Constitution, as interpreted by the Supreme Court, the police power permits state governments to enact enabling legislation under which municipalities may enact ordinances establishing zoning. *Euclid v. Ambler Realty Co.*, 272 U.S. 365 (1926). An ordinance restricting land use to "family" dwellings is valid land use legislation addressed to family needs. *Village of Belle Terre v. Boraas*, 416 U.S. 1 (1974). Under the zoning ordinance of the Borough of Meadow View, multi-family residences are prohibited in all zones. A multi-family dwelling is defined as "a building designed for or occupied by more than one family." A one-family dwelling is defined as "a separate building designed for or occupied exclusively by one family." The term "family" is defined as "one or more persons living and cooking together as a single housekeeping unit, exclusive of household servants." This is the same definition as in *Belle Terre*.

Here, the Homeowners and Mrs. Homeowner's mother are a family. The small kitchen in the addition for Mrs. Homeowner's mother does not mean that separate cooking is planned. If there were no kitchen, however, there would be no issue at all.

Therefore, to make conformity to the ordinance clear, there are two solutions. First, that the addition be changed so that there are no cooking facilities. Second, the Homeowners may ask the court for a declaratory judgment that the permit the building inspector issued is valid.

Where a building inspector is charged with interpretation of the zoning ordinance, the proper standard of review for his action is governed by statute and is often abuse of discretion. Here, the building inspector found that the proposed addition was within the meaning of single-family dwelling given the structure proposed and the uses intended. There is no evidence that the inspector abused his discretion.

Therefore, the court may rule that as there is no evidence of the building inspector's having abused his discretion, the permit is valid, the ordinance is valid, and Watchful's suit is without merit, and summary judgment should issue for the defendants.

Watchful has standing to seek enforcement of the zoning ordinance. The proper action to compel a zoning authority to enforce a zoning ordinance is established by statute. It is often mandamus or a similar suit.

Under the [state] rules of civil procedure and the law of [state], a citizen aggrieved by the failure of a zoning authority to enforce zoning regulations may bring suit. Here, assuming that Watchful is such a citizen, his suit is permissible.

The amendment of the zoning ordinance while the case was before this court, so that it now permits so-called mother-daughter dwellings, is relevant only if it "grandfathers in" previous structures so that those structures are not in violation of the law. Here, if the new Meadow View ordinance does "grandfather in" the Homeowners' addition to their house, then it renders this case moot. If it does not, it is irrelevant.

Homeowners can rely on the permit issued to them by the building inspector. Under the statutory rules of review in most jurisdictions, where a permit is issued, it may be overturned only on a showing of abuse of discretion. Here, the record does not contain facts indicating an abuse of discretion. Therefore, the permit cannot be voided.

While some courts have redefined "family" in the context of zoning laws, the present case does not present an appropriate case for considering that issue. Under the equal protection clause of the fourteenth amendment, as interpreted by the Supreme Court, zoning ordinances may define "family" in such a way as to exclude "non-traditional" families.* Here, the zoning ordinance defines "family" in a functional, not relational, way, allowing those who live and cook together to be counted as one family. Therefore, the definition of "family" in the Meadow View ordinance is not vulnerable to constitutional challenge on equal protection grounds.

Answer Fifty-seven: Torts

To: JUDGE

From: LAW CLERK

Re: *Jason v. Mothers* and *Bart v. Mothers*

In these cases, the court should find both of the mothers negligent. In all likelihood, under the law of this state, each mother may claim family immunity as to the suit by her own child, however.

I. *Bart's Mother*

    A. *Negligence.* Under the law of the State of _____, the elements of negligence are (i) duty of care, (ii) breach of duty, (iii) actual cause, (iv) proximate cause, and (v) damages. *See* W. Prosser and W. Keeton, *Prosser and Keeton on the Law of Torts* sec. 30 (1984). Here, there are several different theories on which Bart's mother is liable. As a parent, and as the hostess for the party, Bart's mother had a duty of care to the small children in the house. At the least, she had the duty of a reasonable person entrusted with small children. She breached that duty, however. A reasonable per-

---

* *Village of Belle Terre v. Boraas*, 416 U.S. 1 (1974).

son would not let a five-year-old play with a toy she had not inspected carefully. A reasonable person would not let five-year-olds play unattended with a toy with warning labels. A reasonable person would not rely on another person to make the decision as to whether a toy was safe for small children to play with. A reasonable person would not leave potentially dangerous materials where an 18-month-old could interfere with them. Bart's mother's negligence was the actual cause of the injuries. "But for" her negligence they would not have occurred. In addition, it was the legal cause. All plaintiffs were foreseeable. There is no question about the injuries suffered. Therefore, Bart and Jason can establish a *prima facie* case in negligence against Bart's mother.

Defenses. Bart's mother may defend on the grounds that the acts of the 18-month-old were an intervening or superseding cause, that Bart and Jason were contributorily negligent or had assumed the risk, or that her own acts were not negligent at all. However, as it was also her duty to supervise the 18-month-old, no defense can succeed that rests on his acts. Bart and Jason were only 5 years old, too young to assume the risk and, regardless of the law in this jurisdiction on comparative and contributory negligence, too young for contributory negligence. Nor is there any defense based on her reasonableness: she did not act reasonably. Therefore, these defenses will fail.

Under the law of most states, the common law doctrine of intrafamilial immunity has been reduced or eliminated. [State the law of the jurisdiction, and apply it.] In any event, immunity will be a defense only for Bart's suit against his mother. Bart's mother has, as demonstrated above, no adequate defense against the action in negligence brought by Jason.

B. *Other Causes of Action*

Under the law of this state, battery requires proof of a harmful or offensive intentional touching, or apprehension thereof. Strict product liability requires that the defendant be in the business of providing products of the sort involved. Bart's mother did not intend to hurt Jason and Bart. She is not in the business of selling toys. Neither theory is appropriate here.

II. *Jason's Mother*

A. *Negligence.* The elements of negligence are set out above. Again, a *prima facie* case can be proved against Jason's mother by both Bart and Jason. Jason's mother had the duty of a reasonable person, and a reasonable parent, entrusted with responsibility for a small child. Jason's mother breached that duty. A reasonable person would not rely on the warning label on a potentially dangerous toy. Jason's mother's breach of her duty of care was the actual cause of the boys' injuries: "but for" her buying the toy and giving it to the children, the injuries would not have occurred. Her breach of duty was the legal cause of the injuries: both boys were foreseeably within the zone of danger. Finally, there was harm, namely, the injuries to Bart and Jason. Therefore, Bart and Jason can establish a *prima facie* case in negligence against Jason's mother.

Defenses. Jason's mother may argue that her actions were not the actual cause of the boys' injuries, but that Bart's mother's and brother's actions were the actual cause. To cut off the original liability, however, the superseding cause must be an act of a special kind—intentional, criminal, grossly negligent, or an act of God. Bart's mother's actions are probably not grossly negligent, and are certainly not intentional or criminal. As for the 18-month-old, since he was under four, he cannot be held to have committed even a negligent act. In any event, the fact that others may have been negligent does not cut off Jason's mother's liability.

Under the laws of the State of _____, as pointed out above, there is an issue of intrafamilial immunity. [Draw conclusion based on applicable state law.] In any event, again, immunity will be a defense for Jason's mother only as to Jason's suit against her. Jason's mother has, as demonstrated above, no adequate defense against the action in negligence brought by Bart.

B. *Other Causes of Action*

For the reasons stated above, in discussing the causes of action against Bart's mother, there is no action in battery against Jason's mother, because she did not apparently intend to hurt Jason and Bart. There is no action in strict product liability because Jason's mother is not in the business of selling toys. Neither theory is appropriate here.

C. *Contribution in a Case of Joint and Several Liability, and Satisfaction of Claims.* [Briefly set out applicable state rules, in one or two sentences.]

A Note on Answering This Question

This is a typical, and ideal, torts question. The writer simply sets out the elements of a *prima facie* case, plugs the facts into the elements, and draws a conclusion. This is the clearest sort of application of the model paragraph. The skill that is required here is the skill of reading the facts carefully enough to discuss intelligently whether or not they fit the elements of the tort.

Note that there is a great deal more that can be said here, for example, about whether the children were themselves negligent. Depending on the law of the jurisdiction, there is much to be said about the application of rules of contributory or comparative negligence. The answer provided here is a good, clear answer, and certainly a passing answer.

The interrogatory asks for a memorandum from a law clerk to the judge preparing an opinion in the case. Give the examiners what they ask for.

Answer Fifty-eight: Criminal Law

1. The possible charges are murder, conspiracy to commit murder, solicitation, and accessory before the fact, to murder.

2. Sally can assert the defenses of self-defense and withdrawal. Frankie can assert defense of a third party, using the standard for self-defense.

1. *The Possible Charges.* Murder: Frankie can be prosecuted for murder. Under the common law of crimes, murder is the unlawful killing of another with malice aforethought. W. LaFave and A. Scott, *Substantive Criminal Law* sec. 7.1 (2d ed. 1986).

Conspiracy to Commit Murder: Both Frankie and Sally can be prosecuted for conspiracy to commit murder. Under the common law of crimes, conspiracy requires proof that there is a confederation of two or more people who have formed an agreement for a common unlawful purpose. In many jurisdictions there must also be an overt act committed by one or more of the conspirators to further the agreement. *Model Penal Code* sec. 5.03; *People v. Albers*, 196 Colo. 66, 582 P.2d 667 (1978); R. Perkins, *Criminal Law* 661 (2d ed. 1969). Here, Frankie and Sally agreed to commit the murder of Joe, and Frankie went to Joe's karate club to kill him. Therefore, both Frankie and Sally can be prosecuted for conspiracy.

Solicitation: Sally can be prosecuted for solicitation. Under the common law of crimes, solicitation occurs when one urges, advises, requests, counsels, tempts, commands, or otherwise entices another to commit a crime. Perkins, *supra* at 583. Here, Sally induced Frankie to commit the crime of killing Joe. Therefore, Sally can be prosecuted for solicitation.

Complicity/Accessory Before the Fact: Sally also can be prosecuted for complicity, or as an accessory before the fact, to murder. Under the common law, an accessory before the fact is one who is guilty of a felony by reason of having aided, counseled, commanded, or encouraged the commission thereof, without having been present either actually or constructively at the moment of perpetration. Perkins, *supra* at 663. Here, Sally counseled and encouraged Frankie to murder Joe, but she was not present when he did so. Therefore, Sally can be prosecuted as an accessory before the fact, to murder.

2. *Defense*. Self-Defense: Sally can assert the defense of self-defense. However, she will have to establish that she was not the aggressor, and that she reasonably believed that such force was necessary to combat imminent deadly force by Joe. *United States v. Noland*, 700 F.2d 479 (9th Cir. 1983); *United States v. Peterson*, 483 F.2d 1222 (D.C. Cir. 1973). Frankie could use the same standard to assert the same defense, as a third party. Their success is doubtful.

Withdrawal: Sally can assert the defense of withdrawal. Under the common law, withdrawal from a crime is an affirmative act communicating the fact of withdrawal to confederates, made in time to abandon the crime in a way sufficient to inform a reasonable person of the withdrawal. *Loser v. Superior Court*, 78 Cal.App.2d 30, 177 P.2d 320 (1947); *Wrecks v. Whitehouse*, 1 D.R.L. 683 (1940).

A Note on Answering This Question

The criminal law areas most frequently tested include solicitation, attempt, conspiracy, and accomplice liability.

This question calls for straightforward application of the method you have just learned. First, in the outline, list every criminal charge that might apply and every defense that might apply. In the essay, write one paragraph for each charge and one paragraph for each defense. The statement of the definition of the criminal offense, for example, is the *Rule*. The application of the elements to this fact pattern is the *Application*. The statement of whether or not this fact pattern fits the definition of the crime is the *Conclusion*.

Answer Fifty-nine: Contracts

1. If Bob seeks an injunction, Dan can assert (a) the statute of frauds; (b) the unreasonableness of the covenant not to compete as to duration and geographic scope; and (c) mistake.

2. Dan is likely to succeed in avoiding the injunction.

3. Dan has no claim against Bob beyond a claim for services rendered until his termination.

4. Dan is entitled to be paid for his work at the rate of $25,000 per year.

1. *Injunction.* Statute of Frauds: Under the statute of frauds, a contract that cannot be performed within one year must be in writing, signed by the party to be charged, and be otherwise enforceable. Here, the 15-year covenant not to compete could not be performed within one year, and was oral. Therefore, the covenant not to compete is unenforceable.

Unreasonableness: Under the laws of the states in which noncompetitive employment covenants are enforceable, courts will scrutinize the terms of such covenants to assure that they do not unreasonably interfere with the right to exercise a trade or engage in commercial activity. In particular, courts will scrutinize the reasonableness of the restrictions as to duration and geographic scope. Here, Dan can argue that the 15-year restriction is unreasonable. Dan never had time to develop his own clientele. His threat of competitiveness to Bob or the Club was therefore nonexistent. Even if the restriction as to distance is supportable, a court sitting in equity will look to general equitable principles of fundamental fairness. Therefore, it is unlikely that a court will enforce the covenant not to compete.

Mistake: Under the law of this state, mistake can sometimes be used to set aside a contract in unusual circumstances that would make enforcement of the contract manifestly unjust. Here, Dan may argue that he should be relieved from the covenant because he thought that the only two golf courses within 75 miles of Rolling Hills were both about 30 miles away. He did not know at the time of entering into the agreement that Eagle's Nest Country Club was in fact only 24 miles from Rolling Hills, and so within the 25-mile limit set in the covenant not to compete. Unilateral mistake, however, will generally not provide a basis for relief from a contract. Dan is unlikely to prevail on this argument.

2. *Standards for Granting Injunction.* The court will grant injunctive relief where the moving party demonstrates that irreparable loss will otherwise occur, there is no adequate remedy at law, and there is a demonstrated likelihood that the moving party will prevail on the merits. Here, Bob is unlikely to be able to demonstrate that he is entitled to an injunction. His suit will in any event fail, as the covenant not to compete is unenforceable as not satisfying the statute of frauds.

3. *Dan's Claims Against Bob.* Dan will not succeed in any claim against Bob beyond a claim for services rendered until his termination.

Bob might assert claims against Dan based on (i) his seeking $30,000 per year, not $25,000 per year; (ii) Dan's breaching the contract by terminating it after only three weeks; (iii) the statute of frauds; (iv) fraudulent inducement. In fact, however, (i) Dan accepted $25,000 per year by his conduct when he moved to Ames and started work; (ii) Bob did not breach the contract by terminating Dan's employment, since Dan's employment was only for as long as Bob was head pro at Rolling Hills; (iii) there is no violation of the statute of frauds, since the contract not only could be completed within one year, but in fact was; (iv) there is no factual basis for claiming fraudulent inducement, as no facts indicate that Bob was aware of the job possibility at Lakeview before employing Dan.

Note: Should the court take the view that the entire agreement is unenforceable because the covenant not to compete fails to satisfy the statute of frauds, Dan will recover the reasonable value of the services he performed, under *quantum meruit*.

Answer Sixty: Evidence

1. The neighbor's testimony that Vicki yelled "My God, darlin', you're killing me," is admissible.

2. Vicki's statement to the paramedics is hearsay not falling within any exception, and is inadmissible.

3. Vicki's statement to the physician may be admissible for the truth of what it asserts, to the extent made for medical diagnosis.

4. Vicki's signed statement to the police is inadmissible.

5. Vicki's last three statements are admissible for purposes of impeachment.

1. Under the Federal Rules of Evidence, hearsay is a statement other than one made by the declarant while testifying at the trial or hearing, offered in evidence to prove the truth of the matter asserted. Fed.R.Evid. 801(c). Hearsay is not admissible except as provided by rule. Fed.R.Evid. 802. One such exception is for excited utterances. Fed.R.Evid. 803(2). Here, Vicki yelled, "My God, darlin', you're killing me." It is an excited utterance. Therefore, the neighbor's testimony that Vicki yelled "My God, darlin', you're killing me," is hearsay, but nonetheless admissible.

2. Vicki's statement to the paramedics is hearsay not admissible within any exception. Under Rule 804(b)(2), where the witness is unavailable in a prosecution for homicide or in a civil action or proceeding, a statement made by a declarant while believing that his death was imminent, concerning the cause or circumstances of what he believed to be his impending death, is admissible as an exception to the hearsay rule. Here, the witness is not unavailable. This is not a prosecution for homicide. Therefore, the statement is hearsay and is inadmissible.

3. Vicki's statement to the physician may be admissible. Under Rule 803(4), Fed.R.Evid., a statement made to a physician for purposes of medical diagnosis or treatment may be admissible even though it is hearsay, to the extent that it was made for the purpose of medical diagnosis or treatment and described medical history, past or present symptoms, pains or sensations, or the inception or general character of the cause or external source, so far as pertinent to diagnosis or treatment. Courts, however, have limited the exception, holding it not to include a statement of cause or an accusation regarding the perpetrator, where the aim is to assign fault, not to aid in medical diagnosis. *See, United States v. Narcisco*, 466 F.Supp. 252 (E.D.Mich. 1977); *W.C.L. v. People*, 685 P.2d 176 (Colo. 1984). Therefore, Vicki's statement to the physician, to the extent that it was made for diagnosis and treatment, may be admissible. Her statement that it was David who stabbed her is inadmissible.

4. Vicki's signed statement to the police is inadmissible. Under the Federal Rules of Evidence, hearsay is not admissible except as it falls under a recognized exception. Rule 802, Fed.R.Evid. Here, Vicki's statement does not fall within any exception. The facts suggest that it might be considered "former testimony," admissible under Rule 804(b)(1). However, first, the former testimony exception applies only where the witness is unavailable, while Vicki is available. And in any event, a notarized statement is not former testimony within the definition in the rule. Therefore, the notarized statement is inadmissible.

5. Vicki's last three statements will be available for impeachment purposes should she continue to deny the neighbor's testimony that she yelled "You're killing me," to David. Under Rule 613, Fed.R.Evid., prior inconsistent statements may be offered solely for the purpose of impeaching a witness. The credibility of any witness may be attacked by any party, including the party calling him. Fed.R.Evid. 607. Where a witness denies making a prior inconsistent statement, extrinsic evidence proving the utterance of the prior statement is admissible, not for the truth of what it asserts, but solely for the purpose of impeachment. Therefore, even where themselves inadmissible, the last three statements may be admissible for purposes of impeaching Vicki.

Answer Sixty-one: Real Property

1. Slick has an enforceable contract. He is equitable owner of the property. Dion has a voidable deed.

2. Slick would assert his rights under his prior contract for purchase of the land. He would claim that Dion was on notice of his prior interest, and so is not a bona fide purchaser.

3. Dion might argue the equitable defenses: unclean hands, laches, estoppel. However, these defenses would be unsuccessful.

4. Slick can have the deed to Dion set aside. He can sue for damages and for specific performance. If Slick prevails, Dion has an action against Seller for damages.

1. *Slick Has an Enforceable Contract.* Slick and Seller had a valid and enforceable contract. Under the common law of contracts, a contract requires offer, acceptance, and consideration. Under the statute of frauds, a contract for the sale of land must be in writing, be signed by the parties, and specify the land. Here, there was offer and acceptance: Slick offered to buy, and Seller agreed to sell. There was consideration: Slick promised to pay and Seller promised to deliver good title and the deed. The fact that Slick paid a deposit of only $50 does not affect the enforceability of the contract. Therefore, Slick has a valid and enforceable contract.

2. *Slick Acquired Equitable Title; Dion Is Not a Bona Fide Purchaser.* Slick acquired equitable title to the property when he entered into the contract with Seller. Dion is in any event on notice of another person's interest and so is not a bona fide purchaser. Under the common law of real property, the buyer acquires equitable title to the property upon signing the contract of sale. The seller retains legal title until the closing. Equitable title must be respected by everyone who has notice of it. To qualify as a *bona fide* purchaser for value, however, a buyer must take without notice of anyone else's interest, in good faith, and for value. Here, Slick acquired equitable title to the property when Seller endorsed their acceptance on the offer of purchase on January 10 and had it delivered to Slick's attorney. In addition, Mr. Dion had notice of Slick's interest. First, Mrs. Dion noticed the surveyor working, which might be notice by itself, and learned from him of someone else's interest in the property. Second, Slick's attorney told Mr. Dion that he had been hired to abstract the title. Given this notice of another interest in the land, Mr. Dion was at least obliged to make further inquiries before proceeding to closing. Therefore, Slick had equitable title, and Mr. Dion was in any event not a *bona fide* purchaser for value.

3. *Dion Has No Equitable Defenses Available.* Dion cannot successfully assert the equitable defenses of unclean hands, laches, or estoppel. Under the principles of equity, first, unclean hands is available only to someone who himself has clean hands: he who seeks equity must do equity. Second, laches is based not simply on delay, but on unreasonable delay. Third, in order to assert estoppel, a party must show that he was misled, and relied on the misrepresentations to his detriment. Here, first, Dion does not have clean hands himself, and so cannot assert clean hands against Slick: Dion purchased the property knowing that Slick had a prior interest. In any event, Slick in fact does have clean hands, since he learned of the marble deposits by lawful means. Second, while it is true that Slick might have tried to prevent the sale to Dion, nonetheless, the sale came less than two weeks after Dion's meeting with Slick's lawyer. Two weeks does not seem like an unreasonable time to wait for further developments. Third, to assert estoppel, Dion would have to show that Slick misled him, and that he relied on the misrepresentations to his detriment. In view of Slick's lawyer's having told Mrs. Dion she should see her own lawyer, however, Dion had clear notice that there was a problem. He was in no way mislead. Therefore, Dion has no equitable defenses, whether of unclean hands, laches, or estoppel.

4. *The Remedies are Specific Performance, Damages, and Declaring the Deed Void.* Slick may bring suit to have the deed to Dion declared void. He may sue Seller for specific performance, and for damages. If Slick prevails, Dion may sue Seller for damages.

Answer Sixty-two: Constitutional Law

The Northwest statute is unenforceable. First, it has been preempted because there is a conflict between the federal and state statutes. Second, it violates the commerce clause.

1. *Preemption.* Under the supremacy clause of the Constitution, art. VI, cl. 2., federal law is the supreme law of the land. *E.g., Gibbons v. Ogden*, 22 U.S. (9 Wheat.) 1 (1824). The federal law preempts state law. Where Congress has intended to "occupy a given field, [then] any state law falling within that field is preempted." If Congress has not entirely displaced state regulation over the matter in question, state law is still preempted to the extent it actively conflicts with the federal law; that is, when it is impossible to comply with both state and federal law, or the state law stands as an obstacle to the accomplishment of the full purposes and objectives of Congress. *California Coastal Comm'n. v. Granite Rock Co.*, 480 U.S. 572, 107 S.Ct. 1419, 1425 (1987). *See generally Rice v. Santa Fe Elevator Corp.*, 331 U.S. 218 (1947); *Florida Lime & Avocado Growers, Inc. v. Paul*, 373 U.S. 132 (1963); *Hines v. Davidowitz*, 312 U.S. 52 (1941); *Warren Trading Post Co. v. Arizona State Tax Comm.*, 380 U.S. 685 (1965).

The facts presented indicate that the Northwest statute is unenforceable, having been preempted both as a matter of congressional intent and because of actual conflict between the federal and state statutes.

First, under the statute, Congress expressly declared that any inconsistent state law is unenforceable. Here, the 100-mile restriction imposed by Northwest is apparently inconsistent with the federal statute, even though the state legislature says it is "intended to complement and be consistent with" the federal law.

The state statute effectively precludes any transportation of nuclear waste through Northwest. Thus the state statute is expressly preempted. *See, e.g., Jersey Cent. Power & Light Co. v. Township of Lacey*, 772 F.2d 1103 (3d Cir. 1985), holding unconstitutional a town ordinance prohibiting importation or storage of spent nuclear fuel. *See also, Hartigan v. General Elec. Co.*, 461 U.S. 913 (1983); *Washington State Bldg. & Construction Trades Council v. Spellman*, 684 F.2d 627 (9th Cir. 1982), *cert. denied*, 461 U.S. 913 (1983). *See generally Annot.* 82 A.L.R. 3d 751 (1978). The statute probably is preempted by The Atomic Energy Act, 42 U.S.C. sec. 1801 *et seq.* and the Hazardous Materials Transportation Act, 49 U.S.C. sec. 1801 *et seq.* Similarly, even if Congress had not declared inconsistent state laws unenforceable, because Northwest's statute effectively bars any transportation of spent nuclear fuel through the state, contrary to Congress's objective, the state law would be preempted on that basis alone. *Id. (Cf., National Tank Truck Carriers, Inc. v. Burke*, 535 F. Supp. 509 (D.R.I. 1982).

If a "scheme of federal regulation is so pervasive as to make reasonable the inference that Congress left no room to supplement it . . .," then preemption is implied. *E.g., Pacific Gas & Elec. Co. v. State Energy Reserves Conservation & Dev. Comm'n.*, 461 U.S. 190, 204 (1983). Here, although the facts indicate the federal statute is "comprehensive," the statute also expressly states that only "inconsistent" state laws are void; therefore, states are authorized to adopt supplemental laws. *Accord, id.; National Tank Truck Carriers, supra.* Therefore, there is no preemption implied by the scope of the federal legislation.

2. Commerce Clause. Under the commerce clause, U.S. Const., art. I, sec. 8, cl. 3, states are prevented from enacting laws that unduly burden commerce. *Raymond Motor Transp. Inc. v. Rice*, 434 U.S. 429 (1979). States can adopt laws that affect interstate commerce, provided the laws serve a legitimate state interest and do not discriminate against interstate commerce. *Id.* "[W]here the statute regulates evenhandedly to effectuate a legitimate local public interest, and its effects on interstate commerce are only incidental, it will be upheld unless the burden imposed on such commerce is clearly excessive in relation to the putative local benefits." *Pike v. Bruce Church, Inc.*, 397 U.S. 137, 142 (1970). A balancing test is applied, weighing the local interests against the degree of interference with interstate commerce.

Here, clearly Northwest has a legitimate local interest (to provide a safe distance between nuclear waste in transit and populated areas), which Northwest defines more cautiously than Congress. But the state statute disproportionately affects interstate commerce by simply keeping nuclear waste out of the state. *Cf. National Tank Truck Carriers, supra.* Protectionism is met with a virtual *per se* rule of invalidity. *See generally, Philadelphia v. New Jersey*, 437 U.S. 617 (1978); *H.P. Hood & Sons, Inc. v. Du Mond*, 336 U.S. 525 (1949); *Lewis v. BT Inv. Mgrs.*, 447 U.S. 27 (1980). Therefore, the Northwest statute is unenforceable as violating the commerce clause.

Answer Sixty-three: Torts

1. Driver and Passenger have a cause of action against Hauler for negligence, and may have one under a theory of negligence *per se*.

2. Driver and Passenger have a cause of action against XYZ on a theory of vicarious liability.

3. Hauler has a cause of action against Driver for assault.

4. If there is an applicable guest statute, Passenger may have a cause of action against Driver for negligence.

5. Driver has a cause of action against Hauler for battery.

1. *Driver and Passenger v. Hauler: Negligence.* Under the common law of torts, to make out a *prima facie* case in negligence, plaintiff must show (i) defendant's duty of care; (ii) breach of duty; (iii) actual cause; (iv) proximate cause; and (v) his own damages. W. Prosser and W. Keeton, *Prosser and Keeton on the Law of Torts* sec. 30 (1984).

Here, Hauler had a duty under state law to drive the truck in a careful, prudent manner and not to stop his truck in that area of the road. Hauler breached his duty by stopping. But for his having breached his duty, the accident would not have occurred. Driver and Passenger were foreseeable plaintiffs. They suffered injuries or damages.

Therefore, Hauler is liable to Driver and Passenger in negligence.

Driver and Passenger may also have a cause of action against Hauler on a theory of negligence *per se*, if they can prove that he violated the statute prohibiting stopping, that the purpose of the statute was to protect against the type of injury they sustained, and that they are members of the group that the statute was intended to protect. *Restatement (Second) of Torts* sec. 286 (1965); W. Prosser and W. Keeton, *Prosser and Keeton on the Law of Torts* sec. 36 (1984).

2. *Driver and Passenger v. XYZ Trucking Company: Negligence.* Under the law of torts, where an employee at the time of his negligence acts is acting within the course and scope of his employment, his negligence may be imputed to his employer. *Id.* sec. 69. Here, it would be a question of fact whether Hauler was acting within the course and scope of his employment. If so, Driver and Passenger could recover against XYZ Trucking Company under a theory of *respondeat superior*.

3. *Hauler v. Driver: Assault.* Under the common law of torts, an actor is subject to liability for assault if he acts intending to cause a harmful or offensive contact with a person or intends to cause an imminent apprehension of that contact, and the other party is thereby put in such apprehension. *Restatement (Second) of Torts* sec. 21 (1965). No actual contact is necessary. Here, Driver lifted the tire iron above her head in a threatening manner, intending to put Hauler in fear that she would strike him. Hauler was, in fact, put in fear. Therefore, Hauler has a cause of action against Driver in assault.

4. *Passenger v. Driver: Negligence (Guest Statute).* Under the law of many states, statutes provide for claims of guests in automobiles. The statutes are highly variable. However, a claim is possible, depending on state law.

5. *Driver v. Hauler: Battery.* Under the law of torts, in order for a plaintiff to recover on a claim for battery, he must show that the defendant acted with the intent of making harmful or offensive contact with the plaintiff's person and that the defendant's conduct resulted in harmful or offensive contact with the plaintiff. *Restatement (Second) of Torts* sec. 13 (1965). Here, Hauler intentionally punched Driver in the face, breaking her nose. Hauler acted with the intent of, and did in fact cause, harmful or offensive contact with the plaintiff. Therefore, Driver has a cause of action against Hauler for battery.

Answer Sixty-four: Contracts

1. Ford does have an enforceable claim against Heber for payment of consulting fees.

2. Welsh does not have an enforceable claim against Ford for payment of his broker's fee.

3. If Ford cashes the check drawn on the Zions Bank there will be no effect on his claims against Heber and his obligations to Welsh.

1. *Ford v. Heber: Consulting Fees.* Where the parties intend to have a single contract, that contract is enforceable even where it is represented in two separate instruments. Under the law of this state, a contract requires offer, acceptance, and consideration. Consideration is any benefit to the promisor or detriment to the promisee. Here, the consulting agreement mentions fees due to Dodge Ford at $350,000 per year. However, it does not require any services from him, unless the Heber Chamber of Commerce requests them. It might be argued that this is a sort of "retainer" agreement, by which Dodge Ford is paid to be available for consulting services. That argument is probably not necessary, however, since the two agreements, viewed as one contract, provide consideration to the Heber Chamber in the transfer of the sports club. That contract, viewed as a whole, is enforceable. Therefore, the consulting contract is enforceable.

2. *Welsh v. Ford: Broker's Fee.* Under the law of this state, a contract comes within the statute of frauds where it cannot be completed within one year, or is for the sale of goods in an amount over $500.00. Such a contract must be in writing and signed by the party to be charged in order to be enforceable. The writing that satisfies the statute of frauds need only contain the parties, the subject of the agreement, and the basic terms, including price. A finder's fee agreement is not unenforceable, however, merely because of ambiguities in the description of the property to be sold, when the defects can be cured by proof of extrinsic facts. Here, the finder's fee agreement covers a period of 15 months. The fact that it could, however, be completed within one year takes it out of the statute of frauds. However, even supposing it to be for the sale of goods, it is also for an amount over $500.00. It must be in writing. Here, the writing identifies the finder, Welsh, the person who will owe the fee if a buyer is found, the commission rate of one per cent, and the time period of employment, namely, fifteen months. The unclarity as to which sports clubs Ford owns and who possible buyers might be does not render the agreement unenforceable, since that information can easily be supplied. Therefore, the statute of frauds does not make the broker's fee agreement unenforceable.

However, the agreement was entered into as of May 1, 1986, and by its terms lasted for 15 months, that is, until November 1, 1987. The sale of the franchise, however, did not take place until January 10, 1988. Therefore, the agreement had expired, and for that reason it is unenforceable.

3. *Accord and Satisfaction.* [State laws differ on this point.]

Answer Sixty-five: Real Property

In a jurisdiction with a statutory period of 25 years or less for adverse possession, Bill will have acquired title by adverse possession to the disputed 100 feet of land north of the fence line. The verbal contract with Cathy is probably in any event unenforceable, and he can refuse to sell.

The Disputed Land. Cathy will argue that the survey she undertook with Bill's permission reveals that the disputed 100 feet of land just north of the fence line belongs to her.

Under the common law of real property, however, title can pass by adverse possession, without documents of conveyance or a formal agreement. *See* R. Powell and P. Rohan, *Powell on Real Property* sec. 91.2 (1988). The statute in the various states providing for acquisition of property by adverse possession do so negatively, by barring an action to recover title to land when the plaintiff has delayed enforcing his rights for more than the statutory period, and the party in possession has met the criteria for adverse possession.

The statutory requirements for adverse possession vary, but in general possession must be

1. Open and notorious, putting the owner on notice of the claiming party's possession;
2. Continuous, i.e., not interrupted or intermittent (although in certain circumstances successive possessors' interests may be joined together);
3. Under a "claim of right" and hostile, as against the whole world;
4. Exclusive; and
5. Actual.

Powell sec. 91.6

The statutory length of time that must pass before the adversely possessing party gains title varies from state to state. In general, successive adverse possessors can "tack" their times together, to meet the statutory requirement. *Id.* sec. 91.59. Both parties must satisfy all elements of adverse possession, there must be clear intent to transfer the property between the successive adverse possessors, the possession must be continuous, and there must be privity between the successive adverse possessors. *Id.* secs. 91.60 to 91.63.

Here, Alice acquired the property north of the fence line by deed and used all of it for ten years. She then sold it to Bill, employing the same legal description, and Bill used all of the property north of the fence line for another fifteen years. Alice and Bill both made use of the land that was open and notorious, under a claim of right (the deeds) and hostile as against the whole world, exclusive, and actual. Tacking their times together is permissible because both parties satisfied all elements of adverse possession, the property was duly transferred, the possession was continuous, and there was privity between Alice and Bill. Tacking the times together, they have a total of twenty-five years. Therefore, in a jurisdiction where the statutory period for adverse possession is twenty-five years or less, Bill has already acquired the disputed one hundred feet of property just north of the fence line by adverse possession.

The Contract for Sale. Cathy will argue that she and Bill entered into a contract for her purchase of Bill's land, that she has changed her position in reliance on that contract by, among other things, having a survey of the land done, and that she is entitled to enforce the contract.

Under the statute of frauds, however, contracts for the sale of land will be unenforceable unless there is a contract, memorandum or note in writing, signed by the party against whom enforcement is sought, and stating essential terms. The writing must identify the parties, the land, and the purchase price, and must contain mutual promises to buy and sell the land. *Id.* sec. 81A.14. As long as the writing evidences a contract and sets forth the essential terms, it will be enforced. *Restatement (Second) of Contracts* sec. 13 (1982).

Here, Bill and Cathy "verbally agreed" that Cathy would buy all of Bill's property. This is a contract for the sale of an interest in land. There is, however, no written contract, memorandum or note, signed by any party, or stating any terms.

Therefore, the contract between Bill and Cathy for the sale of Bill's property is unenforceable, as failing to satisfy the statute of frauds.

Cathy will argue that under the principles of equity, courts will sometimes enforce contracts that do not satisfy the statute of frauds, where justice so requires. Courts will in appropriate circumstances enforce such agreements where a party has made a substantial change in his position, based on justifiable, good-faith reliance. The court will consider such factors as possession of the land by the purchaser, expenditure of funds by the purchaser, and reliance upon the acquisition by the purchaser, or reliance on the payment of the purchase price by the seller.

Here, Cathy has had a survey of the property made. That is not substantial reliance. There is no evidence of any other reliance by Cathy on the purchase.

Conclusions. Therefore, taking the facts as given as the only facts in the case, Bill has acquired title to the disputed area by adverse possession, there has been no substantial reliance on the contract, and the court will not apply equitable principles to enforce the verbal contract for sale of Bill's property to Cathy.

In view of the fact that there is no enforceable contract between Bill and Cathy and that reliance will not alone suffice to make the contract enforcable, Bill can probably refuse to sell the land to Cathy.

A Note on Answering This Question

This question presents a very common pattern in the structure of essay examination questions. (As always, in property questions where the fact pattern describes disputed property, first draw a map.) Determine whether any of the property has passed other than by deed, here, by adverse possession. After that, determine whether or not the contract for sale of the land is enforceable under the statute of frauds. Finally, where the contract fails to satisfy the statute of frauds, determine whether equity will nonetheless enforce the contract, because of detrimental reliance or part or full performance.

Answer Sixty-six: Contracts—U.C.C.

Buyers have accepted the generator. They can demand that Sam fix the switch. They can seek return of their old generator, if necessary by replevin.

A contract for the sale of goods falls under Article 2 of the U.C.C. Under U.C.C. sec. 2-601, where the goods or tender of delivery fails to conform to the contract in any way, the buyer may choose either to reject the goods or to accept them despite their nonconformity. Under U.C.C. sec. 2-602, the buyer may reject nonconforming goods within a reasonable time after delivery. Under U.C.C. sec. 2-606, acceptance does not occur until the buyer has had a reasonable time to inspect the goods. Under U.C.C. sec. 2-606, the buyer accepts the goods where he takes the goods as his own. He may accept by words, action, or silence when it is time to speak.

Here, the Buyers found that Mrs. Buyer could not start the generator, and Mr. Buyer was barely able to do so. In view of their having explained to the seller that they needed a generator Mrs. Buyer could start, that defect would definitely have entitled the Buyers to reject the generator. Here, too, the Buyers noticed that the Hercules 2000 generator had a defective switch. Even had they noticed that defect before using the generator, that defect might not have entitled the Buyers to reject the generator. However, they accepted it and took it as their own by using it. Therefore, the Buyers accepted the generator, within the terms of the U.C.C.

Under U.C.C. sec. 2-608, the buyer may revoke his acceptance if the goods do not conform to the contract, provided that the nonconformity substantially impairs the value of the goods. Here, the broken switch would not entitle the Buyers to revoke the acceptance, since it does not substantially impair the value of the goods. In addition, under U.C.C. sec. 2-508 and sec. 2-106(2), the seller has a right to cure improper tender or delivery by making or substituting a conforming tender or delivery. Here, Seller could have repaired the switch, and he offered to do so.

The implied warranty of fitness for a particular purpose is probably of some significance here. This warranty arises when a seller has reason to know of a particular purpose for which the goods are required and that the buyer is relying on the seller's judgment to select suitable goods. U.C.C. sec. 2-315. Here Sam Seller had reason to know of the Buyers' requirements; they told him what they needed. They also made it clear that they were relying on him to order a suitable generator. In addition, Seller's specific assurances that the generator would be "just the thing for them" may constitute an express warranty. This can be based on any promise made to the buyer about the goods that is part of the basis of the bargain. U.C.C. sec. 2-313(a). Seller would presumably argue that his statements were just sales puffing, and not a warranty at all.

Assuming that there was a breach of warranty by Seller, the Buyers have a number of remedies available to them. They are entitled to revoke their acceptance and receive their money back (sec. 2-712) or they can recover damages under sec. 2-713, which would be the difference between the contract price and the market value of the generator. These damages are in addition to consequential and incidental damages, if appropriate under sec. 2-715. Under the facts presented here, there is no showing that Buyers are entitled to either consequential or incidental damages. The Buyers have no right to specific performance; the goods must be unique, or there must be other special circumstances. U.C.C. sec. 2-716(a).

There may be other causes of action available to Buyers. By refusing to return the generator on the Buyers' demand, Seller may have engaged in conversion. He had no legal security interest in the generator, as this can only be created by specific agreement. U.C.C. sec. 9-204. Additionally, Seller could not claim a mechanic's lien because he was repairing the switch under warranty. In a conversion action, the measure of damages would be the fair market value of the generator at the time of the conversion. Buyers might also be able to seek punitive damages.

Seller's conduct, especially his refusal to refund Buyers' money after their rejection (or rightful revocation) may be a violation of this state's Consumer Fraud Act. A violation of this statute requires an unfair or deceptive act by Seller. If there is a violation, Buyers would be entitled to attorney's fees and possible treble damages.

Answer Sixty-seven: Real Property

1. *Cal's Rights. Rights on the Contract*: Under the common law of contracts, every contract requires offer, acceptance, and consideration. Here, Bob made an oral offer to buy both Blackacre and Whiteacre, and to pay $20,000 for the two properties. He offered to pay $10,000 immediately and $10,000 in one year. Sam accepted the offer. The consideration was the exchange of one promise for another. Therefore, there was an oral contract.

Under the statute of frauds, however, for a contract for the sale of an interest in land to be enforceable, it must be in writing and signed by the party to be charged. Here, Bob and Sam reduced their agreement to a writing, which both signed. Therefore, the contract is enforceable as satisfying the statute of frauds.

Under the principles of equity, a court will reform a contract where the parties came to an understanding, but in reducing it to writing they omitted something they had agreed upon, or the writing otherwise fails to reflect their oral agreement. Parol evidence is admissible to reform a contract. Here, the parties agreed that the land called Blackacre and Whiteacre would be sold by Sam to Bob. The contract, however, describes the land as "Blackacre, containing 20 acres, more or less," and does not mention Whiteacre. The intention of the parties, however, was that the land approximating 20 acres, called both Blackacre and Whiteacre should be sold. Therefore, a court sitting in equity might reform the contract to include both Blackacre and Whiteacre.

Likewise, where the parties agreed on the land to be sold, the fact that both were mistaken about the exact size of the parcels in acres will not void the contract. The intention of the parties was that the land called Blackacre and Whiteacre, of approximately 20 acres (in fact, 17 acres), should be sold by Sam to Bob.

Under the common law of contracts, assignment occurs where a party to a contract transfers to someone else a contract right or benefit, ending his own rights to that benefit under the contract. He may assign his rights, but he may only delegate his duties, remaining liable as a surety for his duties under the contract. Here, Bob sold his rights under the contract to Cal, for $10,000, ending his own rights under the contract with Sam. Cal accordingly acquired the right to buy the property. At the same time, Bob delegated to Sam his duty to pay the additional $10,000 at the time due, remaining as a surety by operation of law for the payment of that sum. Accordingly, assignment of Bob's rights has occurred, and Cal steps into Bob's shoes, acquiring Bob's rights under the contract, including the right to demand performance by Sam.

2. *Cal's Remedies. Contract Remedies*: Under the common law of contracts, the usual remedy for breach of contract is money damages. The usual measure of damages is the amount necessary to put the nonbreaching party in as good a position as he would have been in had the contract been performed. Here, Cal is the nonbreaching party. Had Sam performed, Cal would have received title to Blackacre and Whiteacre, however valued. Therefore, strict application of

contract principles would give Cal a sum of money equal to the value of Sam's performance, however evaluated.

Under the common law of real property, each piece of land is considered unique, and the appropriate remedy for breach of a contract to sell land is therefore the equitable remedy of specific performance. A court in equity will award specific performance where the subject matter is unique (as in the sale of land), where there is difficulty in determining plaintiff's damages, and where the item to be conveyed has special intrinsic value. Here, Blackacre and Whiteacre are land, and unique. Therefore, a court will probably award specific performance.

Cal is also entitled to rescind the contract. Rescission would leave him only with the $10,000 originally paid, however. In view of the increase in the value of Blackacre and Whiteacre, that would be an inadequate remedy. Cal might also seek abatement, arguing that he should pay only $7,000 at closing, because the second parcel is only seven acres, not ten. However, the contract requires payment of $10,000, and that is the amount he must pay.

Sam may argue that Cal did not produce $10,000, but only $7,000, contrary to the terms of the contract. However, this was a real estate sale, and time was not "of the essence." Therefore, Cal's failure to perform completely on the date due does not alone constitute material breach.

Sam may argue that he should be entitled to rescission based on mutual mistake, since the parties did not know about the increase in the value of the land when they signed the contract. Mutual mistake is based on the equitable consideration that neither party should profit from an error both made. Here, however, the increase in the value of the property was not a fact as to which Sam and Bob were in error. On the contrary, it was a risk Sam bore, and it was equally foreseeable by both parties. Therefore, the defense of mutual mistake will probably fail.

Therefore, Cal is entitled to specific performance of the contract. In the alternative, he may be awarded money damages.

A Note on Answering This Question

A person who is good at "issue spotting" will see a large number of issues while reading the fact pattern, making the question appear to be much more formidable than it in fact turns out to be. If you simply concentrate on handling the fundamentals (Is there a contract? Is it enforceable? What is the basic remedy for breach of contract in a sale of real property?), the question becomes manageable. This is another demonstration of the fact that if you use the Key Outline and Model Paragraph strategies, you will write competent essays.

Answer Sixty-eight:
Criminal Procedure

(Performance Test)

The New Jersey examiners have reprinted two briefs on each side of this question. All four briefs appear below. All were written by candidates for the New Jersey Bar. They are not "model" answers; they are actual candidates' answers. They demonstrate the level of performance expected of a bar candidate on a portion of an essay or performance examination asking him to step into the shoes of a practicing attorney.

Answer A (for Defendant)

Defendant's Brief Sample 1

Motion of Defendant Witker to Suppress Evidence

Defendant's Motion Should Be Granted

A. The Government Illegally Obtained All of the Evidence Identified Herein In Violation of the Defendant's 4th and 5th Amendment Rights

1. The Department of Defense Investigator is a Government Agent.

Under the 4th and 5th Amendments of the Constitution, the government cannot conduct unreasonable searches and seizures of property, or obtain incriminating statements from suspects in violation of their privilege against self-incrimination. The Supreme Court has fashioned a judicial remedy to address such breaches—the exclusionary rule. The rule serves to require exclusion of the illegally obtained evidence, and all evidence flowing from that illegal act, at the subsequent prosecution of the person from whom the evidence was seized (and others who have "standing"). The rule is intended to protect against "overzealous" governmental intrusion into the basic rights of citizens; accordingly, it is only applied when the evidence was obtained by a government agent, such as, in state matters, the police.

The threshold question here is whether the DOD investigator was a government agent for law enforcement purposes. While the government will argue that a DOD investigator is not an agent of the prosecution, it is clear from the facts that he was given the task of investigating and gathering evidence against Witker that the Government could use to deprive Witker of property and liberty rights. Thus, any evidence obtained by the DOD investigator must be considered in the context of the constitutional privileges that Witker is entitled to enjoy. As discussed below, *all* such evidence was illegally obtained and must be suppressed.

2. The Bugging of Witker's Apartment and Office Without a Warrant Was Unreasonable and Unlawful

The procedural safeguards in the criminal process designed to protect against unreasonable searches and seizures include the warrant requirement. A warrant to bug a person's home or office, wherein he enjoys an expectation of privacy, must be premised on reliable information that a crime is being or has been committed. No warrant was obtained to bug Witker's home and office and, indeed, none could have obtained, since the government has articulated no reliable basis beyond "mere suspicion" of Witker's offensive conduct. Moreover, no crime was or had been taking place—being a homosexual is not illegal in this country. Thus, the absence of a warrant (and the lack of any underlying basis to even conceive of a warrant's being issued) provides a sound basis for suppression of the tapes produced from the bugs in the house and office.

While it is clear that persons have an expectation of privacy in their own homes, the government will no doubt argue that Witker has not comparable expectation of privacy in his office. That is not so. The facts reveal that Witker was accorded a private office and, especially since he was a lawyer engaged in counseling his government clients, he had a reasonable expectation that his office was private. Accordingly, the tapes from both his home and office conversations must be suppressed.

3. The Tapping of Witker's Home and Office Phones Was Likewise Illegal Without A Warrant and the Tapes Should be Suppressed

Similarly, a warrant was required to tap Witker's home and office phones. For the reasons stated in section 2, *supra*, no warrant was or could have been issued. Nor do the facts indicate that *consent* of one party was given for any or all of the conversations contained in the tapes. In this regard, although the Government could argue that, since national security interests were at stake (*i.e., homosexual government employees could easily be compromised by foreign agents*), *exigent circumstances as obviated the need for a warrant, the facts do not justify a conclusion that this was the reason not to seek a warrant and, indeed, the revelation of Witker's alleged involvement with foreign agents was not* the purpose of the bugging. (The purpose, according to the facts, did not go beyond determining whether Witker was a homosexual.) Thus, absent consent or a warrant, the tapes of phone conversations at Witker's home and office were illegally obtained and must be suppressed.

4. The Tapes of Private Activities in the Defendant's Home And Office Were Also Illegally Obtained and Must Be Suppressed

Again, no warrant was issued to conduct the unreasonable and distasteful intrusion of TV cameras through peepholes in Witker's home and office. As noted in section 2, *supra*, Witker reasonably had an expectation of privacy at both locations, and the intrusion into such privacy without a warrant constituted an unreasonable search and seizure. Therefore, the TV tapes must be suppressed.

5. The Defendant's Oral Confession Was Made Under Duress and Must Be Suppressed

The investigator's intrusion into Witker's home at 10:00 PM, unannounced with the purpose of badgering, taunting and humiliating Witker was unreasonable, and violated Witker's 4th and 5th Amendment rights. The facts indicated that the investigator did not have a search or arrest warrant, yet he entered Witker's apartment with a heavy-handed, domineering demeanor intended to intimidate Witker. The Court can and should reasonably conclude that Witker felt confined, unable to retreat (he was, after all, "invaded" in his own home), and felt himself to be under arrest. The investigator did not inform Witker, in these circumstances, of his *Miranda* rights. Given the totality of these circumstances, the Court must conclude that the oral confession was coerced and, therefore, invalid.

The government will no doubt argue that Witker did not have to let the investigator in; the investigator did not bring Witker to a police station or other location of detention, and Witker could not be found to have been under arrest or a prime suspect of any particular crime. The defense submits that, when viewed in context, the restraining and overbearing nature of the investigator's presence amounted to a detention that required *Miranda* warnings.

6. The Defendant's Written Confession, Being the Fruit of the Poisonous Tree, was Tainted and Must Be Suppressed

The written confession was prepared immediately after the oral confession. No significant time period passed, according to the facts, and no intervening events occurred to remove the circumstances surrounding the oral confession from the written confession. The same illegal coercion and duress that prompted the illegally obtained oral confession still existed. Thus, the written confession was, for those same reasons, illegally obtained. This is so despite the fact, as the government will no doubt point out, the investigator merely "suggested" that Witker write his confession down.

Moreover, despite the "mere suggestion" or "voluntary" nature of the written confession, it was a product of the illegally obtained confession. As a "fruit of the poisonous tree," it suffers from the taint of illegality of the oral confession and must, too, be suppressed.

B. The Government Can Claim No Exception to the Applicability of Constitutionally Based Procedural Safeguards Because the Defendant Allegedly Breached Legal and Ethical Obligations.

An attorney is charged with the highest degree of responsibility over the confidential communications of his clients. Witker, as a government attorney, was privy to confidential client information known to him from his DOD clients. Despite any suspected or alleged breach of that trust, which the government has not claimed to have substantiated at all *prior* to undertaking this shocking series of illegal activities, this does not justify the wholesale abandonment of the constitutional safeguards discussed above.

For all the above reasons, the Court should—and must—suppress the evidence, oral, written and recorded, described above.

Answer B (for Defendant)
Defendant's Brief Sample 2
Brief In Support Of Motion To Suppress

Summary of Argument

The Fifth Amendment assures that every citizen will be secure in their person and property from unreasonable searches and seizures. To the end of enforcing the Constitution, the rule is that evidence obtained in violation of a defendant's rights will be suppressed and will not be permitted in evidence against him. In addition, a person may not constitutionally be required to be a witness against himself. Thus, statements obtained by the state absent a knowing and voluntary waiver of the right to remain silent are inadmissible in an action against the defendant. Finally, federal law provides that law enforcement agents must obtain a court order to conduct electronic surveillance of an individual suspect. The warrant will be issued for a distinct time and place only upon the appropriate application. Here, because no such application was made, and no warrant issued, the evidence was obtained in violation of law and therefore must be suppressed.

ARGUMENT ONE. THE AUDIO AND VISUAL TAPES WERE OBTAINED IN VIOLATION OF THE CONSTITUTIONAL PROTECTION AGAINST UNREASONABLE SEARCHES AND SEIZURES

The government wrongly urged at oral argument that the DOD investigator did not "search" and "seize" within the meaning of the fifth amendment. The Supreme Court has held that any investigatory intrusion by electronic means, which would be illegal if personally conducted, is an illegal search. Thus, attaching electronic "beepers" to cargo in public places is lawful, but as to materials which are transported to protected "private" areas, electronic monitoring is an illegal search if accomplished without a warrant.

If a defendant has an expectation of privacy, a search may not be conducted absent exigent circumstances. The Constitution specifically refers to one's home as one such area. Case law has also established a right to privacy, from *intentional* intrusion, in telephone conversations.

The government is correct that an office has a somewhat lower expectation of privacy. It is in error, however, to suggest that an office is fair territory for warrantless searches. Here Witker's office was private, it was his alone. To the extent that the office is therefore inaccessible to public view and travel, Witker maintains a degree of privacy expectation which is constitutionally protected. That expectation goes, at very least, to visual search such as the video tapes.

While it is true, as the government puts forth, that an office is susceptible to casual viewing from the outside when the door is open, it is equally true that an office is also easily secured from such view. Case law has established that the private office is an extension of the person's home to the extent that the office is served him from public access.

Thus, the wiretapping, bugging, and taping of the defendant's phone, office, and home, were warrantless searches of areas where the defendant had a reasonable expectation of privacy.

No exigent circumstances obtain which would obviate the warrant requirement. The government's invocation of "national security" is pretext. First, an emergency cannot be said to exist where the illegal searches continued for a *year*. Second, the searches were begun not because of national security, but, by the government's own account, to gather evidence of the defendant's sexual habits.

Finally, there was here no probable cause justifying the warrantless search. The government necessarily concedes that homosexuality is not the crime. The argument that homosexuality makes the government attorney vulnerable to espionage efforts of foreign governments is ludicrous, make weight, and pretextual. First, heterosexual activity conducted in private may be embarrassing to one if presented for public view. Thus, heterosexual attorneys who wish their sex habits to remain private are equally vulnerable to foreign agents. Second, there was absolutely no evidence before the surveillance that led the government to believe there was "a problem" with Witker. Third, even after a year-long illegal scrutiny of Witker, the government was unaware of this activity until the incriminating statements were coerced by the DOD investigator.

Accordingly, because the evidence was the result of illegal searches, absent probable cause, exigent circumstances, and a warrant, it must be suppressed in the trial of the defendant.

ARGUMENT TWO. THE INCRIMINATING STATEMENTS WERE OBTAINED WITHOUT *MIRANDA* WARNINGS AND WERE COERCED

There is no question that the DOD investigator's "session" with Witker was a custodial session. With the force of the Department of Defense behind him, the investigator descended upon Witker late one evening and badgered him for hours in his own home. A custodial situation in which *Miranda* rights attach may be something less than an actual arrest. The government wrongly argues there was no custody here for *Miranda* purposes. The investigator was uninvited and unwelcome, and acted under the authority of the DOD. Witker was in his custody.

In such a situation, *Miranda* rights attach. The investigator did not inform Witker of his rights under the *Miranda* decision. The government accuses the defendant of placing form over substance because Witker was an attorney and presumably knew his rights. First, when dealing with its citizens, the government *should* be held to the proper form; as is often said, the government should be made to "turn square corners" when it brings its power to bear on the individual. Second, it is the government that is ignoring the substance here. Witker never waived his constitutional rights to silence and counsel. Into the late evening and early morning hours, the investigator badgered, taunted, and humiliated the defendant.

Confessions are admissible only when voluntary. They are only voluntary when they are made pursuant to a knowing and intelligent waiver of the *Miranda* rights. No such waiver was possible here, where the defendant was mentally and physically worn down hour after hour. Finally, the investigator obtained the incriminating statements. Under these conditions, the government shamefully claims the confession was voluntary. It was not and it must be suppressed.

ARGUMENT THREE. THE TAPES WERE OBTAINED IN VIOLATION OF THE FEDERAL ELECTRONIC EAVESDROPPING STATUTES

Federal law forbids the electronic search of a person's phone or private areas without a warrant. Here no warrant existed; no application was made. Accordingly, this court should refuse to allow entry of this evidence against the defendant.

Respectfully submitted,

Answer A (for Government)

Government Brief Sample 1

(b) Opposition to Defendant's Motion to Suppress

The United States of America, by and through its attorneys, opposes Defendant's Motion to Suppress in the above-captioned matter and avers in support thereof the following:

The Defense Department Investigator Did Not Violate Defendant's Fourth Amendments Rights As He Was Not A Law Enforcement Officer

The fourth amendment rights of the United States Constitution are violated only by state, local or federal law enforcement officers. When the constitutional amendments were drafted, the purpose was to protect citizens from the law enforcement officials, federal and state, who may conduct unreasonable searches and seizures.

The courts have long upheld these constitutional guarantees against encroachment. To deter law enforcement officials from overstepping the bounds of the 4A protections, the courts have refused to admit evidence (real or testimonial) which was obtained as a direct or indirect result of abridgement of 4A rights. Thus when a police officer arrested someone and failed to advise him of his *Miranda* rights, the defendant could move to suppress any statement (incriminating) made as a result thereof.

In the instant matter, defendant seeks to suppress audio plus visual tapes and a confession allegedly obtained in violation of 4A rights. However, none of this evidence was obtained in that manner. An investigator for the Department of Defense who is not a law enforcement officer nor has any authority regarding the law, was responsible for obtaining the audio plus video tapes and the statement regarding defendant. As the investigator is not the same as a police officer, the 4A restrictions do not apply. As the purpose of the unreasonable searches plus seizures in violation of 4A is to deter unlawful police/law enforcement conduct, the same would not be advanced by suppressing the evidence. The courts have not refused to admit evidence seized by a private person and forwarded to police regardless of the alleged 4A violations. The investigator in this instance is akin to a private citizen who has come across evidence of a crime against the United States and therefore forwarded to the appropriate law enforcement powers. He is not an agent of the United States for this purpose.

Therefore, as the investigator as a non-law-enforcement officer did not violate defendant's 4A rights, the Motion to Suppress should be denied and all said evidence admitted in the espionage trial.

Defendant had no reasonable expectation of privacy regarding his telephone conversations nor in his office.

Assuming, arguendo, the investigator is deemed to be a law enforcement officer for purposes of 4A, the evidence is still admissible as defendant had no reasonable expectation of privacy.

The basis for the unreasonable searches under 4A has been whether the person had a reasonable expectation of privacy. Where such expectation exists, 4A rights will be violated generally if the police (investigator) invades that area or object.

It is asserted defendant had no reasonable expectation of privacy regarding his telephone conversations in his office. Because of the sensitive nature of his duties as an attorney for the defense department, he should have expected the possibility of listening devices placed on his telephone. The defendant argues he did have some expectation of privacy.

Furthermore, defendant argues that a warrant issued by an independent and neutral magistrate on the basis of probable cause must be obtained prior to wiretapping. The department of defense had authority to authorize the wiretapping under its powers regarding the national security of this country. As noted earlier, defendant was engaged in or privy to confidential and extremely sensitive information regarding national defense and it was felt there was reason to doubt defendant's loyalty to the U.S.

This was proven by the audio plus video tapes. The fact that defendant's homosexuality was the starting point for the investigation does not invalidate same. Because of his homosexuality, defendant would be vulnerable. The fear of exposure, as was admitted by defendant, made him more likely to be controlled by others to the detriment of the United States.

Likewise, defendant had no reasonable expectation of privacy in his office as to the video tapes. One's office is not the same as one's home or the men's room where private acts would be expected to take place.

As noted above, defendant's actions played an important role in his loyalty to the United States and therefore the necessity to videotape him in his home overruled whatever expectation of privacy defendant had in his office.

Defendant's Expectation of Privacy At Home Was Outweighed By The Potentially Dangerous Defense Leak

Although, generally, citizens have a reasonable expectation of privacy in their own homes from cameras and tape recorders, the circumstances here warranted the intrusion. Thus defendant had to be observed to confirm that fact, as he would not admit it.

Therefore, the Motion To Suppress regarding the video tape at home should be denied. Furthermore, the use of the audio tapes is much less intrusive than video tapes and if the latter should be excluded, the former should not, because the less intrusive means was used.

Although the investigator did not have a warrant to tape plus record defendant's activities, permission was given by the Department of Defense. To avoid intruding on the separation of powers, the courts may not set rules and standards for the Department of Defense as a separate branch of government. The court therefore should not suppress the evidence on 4A grounds because the Defense Department is not bound by same.

The Statement is Admissible Despite the Lack of *Miranda* Warning as Defendant Was Not In Custodial Interrogation

The test for the application of *Miranda* warnings is when defendant is placed in custodial interrogation. At this time, the atmosphere is one of inherent pressure and disadvantage on the defendant which may force him to make a statement that he would not normally make. Therefore statements made while in custodial interrogation are inadmissible if Miranda warnings were not given first and the rights knowingly voluntarily waived.

In the instant case, defendant was questioned in his home. The defendant could have asked the investigator to leave at anytime—he did not. If the investigator did not leave, he could have summoned the police—he did not. The unfamiliar surroundings plus lack of freedom inherent in custodial interrogation were not in existence at defendant's house. Therefore, *Miranda* warnings were not necessary. The statement made by defendant can therefore be admitted into evidence as same is not violation of his 4A rights.

Wherefore, for all the above state reasons, the United States of America requests this Honorable Court to deny defendant's Motion to suppress and allow the evidence into the trial.

> *JANE DOE*
> *Attorney For U.S.A.*

Answer B (for Government)

Government Brief Sample 2

Argument

1.) Defendant Witker's motion to suppress the audio and visual tapes should be *denied; even if* defendant's motion is granted as to the visual tapes, it should be denied as to the audio tapes and as to visual tapes made at defendant's office.

2.) Defendant Witker's motion to suppress his oral and written statements should be denied.

1.) Although the U.S. Department of Defense obtained the audio and visual tapes of Witker without a Warrant, this was accomplished with a *minimal intrusion* on Witker's constitutionally *guaranteed* right of *freedom from unreasonable searches and seizures,* and equally minimal *invasion of his privacy.*

> Because of the sensitive nature of defendant's work as a Dept. of Defense employee, the Department has a compelling duty to protect the public interest and welfare by controlling and monitoring its employees, especially those whose personal behavior proclivities and lifestyle put them at greater risk of being compromised. As a *long-time* government attorney, defendant knew or should have known that this conduct, both personal and professional, would be subject to greater scrutiny than that of a privately employed person; there can be no doubt here that defendant therefore had a *lesser expectation of privacy* than he would have enjoyed as a purely private citizen. *See Bivens v. Six Unknown Agents.* It is well-established that government employees who actively engage in homosexual activities are at greater risk of blackmail and compromise than similar employees who do not actively engage in such activities. The Department therefore had a *legitimate and compelling interest* in investigating the defendant, and conducted its investigation in a way that

did not offend the U.S. Constitution. The tapes obtained pursuant to this valid investigation should therefore not be suppressed.

It is well-established case law that, although defendant may argue that he had a valid expectation of privacy in his apartment, *one's office is not an extension of one's home.* An office is an active center of business activity, and the Supreme Court has held that a defendant is not entitled to the same expectation of privacy, especially where the defendant is employed by *others*, and works daily with others who are also authorized to use the office. While it is true that a defendant may have a valid right to privacy in a personal, locked file cabinet or brief case, this is not the issue here. Here, defendant worked in an office owned and operated by the Department, and the Department clearly has the right to supervise and observe, even secretly, its employees there as long as the intrusion is not unreasonable. Here the intrusion was small and indirect (defendant did not even know he was being observed) and it was important to the greater welfare of the Department and the entire country. Plainly, in the case at hand the interest of the government and the nation in peace and security *outweighed* defendant's personal rights.

Even if the *apartment video tapes* are suppressed, the court should not suppress the *apartment audio tapes* obtained from the telephone wiretap. It is well-established that one who uses the telephone has a lessened expectation of privacy. Because of the very nature of the telephone as a *machine*, defendant's argument on this point must *fail*. When defendant used the telephone, he really had no sure way of knowing who would answer, or who might be listening (*i.e.*, on another extension). The pertinent case law is replete with examples involving a *reduced privacy interest* in regard to telephones. Simply because one dials a number does not guarantee that one has an uncontroverted *right to confidentiality* regarding his conversations. This argument is even more compelling in regard to defendant's office telephone calls. As discussed *supra*, defendant, given his sensitive position, could really not have had *any* expectation of privacy in his office telephone conversations. Also, although employees commonly use office telephones for non-business, private and personal calls, *they clearly do so at their own risk.* The Constitution is not an insurer of confidentiality, (see *Massiah* and *Hoffa* cases) especially regarding conversations where the very instrument used (the telephone) is subject to concurrent use by others.

2.) Case law firmly establishes that a defendant in a custodial setting, or in any setting where he would not feel free to leave, is entitled to *Miranda* warnings prior to *any* interrogation.

Miranda warnings include that the defendant has a right to remain silent, and that he has the right to have an attorney with him during the questioning. If he can't afford an attorney, one will be appointed for him. He is also told that anything he says can and will be used against him.

However, here, the defendant Witker was *not in custody*; he was in his own apartment. Although the investigator's conduct may have somewhat intimidated him and made him feel not free to leave, this issue is not overriding in that the investigator's conduct was not *outrageous or offensive to the ordinary person of reasonable and ordinary sensibilities.* More importantly, *Miranda* does not apply where there is not police interrogation. Thus, if a store detective questions an accused shoplifter, the shoplifter is not entitled to *Miranda* warnings. As long as the store detective's or the security guard's conduct is reasonable (not forceful or executed with undue duress), any statements or admissions freely made can be used against the defendant. Since here Witker was not in custody and not interrogated by a police officer, his statements are not protected by the investigator's failure to issue him *Miranda* warnings and hence should not be suppressed. Even if the *oral statements are suppressed, the court should not suppress* Witker's subsequent written confession. The facts show that this written confession was clearly voluntary, and knowingly done.

Also, *as an attorney*, Witker was or should have been *uniquely aware* of his rights in this regard. Witker voluntarily wrote out a *detailed statement;* he did not merely sign a transcript written by another. To his credit as a citizen, Witker volunteered to do the right and honorable thing, no doubt hoping to somehow mitigate the great and careless harm he had done to his country by betraying defense secrets. There is no doubt that, although he may have been emotionally upset at the time, his distress did not cause him to act involuntarily. He may have acted against his own interest in making the oral and written statements, but the facts show he did so out of the understandable shame and remorse he felt for betraying his country. We assert that both the oral and written statements should therefore *not* be suppressed.

Answer Sixty-nine:
Professional Responsibility

(Code of Professional Responsibility)

The ethical issues are as follows:

1. Payment of referral fee.
2. Duty of undivided loyalty to the client, without undue influence of another person.
3. Duty not to reveal a client's secrets.

Lawyer's payment to Broker appears to be a referral fee. Under the Model Code of Professional Responsibility DR 2-103(B), a lawyer is prohibited from giving anything of value to a person for recommending him as a lawyer or for rewarding the person if the lawyer secures employment from his recommendation. Under DR 9-102(A), a client's funds must be maintained in a separate trust account. The fee retainer must be kept as segregated funds until such time as legal services have been performed. Only after fees are earned and due may the earned portion be withdrawn from the separate account and then only if there is no dispute about the fees. DR 9-102(A)(2). Here, Lawyer has apparently paid a referral fee. He has not kept funds segregated. Therefore, Lawyer is in apparent violation of the Disciplinary Rules of the Model Code of Professional Responsibility.

Perhaps Lawyer's major ethical shortcoming in this case, however, is his failure to recognize clearly that Son, not Father, is the client. Under the Model Code of Professional Responsibility, it is the client to whom a lawyer owes undivided loyalty. A lawyer must avoid being influenced by anyone else. EC 5-1. It is to prevent such influence that DR 5-107(A) requires that a lawyer should not be paid for his services by someone other than the client without consent by the client after full disclosure. *See* EC 5-21 and EC 5-22. Here, even if Son did implicitly consent to Father's payment of fees, Lawyer failed to explain the effect Father's economic leverage might have on Lawyer's representation of Son. Lawyer unethically allowed Father to influence his judgment without regard to Son's desires and best interest. Therefore, having allowed influence by a third party, Lawyer was in violation of DR 5-107(B). He failed in his obligation to seek Son's objectives and to represent Son zealously. DR 7-101.

Son's request that Father not be told of Roommate's involvement is a "secret," that is, information gained during the professional relationship that the client requested be held inviolate. DR 4-101(A). Under the Model Code of Professional Responsibility, except in limited circumstances or with client's consent, a lawyer shall not reveal his client's confidences and secrets. DR 4-101(B) and (C). Here, although Lawyer was obligated to provide an accurate statement of services performed in accounting for the fee retainer, DR 9-102(B)(3), Lawyer's time slips should not have included Roommate's name when Son had specifically requested that his involvement be kept secret. Therefore, Lawyer has revealed a client's secret, and so has violated Disciplinary Rules 4-101(B) and 4-101(C).

Answer Seventy: Wills

(Uniform Probate Code)

1. The 1985 will is ineffective because it had only one witness.

2. The 1979 will is ineffective because the will does not specifically describe the document to which it refers.

3. Where there is no effective will, the estate must be distributed in accordance with the rules of intestate succession.

Under the Uniform Probate Code ("U.P.C."), subsequent wills may by express or implied provisions act to revoke prior wills. U.P.C. sec. 507. *See* 2 W. *Page on the Law of Wills* sec. 21.33. The subsequent will must be properly executed. Signature by mark or initials is sufficient for the execution of a will. Attestation by two witnesses is required. U.P.C. sec. 2-502. Here, the 1985 will had only one witness, the attorney. Therefore, the 1985 will is not effective to revoke the 1979 will.

Under the U.P.C., written instruments may be incorporated into wills. U.P.C. sec. 2-510. However, the incorporation is not effective unless the reference (i) expressly refers to a document that is in existence at the time of execution of the will, (ii) clearly shows the testator's intent to incorporate the written document, and (iii) correctly and with sufficient specificity describes the written document. U.P.C. sec. 2-510. Here, the document is not specifically described. Therefore, the incorporation fails.

Under the U.P.C., where the reference to the written document that specifies distribution is ineffective, the will is ineffective, and an estate, or any part thereof, ineffectively disposed of under a will must be distributed according to the rules of intestate succession as defined in the U.P.C. U.P.C. sec. 2-101. Under the U.P.C., the surviving spouse is entitled to (1) the entire estate if (i) there are no surviving issue or parent(s) of the decedent or (ii) the decedent's surviving issue are all issue of the surviving spouse and the decedent is not survived by any other issue of the surviving spouse; (2) the first $200,000, plus three-fourths of the balance of the intestate estate, if there are no surviving issue but the decedent is survived by a parent; (3) the first $150,000, plus one-half the balance of the intestate estate, if there are surviving issue all of whom are issue of the surviving spouse and the surviving spouse has issue surviving not descended from the decedent; or (4) the first $100,000, plus one-half of the balance of the intestate estate, if there are surviving issue one or more of whom are not issue of the surviving spouse. U.P.C. sec 2-102. (The alternate provision for community property states is found in U.P.C. sec. 2-102A.)

Here, by application of the foregoing rules, both wills fail. Therefore, Mr. Will-writer's estate must be distributed in accordance with the law of intestate succession. Therefore, Sarah will take in accordance with these rules, the exact amount depending on whether there are surviving issue and parents of the decedent.

Answer Seventy-one: Corporations

(Model Business Corporation Act)

Under the Model Business Corporation Act, it is clear that property can be consideration for the issuance of shares. Model Business Corp. Act sec. 6.21(b) (1979). Moreover, the uniform law has done away with the idea of "watered" stock. *Id.* sec. 6.21 official comment. Here, the directors have issued shares of stock in exchange for land. Therefore, the directors' determination that the shares were issued for adequate consideration is conclusive. *Id.* sec. 6.21(c).

The directors may still be liable if they violated the business judgment rule. *Id.* sec. 6.21 official comment. Under the business judgment rule, directors must act in good faith (*Id.* sec. 8.30 a(1)), nonnegligently (*Id.* sec. 8.30 a(2)), and in the corporation's best interests (*Id.* sec. 8.30 a(3)). If the directors failed to follow the rule when they issued the stock to Larry Landholder, they are personally liable to the corporation. *Id.* sec. 8.33.

Under the corporation law of this state, if Shareholder wants to pursue this matter, he can file a suit in equity on behalf of himself and other shareholders or he can file a derivative suit. 11 W. Fletcher *Cyclopedia on the Law of Private Corporations* sec. 5228 (rev. perm. ed. 1980).

Answer Seventy-two: Domestic Relations

(Uniform Marriage and Divorce Act)

1. Naming a corespondent in the petition for dissolution is improper.

2. Under these facts, the maintenance provision is probably not enforceable.

3. The child custody provision will not be binding on the court.

4. The claim of adultery will not affect the determination of custody unless the adultery affected the parent's relationship with his child.

1. Under the Uniform Marriage and Divorce Act (U.M.D.A.), the court shall enter a decree of dissolution of marriage if the court finds that the marriage is irretrievably broken. U.M.D.A. sec. 303. The traditional grounds for divorce, which assumed one party had been at fault, are abolished. *Id.* sec. 305 commissioner's note. Here, the petition filed by Wilma asserts adultery, and names a

corespondent, rather than asserting simply irretrievable breakdown. Therefore, the form of the petition is improper.

2. Under the U.M.D.A., the parties to a marriage may enter into a written separation agreement providing for disposition of property, maintenance, child support, custody, and visitation. *Id.* sec. 306. Except for the provisions relating to child support, custody, and visitation, the terms of the separation agreement are binding on the court, unless the court finds, after considering the economic circumstances of the parties and other relevant evidence, that the terms of the separation agreement are unconscionable. In that event, the court may order a modification of the agreement. *Id.* sec. 306. Here, there is an obvious disparity in the incomes of Herb and Wilma. Herb will earn nothing for the next five years, while Wilma will probably earn $60,000 or more. Therefore, the court may find the maintenance portion of the agreement unconscionable and modify the agreement to award maintenance to Herb.

3. Under the U.M.D.A., provisions relating to child custody may be modified by the court. Therefore, the provisions in the agreement here relating to custody of Charles will not be binding on the court. *Id.* sec. 306.

4. Under the U.M.D.A., conduct that does not affect the parent's relationship with the child is not be be considered in determining custody. *Id.* sec. 402. In determining who is to be awarded custody of a minor child, the court must consider the best interest of the child. The court is to look to all relevant factors, including the wishes of the parents, the wishes of the child, the interaction of the child with others at home, in the school, and in the community, and the mental and physcial health of the parties. *Id.* sec. 402.

Here, Herb is alleged to have had an adulterous relationship with his boss. That conduct is not alleged to have affected his relationship with his child.

Therefore, assuming there to be no other allegations in the case, Herb's adultery will not affect the court's determination of custody.

Answer Seventy-three: Professional Responsibility

(Code of Professional Responsibility)

The ethical issues are as follows:

1. Threat of criminal charges
2. Customs of courtesy and practice
3. Communication with one represented by counsel
4. Unpermitted payments to witness
5. Unpermitted opinions and allusions of counsel at trial

1. Under the Code of Professional Responsibility, it is unethical for a lawyer to "present, participate in presenting, or threaten to present criminal charges solely to obtain an advantage in a civil matter." DR 7-105. Here, Attorney threatened to present criminal charges solely to get an advantage over Bookkeeper in a civil matter. Therefore, Attorney's conduct is subject to sanction under DR 7-105.

2. Under DR 1-102A, a lawyer shall not "engage in conduct that is prejudicial to the administration of justice." Although there is no disciplinary rule specifically mandating courtesy and responsiveness to contacts by other counsel, the facts invite consideration of misconduct on Pam's part. DR 6-101(A)(3) prohibits a lawyer from neglecting a legal matter entrusted to him. EC 7-38 requires a lawyer to follow local customs of courtesy and practice and instructs the lawyer to be punctual in fulfilling all professional commitments. Here, Pam has not responded to telephone calls or letters from opposing counsel. Therefore, Pam's conduct is subject to scrutiny as violating at least the spirit of the Code.

3. Under the Code of Professional Responsibility, a lawyer is prohibited from causing another, including his own client, to communicate on the subject of the representation with a party he knows to be represented by a lawyer, without the prior consent of counsel. Here Attorney caused his client to communicate with Bookkeeper, whom he knew to be represented by counsel, without counsel's consent. Therefore, Attorney violated DR 7-104.

4. Under the Code of Professional Responsibility, DR 7-109(C), a lawyer is prohibited from offering to pay compensation to a witness contingent on the testimony the witness gives or on the outcome of the case. Under DR 7-109(C)(1), the lawyer may pay those expenses *reasonably* incurred by the expert in attending or testifying. Here, the fingerprint expert was to receive a contingent fee. He was also to receive a limo and a two-room hotel suite, which are arguably not reasonable expenses. Therefore, Attorney's conduct is subject to scrutiny as apparently in violation of DR 7-109(C) and DR 7-109(C)(1).

5. Under DR 7-106(C), in the course of a trial, a lawyer shall not:

1. State or allude to any matter that he has no reasonable basis to believe is relevant to the case or that will not be supported by admissible evidence . . . .

2. Assert his personal knowledge of the facts in issue except when testifying as a witness.

3. Assert his personal opinion as to the justness of a cause, as to the credibility of a witness, as to the culpability of a civil litigant . . . .

Here, Attorney asserted his personal knowledge of the facts in the case, his personal opinion that Bookkeeper was not credible as a witness, and his personal opinion on Bookkeeper's culpability. Therefore, Attorney has violated DR 7-106(C).

Answer Seventy-four: Corporations

(New York Law)

1. Each of the directors other than Jones properly voted to declare the dividend; Jones did not properly vote to declare the dividend.

A New York corporation may declare and pay dividends out of surplus, so that the net assets of the corporation remaining after the declaration and payment of the dividend at least equal the corporation's stated capital, except when the corporation is insolvent or would thereby be made insolvent or when the dividend would contravene restrictions contained in the corporation's certificate of incorporation. N.Y. Bus. Corp. Law ("N.Y.B.C.L.") sec. 510 (McKinney 1986). A corporation is insolvent if it is unable to pay debts as they become due in the usual course of its business. N.Y.B.C.L. sec. 102(8) (McKinney 1986).

In deciding whether there is surplus from which a dividend may properly be declared and paid, the directors of a corporation must determine the value of the corporation's assets, and are entitled to rely on financial data prepared or presented by a public accountant in doing so, as long as they act in good faith in relying on the data. *Randall v. Bailey*, 23 N.Y.S.2d 173, 184 (N.Y. Sup. Ct. 1940), *aff'd mem.*, 262 A.D.2d 844, 29 N.Y.S.2d 512 (1st Dep't 1941), *aff'd*, 288 N.Y. 280, 43 N.E.2d 43 (1942); 2 *White on New York Corporations* par. 510.06; N.Y.B.C.L. sec. 717(a) (McKinney Supp. 1988). A director is not considered to be acting in good faith if the director has knowledge concerning the matter in question that would cause reliance on the data to be unwarranted. N.Y.B.C.L. sec. 717(a).

Here, the directors other than Jones had no knowledge concerning DeskCo.'s assets that would have caused reliance on the accountant's report to be unwarranted, and thus were entitled to rely on the report in determining whether to declare a dividend. [Credit was also given to candidates who argued that the directors' vote was improper because, had they performed their duties with the requisite degree of care, they would have learned about the sale of the comparable building and the destruction of the furniture inventory.]

There were no relevant restrictions in DeskCo.'s certificate of incorporation, and the accountant's report indicated that DeskCo. had sufficient surplus to support the proposed dividend, was not insolvent, and would not be rendered insolvent by the dividend. The report showed that DeskCo. had $400,000 surplus ($900,000 net assets less $500,000 stated capital) from which a dividend could be declared.

Jones's vote in favor of the motion to declare a $200,000 dividend was not proper. Jones knew that DeskCo.'s assets could be insufficient to support the proposed $200,000 dividend; his reliance on the accountant's report was, therefore, unwarranted. *Cf.* N.Y.B.C.L. sec. 717(a). Jones breached his duty to the corporation by voting in favor of the dividend under these circumstances.

If, in fact, DeskCo. had insufficient surplus to support the $200,000 dividend at the time the vote was taken, the dividend was illegally declared, notwithstanding the proper reliance of the majority of the directors on the accountant's report. *Cf.* N.Y.B.C.L. sec. 510.

    2. GoodSmells' contention was incorrect.

The purpose or purposes for which a New York business corporation is formed must be set forth in its certificate of incorporation. N.Y.B.C.L. sec. 402(a)(2) (McKinney 1986). A corporation generally has the power to make contracts in furtherance of its corporate purposes. N.Y.B.C.L. sec. 202(a)(7) (McKinney 1986). Since DeskCo.'s certificate of incorporation provides that DeskCo.'s sole corporate purpose is to engage in the manufacture of furniture, DeskCo. was in fact powerless to enter into a contract for the purchase of perfume and its contract with GoodSmells was, therefore, *ultra vires*.

The contract was not, however, invalid. Under the B.C.L. a contract entered into by a corporation is not invalidated by the corporation's lack of power or capacity to enter into it. N.Y.B.C.L. sec. 203(a) (McKinney 1986). *See also 711 Kings Highway Corp. v. F.I.M.'s Marine Repair Serv.*, 51 Misc.2d 373, 273 N.Y.S.2d 299 (Sup. Ct. Kings Co. 1966).

Ultra vires may only be asserted in an action by a shareholder to enjoin a corporate transaction, in an action by a corporation against an officer or director to recover for loss or damage due to an *ultra vires* act, or in an action or special proceeding by the Attorney General to annul or dissolve the corporation or to enjoin it from doing unauthorized business. N.Y.B.C.L. sec. 203(a).

3. Green's motion should be denied.

The provisional remedy of attachment is available in an action for money damages where the defendant, with intent to frustrate the enforcement of a judgment that might be rendered in plaintiff's favor, is about to dispose of property. N.Y. Civil Practice Law and Rules ("C.P.L.R.") sec. 6201(3) (McKinney 1980).

On a motion for an order of attachment, the plaintiff has the burden of establishing that there is a cause of action, that it is probable that the plaintiff will succeed on the merits, that grounds for the attachment exist, and that the amount demanded from the defendant exceeds all counterclaims known to the plaintiff. N.Y.C.P.L.R. sec. 6212(a) (McKinney 1980). Green's evidence is insufficient to meet this burden of proof as against Blue or DeskCo.

By offering as evidence the promissory note signed by Blue, and by alleging that the note has not been paid, Green has shown that he has a cause of action against Blue.

Green's evidence in support of his contention that there are grounds for an order of attachment, however, consists solely of the allegation that Blue might transfer substantial assets to others with the intent to frustrate the enforcement of any judgment Green might obtain. Mere allegations of intent to defraud are insufficient to sustain an order of attachment under N.Y.C.P.L.R. sec. 6201(3). *Société Générale Alsacienne de Banque Zurich v. Flemingdon Dev. Corp.*, 118 A.D.2d 769, 772–73, 500 N.Y.S.2d 278, 282–83 (2d Dep't 1986); *Computer Strategies, Inc. v. Commodore Business Mach., Inc.*, 105 A.D.2d 167, 143, 483 N.Y.S.2d 716 (2d Dep't 1984). Thus, on these facts, no order of attachment could properly be granted as against Blue.

Green's evidence is also insufficient as against DeskCo. A plaintiff seeking an order of attachment must satisfy his burden of proof with respect to each defendant as to whom an order of attachment is sought. *See Ford Motor Credit Co. v. Hickey Ford Sales, Inc.*, 62 N.Y.2d 291, 296, 465 N.E.2d 330, 476 N.Y.S.2d 791 (1984); *Société Générale*, 118 A.D.2d at 774, 500 N.Y.S.2d at 282; *Packer v. Caesar's World, Inc.*, 54 A.D.2d 676, 387 N.Y.S.2d 851, 852 (1st Dep't 1976). Green has failed to show that he has a cause of action against DeskCo. The promissory note was signed "Blue"; the fact that Green accepted Blue's note because Blue was the president and majority shareholder of DeskCo. is not sufficient to establish a cause of action against DeskCo. on the note. Green's evidence also fails to show that any ground for attachment of DeckCo.'s assets exists. Green has submitted no evidence to indicate any action or anticipated action to transfer or dispose of assets on DeskCo.'s part with intent to frustrate enforcement of a potential judgment in Green's favor. *See Ford Motor Credit*, 62 N.Y.2d at 302; N.Y.C.P.L.R. sec. 6201(3), 6212(a).

Green's motion for an order of attachment should, therefore, be denied in all respects.

Answer Seventy-five:
Trusts/Property/Contracts

(California Law)

1. B should prevail in the action *B v. T*, and C should prevail in the action *C v. T*.

2. The trustee is personally liable. (Some courts will reimburse the trustee where his actions are found to have been in good faith.)

1. *B v. T*. Under the common law of real property, covenants, including the covenant to repair, run with the land where there is intent, notice, vertical privity of estate, horizontal privity of estate, and the covenant "touches and concerns" the land.

Here, the 10-year lease between A and B contained a clause in which A covenanted to keep the leased premises "in good repair and condition throughout the term of this lease." As the term of the lease was for ten years, the covenant was presumably intended to run with the land. The relationship between A and B, as landlord and tenant, constituted "horizontal" privity. The relationship between A and his successors in interest, including the trustee, constituted "vertical" privity. The covenant to repair by its nature "touches and concerns" the land. As to notice, the term was in the lease. The trustee would have either constructive notice (if he had not read the lease) or actual notice, accordingly.

Therefore, the trustee was bound by the covenant in the lease. He was liable for breaches of that covenant.

Under the law of this state, a trustee is personally liable in damages where he breaches his obligation under the trust. (In some jurisdictions, he must be reimbursed by the trust if he was acting in good faith pursuant to his obligations under the trust.) The trustee also has personal liability for damages arising out of breach of covenant between the time the trust was established and the time he assumed direct responsibility for its management. In either event, the party asserting the breach must sue the trustee, rather than the trust.

Here, B gave prompt notice to the executor of the estate and to the trustee, and both the executor and the trustee nonetheless failed to repair the parking lot. Accordingly, B may sue the trustee personally for damages for the amount B expended to repair the parking lot.

Therefore, the trustee is personally liable for the $1,500 in damages.

Note that the same result is reached where the lease is regarded as a contract, rather than under real property law. Under the law of contracts of this state, duties are delegable in the absence of a prohibition. Here, the covenant to repair imposed a duty on A and his successors. Therefore, B would have a cause of action against A and his successors for breach of contract, and he could recover his actual damages, $1,500.

2. *C v. T*. Under the law of torts, the elements of negligence are duty of care, breach of duty, actual cause, proximate cause, and damages.

Here, T, as successor to A, had the duty to repair the parking lot: the fact pattern states that the parking lot was "exclusively controlled and maintained by A for the covenience of his tenants and their customers." T was in breach of his duty to maintain the parking lot: the fact pattern states that "tenants complained to T about the parking lot, but T refused to repair it."

Under the real property law of this state, someone who comes on the land at the invitation of the landowner, in order to transact business there, is an *invitee*. The landowner owes to that person a duty either to make safe any hazards of which he knows or should know, or to warn of such hazards. Here, C was a customer, and so an invitee. T owed a duty, accordingly, to warn of hazards or to repair them. T breached that duty.

Actual and proximate causation are also present.

Therefore, C can make out a *prima facie* case in negligence against T. In the absence of defenses, C will recover the amount of his damages against T, personally.

3. *Liability of T as Trustee.* Under the common law, a trustee is legal owner of property, while acting as trustee, and he owes a fiduciary duty to the assets and beneficiaries of the trust. (In a number of jurisdictions, however, where the trustee is acting within the scope of his duties as trustee, the trust will indemnify him for recoveries against him, or the plaintiff may sue the trust directly, without naming the trustee as defendant.)

Here, there appear to be no grounds for shifting liability from the trustee to the trust. The breach of duty was substantial and there are apparently no available defenses to it.

Therefore, unless the court finds that T acted in good faith, T will be liable for the breach of duty alleged in both lawsuits, *B v. T* and *C v. T*.

Answer Seventy-six:
Wills/Torts/Procedure

(New York Law)

(a) John's will is valid, but the handwritten bequest to Susan is not valid.

Since John was eighteen years old when he executed his will, he was eligible to make a valid will in New York. Estates Powers and Trusts Law ("E.P.T.L.") 3-1.1 requires that a testator be "eighteen years of age or over" to make a valid will. John, therefore, died testate because the facts expressly state that his will was duly executed.

The bequest to Susan, however, is invalid because it was added after the will was executed. E.P.T.L. 3-2.1(a)(1)(B) provides that "[n]o effect shall be given to any matter, other than the attestation clause, which follows the signature of the testator, or to any matter preceding such signature which was added subsequent to the execution of the will." Since John added the bequest to Susan subsequent to the execution of his will, the bequest to Susan is invalid. The continued presence of the attorney and the witnesses to the will did not validate the added bequest to Susan.

   (b) Two causes of action can be maintained against Tom, a personal injury action on behalf of John's estate, and a wrongful death action for the benefit of John's distributees.

A cause of action can be maintained against Tom for the personal injuries sustained by John as a result of Tom's negligence. E.P.T.L. 11-3.2(b) provides that "[n]o cause of action for injury to a person or property is lost because of the death of the person in whose favor the cause of action existed. For any injury, an action may be brought or continued by the personal representative of the decedent. . . ." The personal injury action, maintainable on behalf of John's estate against Tom, will seek recovery for those damages sustained by John prior to his death, primarily conscious pain and suffering. Pre-judgment interest is not recoverable in a personal injury action (C.P.L.R. 5001). Any recovery in the personal injury action will become an asset of John's estate. Since John died testate, naming his brother, David, as his sole valid beneficiary, any recovery will ultimately inure to the benefit of David.

A second cause of action, for John's wrongful death, may be maintained by John's personal representative for the benefit of John's distributees. This cause of action can be maintained "to recover damages for a wrongful act, neglect or default which caused the decedent's death against a person who would have been liable to the decedent by reason of such wrongful conduct if death had not ensued." E.P.T.L. 5-4.1. The wrongful death cause of action cannot be bequeathed by John's will because it is not an asset of John's estate. Under E.P.T.L. 4-1.1(4), John's sole distributees are his parents, Richard and Marilyn Brown, and they are, therefore, the only persons for whose benefit the wrongful death action can be maintained.

In the wrongful death cause of action, recovery is limited to compensation for "pecuniary injuries resulting from the decedent's death to the persons for whose benefit the action is brought." E.P.T.L. 5-4.3. Thus, any recovery in such action is to compensate statutory distributees for their "pecuniary injuries." *Loetsch v. New York City Omnibus Corp.*, 291 N.Y. 308. Recovery is also allowable for "the reasonable expenses of medical aid, nursing and attention incident to the injury causing death and the reasonable funeral expenses of the decedent paid by the distributees, or for the payment of which any distributee is responsible. . . ." E.P.T.L. 5-4.3. Interest is also recoverable on the principal sum recovered from the date of the decedent's death.

(c) The personal injury action and the wrongful death action can both be brought against Tom in the New York Supreme Court even if Tom remains in State X.

Since Tom is a New York domiciliary, any action can be brought against him in New York by serving him with a summons in State X. C.P.L.R. 313 provides that "A person domiciled in the state. . . . may be served with the summons without the state in the same manner as service is made within the state. . . ."

Answer Seventy-seven: Corporations

(Utah Bar Exam)

1. On the alter ego theory, all of the shareholders are personally liable to Mr. Jackhammer.

2. Depending on state law, the corporation may not be adequately capitalized and, again, the shareholders are liable.

3. If no certificate of incorporation was issued, all shareholders are personally, jointly, and severally liable for all corporate liabilities.

1. *Alter ego*. Under the corporations law of this state, generally the shareholders of a corporation are shielded from personal liability and are not liable for corporate debts and obligations. However, if the corporation is found to be the mere alter ego of the shareholders or officers and directors, the court will pierce the corporate veil and hold shareholders, officers, or directors liable.

The court will pierce the corporate veil upon a finding that:

1. Unity of interest exists, so that the corporation and the individuals no longer have separate personalities.

2. A fraud or injustice would be promoted by adherence to the fiction of separate corporate existence.

In applying the above standards the court will look at the following:

Undercapitalization. Here, the corporation had few assets in relation to the size of the business it was contemplating doing and in relation to the size of the contract with Mr. Jackhammer.

A corporation with only one typewriter and $700 in cash entering into a $50,000 contract is probably undercapitalized. Therefore, it is likely that this part of the test is met.

Failure to follow corporate formalities. Here, there were no shareholder or director meetings nor corporate minutes. There was an intermingling of corporate and business assets. Therefore, it is likely that this part of the test is met.

Personal use of corporate funds. Here, the president took the corporation's funds and spent some of them on personal expenses. Mr. Secretary used the corporate typewriter for personal purposes. Therefore, this prong of the test is probably met.

Sole or substantial stock ownership and domination by defendant. Here, Mr. President held more shares than the others and seems to have had complete control of the corporation. Therefore, it is likely that this part of the test is met.

Sanctioning fraud or promoting injustice. Here, Mr. President misrepresented the corporation's size, assets, and business to Mr. Jackhammer. To shield him from liability would be an injustice to Mr. Jackhammer.

Therefore, it appears that the general standard is met for piercing the corporate veil. Therefore, at least Mr. President will be liable to Mr. Jackhammer for the amount of the contract. It does not appear, however, that the corporation is the alter ego of Ms. Veep, Mr. Secretary, or Ms. Shareholder. Nor did they participate, it appears, in the misconduct towards Mr. Jackhammer. Therefore, it is unlikely that they would be held liable on this theory.

2. *Inadequate capitalization*. Inadequate capitalization may, depending on state law, be an independent ground for finding all of the officers and shareholders liable to Mr. Jackhammer.

Under the corporations law of this state, an agreement to provide future services to the corporation is not adequate consideration for stock. The person making the promise does not thereby become a shareholder. Here, Ms. Shareholder's promise to perform services in the future valued at $300 is not sufficient consideration for stock. Therefore, Ms. Shareholder is not a shareholder of Own a Piece of the Wall, Inc. ("O.P.W.").

Under the corporations law of this state, the transfer of ownership of tangible property may be consideration for stock. However, Mr. Secretary kept the typewriter at home, for his own use, suggesting that he never assigned ownership to the corporation or that the value of whatever was assigned may have been less than $300. Therefore, he may not be a shareholder. This is a fact question.

[The requirements for capitalization of a corporation vary from state to state. Enumerate the requirements for your own state. Then conclude whether this corporation may have been inadequately capitalized.]

3. *Failure to observe formalities in formation of corporation.* Under the corporations law of this state, the corporate existence begins with issuance of the certificate of incorporation. Persons who act as a corporation without authority are jointly and severally liable for all debts and liabilities incurred.

Here, the facts do not state whether a certificate of incorporation was issued. If one was issued, it is conclusive evidence that all conditions precedent have been complied with. The corporation will be effective, despite deficiencies in articles of incorporation and lack of a registered agent. Accordingly, the shareholders will enjoy limited liability.

On the other hand, if no certificate of incorporation was issued, the corporation never came into existence, and the shareholders are jointly and severally liable for all debts and liabilities incurred, including the debt to Mr. Jackhammer. The shareholders can argue that their bona fide attempt to organize a corporation and their doing business as a corporation gave rise to a de facto corporation. This theory, however, is questionable.

Therefore, if no certificate of incorporation was issued, there is no corporation, and the shareholders are jointly and severally liable for all debts and liabilities.

Answer Seventy-eight: Domestic Relations

(New York Law)

(a) All of the court's rulings were correct.

(b) The court should deny Wife's motion to increase Chi's child support

(a) Ruling (1) was correct.

Wife had no cause of action against Hus for annulment.

An action to annul a marriage on the ground that the consent of one of the parties was obtained by fraud may be maintained by the party whose consent was so obtained only if the action is commenced within three years of discovery of the facts constituting the fraud. New York Domestic Relations Law ("D.R.L.") 140(e), C.P.L.R. 214.

The fraud or misrepresentations by the defendant must be material or relate to something vital to the marriage and must be such as to deceive an ordinary person. *Boardman's New York Family Law* sec. 181. A fraudulent promise to embrace the religion of a spouse in order to gain that spouse's consent to the marriage has often been held to constitute grounds for the annulment of the marriage. 47 N.Y. Jur.2d, Domestic Relations sec. 991; *Howardell v. Howardell,*

1 Misc. 2d 941, 151 N.Y.S.2d 265. Where, as here, the evidence showed only that Hus had changed his mind and there was no proof that Hus had made a false and fraudulent promise to Wife prior to marriage to induce her to marry him, Wife is not entitled to an annulment.

Additionally, Wife is not entitled to an annulment because she and Hus continued to live together as husband and wife from May 1984 to February 1985. A marriage will not be annulled on the ground of fraud if it appears that, at any time before the commencement of the action, the parties voluntarily cohabited as husband and wife with full knowledge of the facts constituting fraud. D.R.L. 140(e).

Ruling (2) was correct.

The court had no power to equitably distribute the parties' marital property. D.R.L. 236B(5)(a) directs a court to determine the respective rights of the parties in their marital (and separate) property and mandates disposition thereof in the final judgment only in an action wherein all or part of the relief granted is a divorce, or the dissolution, annulment, or declaration of the nullity of a marriage. *Berman v. Berman*, 111 A.D.2d 141, 489 N.Y.S.2d 519. Because the annulment was denied, Wife was not entitled to equitable distribution.

Ruling (3) was correct.

Wife is seeking temporary maintenance. She is not asking the court to modify the terms of the separation agreement. During the pendency of an action, the court may order temporary maintenance to meet the reasonable needs of a party in such amount as justice requires, having regard for the circumstances of the case and of the respective parties. D.R.L. 236B(6)(a). The predominant consideration is the financial need of the moving party, and if the applicant is in genuine need of support pending trial, an award may be made. *Jorgensen v. Jorgensen*, 86 A.D.2d 861, 447 N.Y.S.2d 318. However, the court may not order maintenance, temporary or otherwise, where the parties have entered into a separation agreement providing for maintenance pursuant to Part B, subdivision 3. D.R.L. 236B(6)(a). This codifies the settled rule of case law that alimony *pendente lite* is not allowed until a separation agreement is set aside or breached by the parties. 48 N.Y. Jur.2d, Domestic Relations Section 1270. *Gotthainer v. Gotthainer*, 107 Misc. 2d 221, 435 N.Y.S.2d 444; *Wilkinson v. Wilkinson*, 10 A.D.2d 937, 200 N.Y.S.2d 879.

Ruling (4) was correct.

Wife was entitled to a judgment of divorce from Hus upon proof that she and Hus lived separate and apart pursuant to their separation agreement for a period of one or more years after the execution of such agreement and satisfactory proof by Wife that she had substantially performed all of the terms and conditions of such agreement. D.R.L. 170(6).

The fact that Hus and Wife cohabited together on one occasion does not abrogate their separation agreement. *Farkas v. Farkas*, 26 A.D.2d 919, 274 N.Y.S.2d 842. There must be proof of an intention to abandon the agreement to reconcile, and to manifest an intention to permanently resume the marital relationship. 47 N.Y. Jur. 2d, Domestic Relations Section 807. Such proof is lacking here.

(b) The court should deny Wife's motion to increase Chi's child support.

Both a father and mother are liable for the support of their child in accordance with their needs. D.R.L. 32; F.C.A. 413. The Court of Appeals has held that the child support provisions of a separation agreement should not be disturbed absent a showing of unanticipated and unreasonable change in circumstances. *Boden v. Boden*, 42 N.Y.2d 210, 397 N.Y.S.2d 701. One commentator suggested that this doctrine did not appear to be affected by D.R.L. 236(9)(b), which provides that the court has the authority to modify a prior judgment as to child support upon a showing of substantial change in circumstances, including financial hardship. 1981 Practice Commentary to D.R.L. 236, C236B:28.

The child support provisions of a separation agreement remain subject to the court's supervisory powers as set forth in D.R.L. 240. 1981 Practice Commentary to D.R.L. 236, C236B:28. However, the Court of Appeals itself has severely limited the *Boden* doctrine. The court held in *Brescia v. Fitts*, 56 N.Y.2d 132, 451 N.Y.S.2d 68, that the *Boden* rule applies only where the child's needs are being adequately provided for and the dispute involves an effort to obtain a readjustment of the parents' respective obligations, i.e., one parent seeks to have the other pay a greater percentage of the child's needs. In other words, an upward modification of child support may be obtained if the child's needs are not being adequately met because of a change in circumstances. 1982 Practice Commentary to D.R.L. 236, C236B:28. Wife has not shown that Chi's needs are not being adequately met. It is not a matter of the child's right to receive adequate support that is being asserted, as in *Brescia v. Fitts*, supra. Hus' increased earnings, arguably not even an unanticipated change in circumstances, have no bearing on Chi's needs. *Rubin v. Rubin*, 69 N.Y.2d 702, 512 N.Y.S.2d 364 *affirming* 119 A.D.2d 152, 506 N.Y.S.2d 44; *Sassian v. Sassian*, 126 A.D.2d 984, 511 N.Y.S.2d 760. Wife's motion, therefore, should be denied.

Answer Seventy-nine: Community Property

(California Law)

The following are subject to execution in satisfaction of Victor's judgment:

1. The savings bonds
2. The stock portfolio (if the court treats it as community property ("CP") for purposes of satisfying a judgment debt)
3. Wendy's one-half interest in the condominium
4. The CP portion of the increase in value of the business

Liability of Wendy or Harry to Victor. Under the California law of community property, the judgment creditor can reach the separate property ("SP") of the tortfeasor, all of the CP, and, although there is a question of constitutionality, the quasi-community property ("QCP"), as well. Quasi-community property is property one of the spouses earned outside California which, had it been earned inside California instead, would be community property. (With the exception of the ability of the judgment creditor to reach it, this property is otherwise treated as SP during the marriage.)

Here, Victor has obtained a judgment in tort against Wendy. Therefore, Victor can reach Wendy's SP and all of the CP. He may also be able to reach the QCP.

Under California law, the tort claim is paid first out of the CP when the defendant was acting for the community, and only then out of the SP. Conversely, when the defendant was acting on his own behalf, the judgment comes first out of the SP, then out of the CP.

Here, Harry and Wendy own the condominium as joint tenants, and it may be argued, accordingly, that when Wendy went to the condominium owners' meeting at which she committed the tort against Victor, she was on community business. However, it may be argued on the other side, that as Wendy went to the meeting over Victor's objection, she was on her own business and not that of the community.

1. *The Savings Bonds.* Under California law, the proceeds of a personal injury recovery are usually CP. However, where the other spouse is the tortfeasor, they are SP. Under California community property law, assets purchased with SP become SP.

Here, Wendy received the funds with which she purchased the savings bonds as a tort recovery. Harry was the tortfeasor. Therefore, the savings bonds are Wendy's SP. Victor can reach them to satisfy his judgment against Wendy.

2. *The Stock Portfolio.* Under the California law, property acquired during the marriage that would be CP under California law, but that was SP in the state in which it was acquired, becomes QCP for purposes of satisfying judgments when the couple comes to live in California.

Here, the stock portfolio was purchased out of Harry's accumulated earnings while the couple lived in State X. There, a spouse's earnings are his or her SP. Under California law, the earnings and assets purchased therewith would be CP. Now Harry and Wendy live in California.

Therefore, the earnings and the stock portfolio purchased therewith are QCP for purposes of satisfying Victor's judgment against Wendy. Therefore, it is subject to execution in satisfaction of Victor's judgment against Wendy.

3. *The Condominium.* Under California law, title controls the treatment of real property. Where property is owned by a husband and wife as joint tenants with right of survivorship, that characterization will be controlling. The court will not inquire into the sources of the assets with which the property was acquired. A judgment creditor can attach only the one-half interest of the judgment debtor in joint property.

Here, Harry and Wendy own the condominium as joint tenants with right of survivorship. Although in this case the condominium was in fact purchased with funds earned by Harry in State X, where they were SP, the court will not inquire into the source of the funds with which Harry and Wendy purchased the condominium.

Therefore, Victor as a judgment creditor can attach only Wendy's one-half interest in the condominium.

4. *The Auto Repair Business.* Under California law, assets purchased with SP become SP. The courts have devised two different formulas for valuing the respective spouses' interests in a business operated during the marriage. Under the *Van Camp* formula, used where it was the market and not the contribution of the spouse that accounted for the increase in the value of the business, the

court will subtract the spouse's reasonable earnings, as SP, and will treat the residue of the increase in the value of the business as CP. Under the *Pereira* formula, on the other hand, the spouse's SP is calculated not on the basis of his potential salaried earnings, but rather as though his original SP contribution had been a simple investment. The court looks at the reasonable return on that investment over the period of years and treats the residue, the growth in value of the business, as CP. *Pereira* is used where it was the spouse's contributions to the business more than simply market conditions that contributed to the growth of the business.

Here, Harry purchased the auto repair business when the couple moved to California. He used money he had inherited, which was SP. There is no indication of whether the increase in value of the business, assuming its value has increased, is due primarily to Harry's contributions or primarily to market conditions. Harry does, however, deposit an amount equal to his previous salary as an auto mechanic into a joint checking account, from which the couple pay their monthly living expenses. Applying the *Van Camp* formula, Harry's salary deposits into the joint checking account are CP, but since he may be more valuable to the business as a manager than as a mechanic, this may not alone reflect the amount of CP; in any event, the residue of the value of the business is SP. Applying the *Pereira* formula, on the other hand, the increase in the value of the original investment at normal market rates of return is SP, and any value of the business over and above that is CP.

Therefore, depending on which formula is applied, Victor can reach more or less of the increase in the value of the auto repair business.

Under California law, the spouses may make an agreement (which since January 1, 1985, must be in writing), to change the character of community property. A spouse may not unilaterally change the character of community property by the way he describes the property in his will. Here, Harry executed a will describing the auto repair business as community property. That is insufficient alone to change the community property character of the business.

Answer Eighty: Trusts

(New York Law)

(a) The first issue presented deals with the validity of Mom's exercise of the power of appointment, particularly as it relates to the rule against perpetuities. There were no restrictions placed upon Mom in naming appointees of the power. Thus, she had a general power of appointment (E.P.T.L. sec. 10-3.2), meaning that it was exercisable wholly in favor of Mom, her estate, her creditors, or the creditors of her estate. The power was presently exercisable (E.P.T.L. sec. 10-3.3) because it could be exercised by her at any time during her life or at her death. For perpetuities purposes, sec. 10-8.1 establishes that, with a presently exercisable general power, the period begins to run on the effective date of the instrument of exercise. If the power was anything other than a general power, presently exercisable, the period would begin to run at the time of creation of the power (i.e., at Dad's death).

The basic New York rule against perpetuities is found in E.P.T.L. sec. 9-1.1. The rule provides that (a) every present or future estate shall be void in its creation which shall suspend the absolute power of alienation by any limitation or condition for a period longer than lives in being at the creation of the estate plus a term of not more than 21 years, and (b) no estate shall be valid unless it must vest, if at all, within a period of lives in being at the creation of the estate, plus a term of not more than 21 years. Mom's exercise created a trust that could last for longer than lives in being plus 21 years, inasmuch as Biz could have more children after Mom's death, who would be required to attain the age of 25. At common law, such an exercise was invalid. Under E.P.T.L. sec. 9-1.2, however, the age contingency is reduced to age 21 for all persons subject to the contingency. Thus, the New York reform legislation would save the interest, and the exercise of the power is valid. It is noteworthy that the exercise would have been valid even if we were required to measure the perpetuities period from Dad's death. In that case, the measuring life, Biz, was in being at the creation of the power. Thus, with the statute reducing the age contingency, the exercise would be valid.

(b) A trust contemplates the holding of property by one person for the benefit of another. Thus, one person cannot be sole trustee and sole beneficiary (*In re Will of Phipps*, 2 N.Y.2d 105). A trust instrument naming one person as sole trustee and sole beneficiary will fail. *Rose v. Hatch*, 125 N.Y. 427; E.P.T.L. sec. 7-1.1. Here, the Bank is named as co-trustee. The law is settled that one of two or more trustees may be the beneficiary. *Robertson v. de Brulatour*, 111 A.D. 882, aff'd 188 N.Y. 301. Thus, the appointment of Biz as co-trustee is proper.

If Biz accepts the appointment as co-trustee, he will have a conflict of interest problem. Even though the trust only provides for payment of income to Biz, and does not provide for the distribution of principal to him, Biz would be participating in making investment decisions that could impact upon the amount of income generated and the amount of growth in principal. His interest as an income beneficiary in such decisions would conflict with the interests of the remainderman. This is a source of potential difficulty for him and his estate if it is later claimed that he violated his fiduciary duty to the remainderman by exercising his discretion in favor of himself as income beneficiary.

(c) A surviving spouse's right of election, where decedent has died on or after September 1, 1992, is the greater of $50,000 or 1/3 of the net estate. E.P.T.L. sec. 5-1.1-A(a)(2). This share is subject, however, to reduction in the amount of property received from the estate under the laws of intestacy, testamentary substitutes, and bequests under the will. E.P.T.L. 5-1.1-A(a)(4). While under the 1992 and subsequent amendments to the elective share rules, a spouse dying prior to September 1, 1994 could leave the elective share in trust, this option is not open to spouses dying on or after September 1, 1994. E.P.T.L. 5-1.1-A(5).

Thus, if Biz were to die now, survived by one child, Deb's elective share would be one-third of Biz' net estate. Under E.P.T.L. 5-1.1-A, Deb would have the right to elect her share outright against the principal of the trust Biz proposes to create in his new will.

[If Deb takes the interest instead of her elective share, partial credit would also be given to candidates who properly discussed the potential application of E.P.T.L. sec. 7-1.6(b) to the facts. This section deals with the application of principal for the benefit of an income beneficiary whose support or education is not sufficiently provided for. In such a case the court must be satisfied that the original purpose of the settlor cannot be carried out and that such application of principal would effectuate the intention of the settlor. It is difficult to envision a situation in which the income from a $2,000,000 trust would not be found adequate.]

(d) If Deb takes the interest instead of her elective share , the fourth point deals with the marital deduction for federal estate tax purposes. As proposed, Deb's interest in the trust would constitute a "terminable interest." Prior to changes in the Internal Revenue Code in 1981, Deb's interest would not qualify for the marital deduction.

Under IRC sec. 2056(b)(7), Deb's interest in the trust could qualify as qualified terminable interest property ("QTIP"). In its simplest terms, a trust of income for the spouse for life, remainder at her death to such persons as Biz selects, can qualify to pass tax free under the marital deduction. This occurs only if the executor elects on the decedent's estate tax return to so treat it. The trade-off is that the property will have to be included in Deb's estate at her death. [Thus, a candidate would be correct in stating that under the proposed trust the entire estate can qualify for the marital deduction.]

Note of the Bar Examiners

The better answer would note, however, that qualifying the entire estate would, in all likelihood, be a mistake. Doing so, rather than electing to qualify only part of the trust, would essentially waste Biz's exemption equivalent of $600,000. By way of example, if Biz places $2,000,000 in the trust, his executor could elect to treat only $1,400,000 as qualified for the marital deduction. Biz would pay no federal estate tax ($1,400,000 + his exemption equivalent of $600,000 = $2,000,000), and at her death (assuming she had no other property), Deb's estate would be taxed on $800,000 ($1,400,000 less her exemption equivalent of $600,000). If Biz's executor qualified the entire $2,000,000, his estate would pay no tax, but Deb's estate would later be taxed on $1,400,000 ($2,000,000 - $600,000), thus significantly increasing the tax on the two estates. Through judicious use of the election, the tax consequences on the two estates can be minimized.

Index of Questions

33 Criminal Procedure—New Jersey—60 minutes
34 Contracts & Sales—Michigan—20 minutes
35 Evidence—Utah—40 minutes
36 Real Property—Utah—40 minutes
37 Torts—Utah—40 minutes
38 Contracts & Sales—Utah—40 minutes
39 Real Property—New Jersey—60 minutes
40 Evidence—Utah—40 minutes
41 Federal Jurisdiction & Procedure—Colorado—20 minutes
42 Constitutional Law—Utah—40 minutes
43 Criminal Procedure—Utah—40 minutes
44 Torts—Vermont—60 minutes
45 Contracts & Sales—Colorado—20 minutes
46 Real Property—New Jersey—60 minutes
47 Evidence—Colorado—20 minutes
48 Constitutional Law—Michigan—20 minutes
49 Real Property—New Jersey—60 minutes
50 Contracts & Sales—Michigan—20 minutes
51 Torts—New Jersey—60 minutes
52 Criminal Law—Colorado—20 minutes
53 Evidence—Colorado—20 minutes
54 Constitutional Law—Colorado—20 minutes
55 Contracts & Sales—Michigan—20 minutes
56 Real Property—New Jersey—60 minutes
57 Torts—New Jersey—60 minutes
58 Criminal Procedure—Colorado—20 minutes
59 Contracts & Sales—Vermont—60 minutes
60 Evidence—Colorado—20 minutes
61 Real Property—Vermont—60 minutes
62 Constitutional Law—Colorado—20 minutes
63 Torts—Colorado—20 minutes
64 Contracts & Sales—Utah—40 minutes
65 Real Property—Colorado—20 minutes
66 Contracts & Sales—Vermont—60 minutes
67 Real Property—California—60 minutes
68 Criminal Procedure—New Jersey—60 minutes
69 Professional Responsibility—Colorado—20 minutes
70 Wills—Colorado—20 minutes
71 Corporations—Colorado—20 minutes
72 Domestic Relations—Colorado—20 minutes
73 Professional Responsibility—Colorado—20 minutes

Index of State Sources

Question 17—Criminal Procedure

Question 18—Contracts & Sales

Question 21—Real Property

Question 26—Contracts & Sales

Question 29—Real Property

Question 31—Constitutional Law

Question 32—Torts

Question 34—Contracts & Sales

Question 48—Constitutional Law

Question 50—Contracts & Sales

Question 55—Contracts & Sales

Nebraska—20 minutes

Question 6—Federal Jurisdiction & Procedure

Question 7—Constitutional Law

Question 9—Torts

Question 15—Constitutional Law

Question 24—Torts

Question 28—Real Property

New Jersey—60 minutes

Question 25—Criminal Procedure

Question 33—Criminal Procedure

Question 39—Real Property

Question 46—Real Property

Question 49—Real Property

Question 51—Torts

Question 56—Real Property

Question 57—Torts

Question 68—Criminal Procedure

New York—50 minutes

Question 74—Corporations

Question 76—Wills/Torts/Procedure

Question 78—Domestic Relations

Question 80—Trusts

Utah—40 minutes (after 1990, Utah questions will be 30 minutes long)

Question 12—Evidence

Question 14—Federal Jurisdiction & Procedure

Question 22—Constitutional Law

Question 27—Evidence

Question 35—Evidence

Question 36—Real Property

Index of Multistate Subjects

THE BEST WAY TO LAND A LEGAL JOB:
AN INTERNSHIP

Internships are the hottest way to get job experience, learn about the legal profession, and showcase your talents before potential employers. *The Experienced Hand* is a wonderful guide that will show you how to find an internship and do your best while there. The book contains worksheets to help you evaluate and accomplish your goals, advice on how to enlist faculty support for academic credit for your internship, a sample learning contract, a sample evaluation form, actual case histories, journals, sample letters and resumes. *The Experienced Hand* is a valuable resource if you are considering work experience as part of your legal education.

THE EXPERIENCED HAND: A Student Manual for Making the Most of an Internship by Timothy Stanton and Kamil Ali, $11.99

PRECISELY WHAT YOU NEED TO KNOW

- **Hanau Charts** Flow charts for organization
- **Case Clips** Facts, issue, and rule for every case
- **Outlines** Concise arrangement of the law
- **Mnemonics** Memory aids and devices

$14.99 per copy, keyed to the following texts:

Administrative Law
Order Code: 1AL1-AC
Bonfield
Breyer
Gellhorn
Cass
Schwartz
Mashaw

Civil Procedure
Order Code: 1CP1-AC
Cound
Field
Rosenberg
Hazard

Civil Procedure
Order Code: 1CP2-AC
Yeazell

Commercial Law
Order Code: 1CL1-AC
Whaley
Jordan
Farnsworth

Commercial Paper
Order Code: 1CL1-AC
Whaley
Speidel
Jordan
Farnsworth

Constitutional Law
Order Code: 1CO1-AC
Brest
Cohen
Ducat
Gunther
Lockhart
Rotunda
Stone

Contracts
Order Code: 1CT1-AC
Dawson
Kessler
Fuller
Murphy
Calamari
Rossett

Contracts
Order Code: 1CT2-AC
Farnsworth 4th Ed.

Contracts
Order Code: 1CT3-AC
Farnsworth 5th Ed.

Corporations
Order Code: 1CP1-AC
Cary
Choper
Hamilton
Henn
Jennings
Solomon
Vagts

Criminal Law
Order Code: 1CR1-AC
Kadish
LaFave
Kaplan
Weinreb
Dix
Johnson
Moenssens

Criminal Procedure
Order Code: 1CP1-AC
Kamisar
Saltzburg
Weinreb/Crim. Proc.
Weinreb/Crim. Just.
Miller

Domestic Relations
Order Code: 1FL1-AC
Areen
Foote
Krause
Wadlington

Evidence
Order Code: 1EV1-AC
McCormick
Green
Weinstein
Kaplan
Cleary

Family Law
Order Code: 1FL1-AC
Areen
Foote
Krause
Wadlington

Income Tax/Corporate
Order Code: 1TC1-AC
Lind
Kahn
Wolfman
Surrey

Income Tax/Personal
Order Code: 1TP1-AC
Klein
Andrews
Surrey
Kragen
Freeland
Graetz

International Law
Order Code: 1IL1-AC
Sweeney
Henkin

Property
Order Code: 1PR1-AC
Browder
Casner
Cribbet

Property
Order Code: 1PR2-AC
Dukeminier

Sales and Secured Transactions
Order Code: 1CL1-AC
Whaley
Speidel
Jordan
Honnold
Farnsworth

Torts
Order Code: 1TR1-AC
Epstein
Keeton
Franklin

Torts
Order Code: 1TR2-AC
Henderson

Torts
Order Code: 1TR3-AC
Wade

ORDER TODAY, Books Shipped Within 24 Hours!
1•800•366•7086

O r d e r   F o r m

SULZBURGER & GRAHAM PUBLISHING Ltd.
PO Box 20058 • Park West Station • New York NY 10025
1(800) 366-7086 • (212) 769-9738 • FAX: (212) 769-9675

Please send me BLOND'S ...

Product Description	Product Number	Casebook You Use	Price

Shipping & Handling $2.50

Total _____

Name _____
Address _____
City/State/Zip _____
Graduation _____
Day Phone _____

○ **Check or money order enclosed (payable to Sulzburger & Graham Publishing)**
   ○ **MasterCard** ○ **Visa** ○ **American Express** ○ **Optima** ○ **DiscoverCard**

_____   _____   _____
Charge Card Number   Expiration   Signature

All orders are shipped UPS same or next business day. Delivery time will vary, based on distance from New York City. Washington/Boston corridor can expect delivery 2 working days after shipment. West Coast should allow 6 working days. Overnight, 2nd day and COD available at extra cost. We cannot deliver to PO Boxes.